How Real Is Hell?

"Until recently, Evangelicals believed that hell was a place of eternal conscious suffering, even if preachers no longer 'dangled the feet' of their congregations over its imagined flames. This is now contested ground, and Steve Barber has helped us understand why this belief is no longer widespread by exploring the biblical texts that shape a range of views. This is an academically rigorous, yet eminently readable and pastorally sensitive book—the fruit of research at Oxford."

—PAUL GOODLIFF, visiting tutor in Christian doctrine, Spurgeon's College, and former general secretary, Churches Together in England

"Arising from and addressing real pastoral anxieties, Steve Barber does outstanding work looking in detail at key biblical texts to help us understand and offer counsel. His work comes as a breath of fresh air into what is often a stale evangelical debate, and will be at turns challenging, comforting, and hopeful. Warmly recommended."

—ROB ELLIS, Principal Emeritus and Senior Research Fellow, Regent's Park College, University of Oxford

"Using his extensive biblical knowledge and ceaseless pursuit of truth, Reverend Barber examines the doctrine of hell with a focus on what the bible says about the eternal fate of those who are not Christians. This book provides an open and clear interpretation of the relevant texts using accomplished exegesis and sound methodology. Pastors and preachers will find it an invaluable tool for comprehending this controversial and complex doctrine of hell."

—HELEN BAKER, Pioneer Baptist Minister

"In his introductory remarks, Steve articulates the book's purpose. This is not merely an academic exercise: it is intended for the broader church. It invites and implores its readers to delve into the subject with the same fervor as the author. Steve's personal engagement with the topic is evident and he desires that others approach it with the same passion and commitment."

—WALE HUDSON-ROBERTS, Baptist minister, and Racial Justice Coordinator, Baptist Union of Great Britain

How Real Is Hell?

A Close Exploration of the Biblical Texts

STEVE BARBER

WIPF & STOCK · Eugene, Oregon

HOW REAL IS HELL?
A Close Exploration of the Biblical Texts

Copyright © 2024 Steve Barber. All rights reserved. Except for brief quotations in critical publications or reviews, no part of this book may be reproduced in any manner without prior written permission from the publisher. Write: Permissions, Wipf and Stock Publishers, 199 W. 8th Ave., Suite 3, Eugene, OR 97401.

Wipf & Stock
An Imprint of Wipf and Stock Publishers
199 W. 8th Ave., Suite 3
Eugene, OR 97401

www.wipfandstock.com

PAPERBACK ISBN: 979-8-3852-2827-0
HARDCOVER ISBN: 979-8-3852-2828-7
EBOOK ISBN: 979-8-3852-2829-4

All Scripture quotations, unless otherwise indicated, are taken from the Holy Bible, New International Version®, NIV®. Copyright ©1973, 1978, 1984, 2011 by Biblica, Inc.™ Used by permission of Zondervan. All rights reserved worldwide. www.zondervan.com. The "NIV" and "New International Version" are trademarks registered in the United States Patent and Trademark Office by Biblica, Inc.™

Dedicated to my brother Phil, who died too soon.

Contents

Introduction 1

CHAPTER 1: Understanding *Géenna* (Hell) Imagery 9

CHAPTER 2: Eternal Punishment and the Age to Come 32

CHAPTER 3: The Language of Destruction, Perishing, and Death 37

CHAPTER 4: The Relevance of the Story of the Rich Man and Lazarus 44

CHAPTER 5: Sulfur, Smoke, Torment and Second Death 50

CHAPTER 6: All Things Reconciled 56

CHAPTER 7: Conclusions to the Descriptive and Synthetic Tasks 61

CHAPTER 8: So What? 64

Appendix: Survey 73

Bibliography 81

Introduction

I HAVE FELT INCREASINGLY uneasy over the past few years about the doctrine of eternal conscious suffering for those who reject Jesus—a doctrine taught by all the churches I have attended. There have been several occasions in youth meetings or seekers' groups where the fate of those who reject Jesus has been raised, and I have felt awkward about presenting a doctrine of hell as eternal conscious suffering even though I believed it was part of orthodox Christian belief and taught in Scripture. My discomfort arose from several theological questions: whether eternal conscious punishment is proportionate; the incongruence of a God of love meting out such a punishment; the idea that God would keep people alive for the sole purpose of punishing them (which became increasingly relevant as I came to understand that the Jewish notion of immortality is based on God continuously breathing his breath into us rather than the idea that the soul was created immortal); the lack of a restorative purpose; and the difficulty of accommodating the doctrine within a cosmic salvation where all things will ultimately be reconciled to Christ.

Recent study for a sermon series on *future things* led me to reexamine the biblical passages often used to support the doctrine. Subsequently, I felt that the biblical case for the doctrine was not as solid as I had previously believed, and alternative readings of the passages, such as conditional immortality, seemed feasible. Around the same time, I spent several hours discussing theology with a woman who was struggling with her faith and questioning several beliefs she had absorbed through her upbringing in an evangelical church, including this doctrine. In an honest and open discussion, we explored the strengths and weaknesses of the evidence for this doctrine and the consequences of believing or not believing such teaching.

Terminology

I shall use the term *traditional* to describe belief in eternal conscious suffering. Within this umbrella term are a variety of views, including different understandings of the physicality of suffering and different interpretations as to the metaphorical aspect of the biblical imagery. In using *traditional*, I do not intend to imply that this belief originates with Jesus and the first apostles. Rather I employ the term because it has been the predominant belief of the Western church throughout history, including evangelicalism, and because it is commonly used in debates on the nature of hell as a summary term for those believing in eternal conscious suffering.[1]

I shall use the term *conditional* for the belief that God's punishment will ultimately involve a cessation of existence for the wicked. This, too, covers a range of beliefs, from those who believe that the wicked will simply remain dead and not be raised, to the belief that they will experience severe and terrifying punishment, but not unending.

The ensuing discussion shall largely consider the merits of these two positions, though some time shall be spent on a third position that has gained interest in recent years in evangelicalism: *universalism*—the view that, in the end, everyone will be brought into God's kingdom. Yet again, there is a range of views covered by this term. Although having gained popularity, this remains a minority evangelical position, and a defense of universalism has only been attempted by a few evangelical theologians.

---

1. E.g., ACUTE, *Nature of Hell*; Gundry and Sprinkle, *Four Views*; Gundry and Crockett, *Four Views*.

Introduction

Methodology

In this book I explore the scope of pastoral theological guidance available to a person disturbed by the traditional belief in hell. This scenario is an amalgamation of various conversations I have had with youth groups, seeker meetings, and, in particular the woman struggling with her faith. All these conversations have taken place in the setting of a free church that is a member of the UK Evangelical Alliance, and so the context envisaged for such pastoral theological guidance is that of an evangelical free church.

The Critical Conversation Method as portrayed by Stephen Pattison shall be used. This involves a three-way conversation between:

i) My own beliefs, ideas, feelings, perceptions, and assumptions;

ii) The contemporary situation being examined; and

iii) The beliefs, assumptions, and perceptions provided by the Christian tradition (including the Bible).[2]

Pattison describes Critical Conversation as "a fairly simple way of trying to understand and think through the complex relationship between situations and theological and other ideas and theories."[3] He suggests that encouraging both the situation and one's beliefs to engage in conversation with traditional beliefs avoids "giving slick and unrealistic answers in complex situations."[4] Furthermore, Critical Conversation allows for traditional theological understanding to be explored and questioned, allowing the voice of each participant to be taken seriously.[5]

So, applying Pattison's model:

i. My own beliefs, ideas, feelings, perceptions and assumptions

These have been outlined in the introduction above.

---

2. Pattison as cited by Woodward et al., *Blackwell Reader*, 139.
3. Woodward et al., *Blackwell Reader*, 135.
4. Woodward et al., *Blackwell Reader*, 142.
5. Woodward et al., *Blackwell Reader*, 139.

ii. The contemporary situation being examined

In 2010, according to a survey published by the UK Evangelical Alliance (EAUK), 37 percent of UK evangelicals "strongly agreed that hell is a place where the condemned will suffer eternal conscious pain," and a further 13 percent "agreed slightly" with this. However, 31 percent of evangelicals said they were unsure and 11 percent strongly disagreed with such a concept of hell. The report claimed this was "the issue where there is the greatest uncertainty" among evangelicals.[6]

The EAUK survey was conducted over ten years ago. Therefore, I decided to conduct my own survey as to the beliefs of committed worshipers within evangelical churches. The survey was designed to enable comparison with the EAUK survey. For this reason, I used the same five-point Likert scale, and asked the same question.[7] I also designed it to enable a comparison between the beliefs of lay members and those of ministers. However, as detailed in the appendix, there is a strong likelihood of sampling bias, and the results only provide an indication of possible changes in beliefs.

There is evidence to suggest that evangelicals today are more polarized in their opinions as to whether "hell is a place where the condemned will suffer eternal conscious suffering" than evangelicals in 2010 (when the EAUK survey was conducted).[8] This polarization is caused by an increase in the proportion of those willing to reject the traditional view[9] and may indicate a growing confidence among UK evangelicals to reject the traditional understanding of hell, though further research is required to overcome possible bias in my research.

---

6. EAUK, *21st Century Evangelicals*.

7. The purpose, design, distribution, and results of the survey are included in the appendix, along with an analysis of the results.

8. Appendix: Hypothesis 3.

9. Appendix: Hypothesis 1. However, there was no evidence to suggest a decrease in the proportion of those strongly agreeing with the traditional view. See hypothesis 2.

INTRODUCTION

Further, I found there is very strong evidence that ministers today are more inclined to firmly reject the traditional view than UK evangelicals in 2010.[10] These ministers are more polarized in their views than evangelicals in 2010. This is not caused by a decrease in the proportion of those adhering to the traditional view,[11] but by less uncertainty about beliefs in hell. Only two of the seventeen ministers who responded to the survey answered in the three middle categories of *slightly agree*, *unsure*, and *slightly disagree*.

There is also a significant difference in the ministers' willingness to reject the traditional view compared to the lay evangelicals I surveyed.[12] The proportion of ministers who strongly agree with the traditional view does not differ significantly from lay evangelicals,[13] but ministers were again more polarized in their beliefs than lay members. It is unclear why this is the case, but it could be because ministers have had opportunity to theologically explore the issue more thoroughly than most in their congregations, or that ministry itself attracts more pastorally inclined people who would by nature be more disposed to reject the traditional position. My survey did not investigate the reasons behind people's beliefs, and further research is necessary to find out why this discrepancy exists.

It is not possible to say there is a clear position held by those surveyed. There are firm convictions among those who believe in a traditional view of hell and those who reject this, particularly among ministers. This lack of consensus ought to inform the minister's pastoral response to the person disturbed by the traditional view. Further, the fact that the majority of ministers in my survey reject this view is a warning against a pastoral response that portrays the traditional view as the only evangelical position.

---

10. Appendix: Hypothesis 4.
11. Appendix: Hypothesis 5.
12. Appendix: Hypothesis 6.
13. Appendix: Hypothesis 7.

iii. *The beliefs, assumptions and perceptions provided by the Christian tradition (including the Bible); an evangelical context, an evangelical approach*

In the introduction of *The Nature of Hell*, ACUTE sets out the basis for its ensuing discussion: "as evangelicals [we are] committed to the supreme authority of the Bible."[14] Similarly, Bebbington observes that evangelical churches share a belief that "all spiritual truth is to be found in its [the Bible's] pages."[15] Therefore, given the evangelical context of our scenario, careful attention must be given to analyzing the relevant Bible passages, and this shall be done using Hays's four step hermeneutical approach.

Hays's first step is the *descriptive task* which involves reading the text carefully[16] and evaluating the validity of different interpretations. Following Hays's encouragement to examine all the available evidence for understanding the original meaning of a text, I shall survey extra-canonical texts from Second Temple Judaism including texts from the Apocrypha and the Pseudepigrapha, as well as the writings of the early church fathers, particularly the apostolic fathers.

Hays's second step, the *synthetic task*, involves fitting the text in the canonical order.[17] In contrast to Meeks, who argues that we can only look at the beliefs and practices of individual communities represented by New Testament documents, claiming them to be a "chaotic cacophony of many voices uncoordinated,"[18] Hays sees the necessity of understanding the New Testament as a "complex polyphonic choral composition scored by God and performed by human voices under the direction of the Holy Spirit."[19] Hays's

---

14. ACUTE, *Nature of Hell*, 8.

15. Bebbington, *Evangelicalism*, 12. Although Holmes helpfully observes that Bebbington's identification of evangelical characteristics is UK-centered, biblicism appears to be a characteristic of evangelicalism across the globe. Holmes, "Evangelical Theology," 23–27.

16. Hays, *Moral Vision*, 3.

17. Hays, *Moral Vision*, 4.

18. Hays, *Moral Vision*, 188.

19. Hays, *Moral Vision*, 188.

INTRODUCTION

approach resonates with evangelical sensitivities, and the evangelical context necessitates the pursuit of harmonizing the different voices in the New Testament. I shall largely tackle issues related to the *synthetic task* as they arise in the *descriptive task*. I deal with both tasks in chapters 1 through 7. They occupy the majority of the book, which is fitting giving the evangelical emphasis on the Bible.

The third step is the *hermeneutical task*, which seeks to relate the text to our situation.[20] This task involves appropriating the scriptural teaching as a word spoken to us. The fourth and final of Hays's steps is the *pragmatic task* which is living the text.[21] Whereas the hermeneutical task is "the cognitive or conceptual application of the New Testament's message to our situation,"[22] the pragmatic task is "the enacted application of the New Testament's message in our situation."[23] Shaped by the contribution of the other conversation partners, both the hermeneutical task and the pragmatic task are tackled in my concluding thoughts where I discuss the scope of pastoral theological guidance that can be offered to a person disturbed by the traditional view.

Although I approach this subject with preconceived notions as to what I believe is theologically acceptable, I hope that my evangelical convictions lead me to follow Sprinkle's advice: "As Christians, we must stand on God's inspired word, even if it leads us to conclusions that are different from what we have previously believed."[24]

---

20. Hays, *Moral Vision*, 5.
21. Hays, *Moral Vision*, 7.
22. Hays, *Moral Vision*, 7.
23. Hays, *Moral Vision*, 7.
24. Sprinkle, "Introduction," 15.

CHAPTER 1

Understanding *Géenna* (Hell) Imagery

The Texts: Descriptive and Synthetic Tasks

In chapters 1–7 I analyze six areas which appear to be central to evangelical textual disputes around the fate of the unrighteous.[1]

POWYS OBSERVES THAT GÉENNA (hell) "became a familiar and common expression during first-century CE Palestine."[2] It was "equated with God's final judgement of the wicked"[3] and "takes its name from the Hebrew *Valley of Hinnom*, just south of Jerusalem,"[4] a notorious site of idolatry involving child sacrifice by fire to Molech in the days of Ahaz and Manasseh.[5] The idea that Jesus was

---

1. E.g., ACUTE, *Nature of Hell*; Gundry and Sprinkle, *Four Views*; Edwards and Stott, *Essentials*; Duke, "Eternal Torment"; Gray, "Destroyed Forever." The first five of these areas correspond to the key exegetical issues identified in ACUTE, *Nature of Hell*, 77–87.

2. Powys, *"Hell,"* 276.

3. Lunde, "Heaven and Hell," 310.

4. ACUTE, *Nature of Hell*, 42.

5. For further background to the development of the Valley of Hinnom in the Old Testament as an evil and cursed place see Lusthaus, "History," 180–82; ACUTE, *Nature of Hell*, 42–43.

How Real Is Hell?

referring to a burning rubbish dump is unattested,[6] though N. T. Wright maintains this belief.[7] Verbrugge's suggestion that "*géenna* came to be applied to the eschatological hell in general, even when it was no longer localized at Jerusalem"[8] reflects the understanding of most writers, regardless of their convictions about the fate of the wicked. *Géenna* (hell) does not appear in the LXX (Septuagint), although the "Valley of Hinnom" occurs eleven times. Furthermore, it is widely accepted that New Testament imagery such as "hell of fire," "their worm never dies," and "fire is not quenched" finds its roots in Isa 66:24 despite not explicitly mentioning *géenna* (hell) or the "Valley of Hinnom."

In the New Testament, the word *géenna* (hell) occurs twelve times, eleven of which are in the Synoptics (all spoken by Jesus).[9] Further, the concept is used widely elsewhere in the Synoptics even when the word itself is absent.[10] ACUTE suggests *géenna* (hell) is used in four contexts: to avoid specified sin which leads to *géenna*; to recognize it is better to enter life maimed than to go whole-bodied to *géenna*; to fear the One who has power to throw you into *géenna*; and to describe the condemnation of the Pharisees.[11] As Pawson and Scharen identify, it is spoken mostly as a warning to the disciples, although on two occasions it is used to pronounce judgment against the Scribes and Pharisees.[12]

---

6. There appears to be no early evidence of this, with the first reference occurring a thousand years after Christ. See Burk, "Eternal Conscious Punishment," 23; Stackhouse, "Terminal Punishment," 63; Scharen, "Hell Part 2," 328; Fudge, *Fire That Consumes*, 160–61; and Lusthaus, "History," 184–85. Scharen suggests the idea first appears in the writings of Rabbi David Kimhi around 1200 CE.

7. Wright, *Jesus and the Victory*, 183; Wright, *Surprised*, 189.

8. Verbrugge, *Theological Dictionary*, 239.

9. Matt 5:22, 29, 30; 10:28; 18:9; 23:15, 33. Mark 9:43, 45, 47; Luke 12:5; Jas 3:6.

10. E.g., Matt 3:12; 8:12; 13:42, 50; 22:13; 25:30, 41; Luke 3:17; and 13:28.

11. ACUTE, *Nature of Hell*, 43. Lusthaus agrees, although divides the final category into two. Lusthaus, "History," 176–77.

12. Pawson, *Road to Hell*, 94–98; Scharen, "Hell Part 1," 330.

Understanding Géenna (Hell) Imagery

Géenna (Hell) Imagery as Metaphorical Language

The second edition of *Four Views on Hell* provides a telling illustration of the development of evangelical opinion from 1996 to 2016.[13] In 1996, the book contained a chapter by Walvoord on "The Literal View." By 2016, presumably due to shifting opinions in the evangelical world, this was replaced by a chapter on "Hell and Purgatory." This is a significant movement, particularly if Moore is correct in claiming "the literal interpretation has been the majority view in Christian tradition."[14] Today, unlike twenty-five years ago, there is widespread agreement that *géenna* (hell) imagery is metaphorical, and that literal interpretation is inconsistent with "the conflicting language used in the New Testament to describe *géenna*."[15] For example, the bodies of the wicked burn and at the same time are rotting away with worms and maggots.

Caird's analysis of biblical language leads him to conclude that "we need to allow for some literalist misinterpretation."[16] He notes that "hyperbole and overstatement are very common in Semitic language," and there is "a tendency to think in extremes without qualification, in black and white without intervening shades of grey."[17] *Géenna* (hell) imagery is widely accepted as hyperbolic and rhetorical by those holding differing beliefs about the fate of the unrighteous,[18] and it seems reasonable to conclude with Powys that the primary function of *géenna* (hell) imagery is to motivate rather than to inform.[19]

---

13. Gundry and Crockett, *Four Views*, compared with Gundry and Sprinkle, *Four Views*.

14. Moore, "Hell," 302.

15. Crockett, "Metaphorical View," 59. See also Edwards and Stott, *Essentials*, 149.

16. Caird, *Language and Imagery*, 256.

17. Caird, *Language and Imagery*, 110.

18. E.g., Wright, *Radical Evangelical*, 92; Crockett, "Metaphorical View," 52; Powys, *"Hell,"* 293; MacDonald, *Evangelical Universalist*, 149. Parry published *The Evangelical Universalist* under the pseudonym MacDonald.

19. Powys, *"Hell,"* 293.

How Real Is Hell?

Furthermore, dealing with texts that are apocalyptic in nature, whose pictorial language would much more readily be understood by a first-century CE audience,[20] Duke argues that less weight ought to be given to these texts compared to "the plain sense of well-known biblical texts."[21] In a little while I shall consider the use of apocalyptic language in Second Temple Judaism, but unless there is overwhelming clarity over the meaning of the apocalyptic imagery, Duke's approach seems sensible.

Before doing so, it is noted that N. T. Wright offers a different perspective contending that Jesus utilized *géenna* (hell) imagery to warn Israel about God's forthcoming judgment through Rome if they resisted his message. It was used not "as a general rule, telling them that unless they repented in this life they would burn in the next,"[22] but as a warning of Jerusalem's destruction. Rome "would turn Jerusalem into a hideous, stinking extension of its own smoldering rubbish heap."[23] Therefore, when Jesus said, "But I will warn you whom to fear: fear him who, after he has killed, has authority to cast into hell. Yes, I tell you, fear him!" (Luke 12:5), he was saying they should fear Rome, not God.[24] Wright concludes it is only "by extension and with difficulty that we can extrapolate from [this] . . . to the deeper question of a warning about what may happen after death itself."[25] If Wright is correct, there is significant reason to tread carefully when using *géenna* (hell) imagery as a basis for understanding the eternal fate of the unrighteous.

---

20. As argued by Crockett, "Metaphorical View," 55.

21. Duke, "Eternal Torment," 237–38. His employment of the term *plain sense* appeals to traditionalist sensibilities.

22. Wright, *Surprised*, 188.

23. Wright, *Surprised*, 189. Even if Wright is wrong in identifying *géenna* as a rubbish tip outside Jerusalem, this does not fatally undermine his argument.

24. Wright, *Jesus and the Victory*, 454–55.

25. Wright, *Surprised*, 189.

Understanding Géenna (Hell) Imagery

Tools for Interpretation

In discussing the limitations faced in interpreting *géenna* (hell) imagery, Moore concludes, "At this juncture in redemptive history, we simply do not possess the categories by which to fully understand the mysteries involved, for *now we see but a poor reflection as in a mirror*."[26] However, I feel there are some interpretative tools which can help us to further our exegetical understanding of these passages. I shall now consider four such tools: The Old Testament; the Apocrypha and Pseudepigrapha from the Greek Hasmonean and early Roman Eras; the other books of the New Testament; and the early church fathers.

Tools for Interpretation: The Old Testament

Fudge helpfully argues that the Old Testament should be the first place to turn for understanding *géenna* (hell) imagery. He refutes the notion that "most of the ideas found in the New Testament writings had their origin in the apocalyptic writings"[27] by emphasizing that, while "much of the New Testament *language* shares that background to be sure, its crucial *ideas* regarding final punishment come from the biblical books of the Old Testament, not from these imaginative writings between the Testaments."[28] I shall mention three areas here, and consider a further area below when considering *fire* and *worm* imagery.

First, the Old Testament concept of Sheol underpins the New Testament understanding of Hades.[29] Predominantly, Sheol was used in the Old Testament neutrally as the place for all the dead, although Powys identifies only eight (out of sixty-five occurrences) where it is "construed as a place of condemnation," all of which are in the wisdom literature.[30] Since "the apocryphal usage largely

---

26. Moore, "Hell," 304.
27. Fudge, *Fire That Consumes*, 122, citing C. T. Fritsch.
28. Fudge, *Fire That Consumes*, 122.
29. See Verbrugge, *Theological Dictionary*, 50.
30. Powys, "Hell," 83.

How Real Is Hell?

reflects Old Testament usage,"[31] we can look to the Old Testament to help us interpret the meaning of Hades in the New Testament.

Secondly, the Old Testament concept of the *Day of the Lord* provides a further interpretive tool for understanding *géenna* (hell) imagery. Kreitzer argues that it was "the standard Jewish expectation that all men and women will be held accountable before God for their lives."[32] While this expectation appears to have developed in the period between the Old and New Testaments, the idea is grounded in the Old Testament, and there seems no reason to disagree with Fudge, who claims, "Jesus' teaching on final punishment is, at every point, agreeable to the Old Testament."[33]

Thirdly, there is the idea of ongoing life. Caird writes, "During most of the Old Testament, Hebrew people had no belief in an afterlife. Sheol, like Hades, was the place of the dead."[34] However, the Old Testament sees the emergence of the idea of a resurrection,[35] which lays the foundation for the New Testament concept. Caird states that originally the language of resurrection "was used metaphorically of national recovery from disaster." However, "centuries later, almost certainly under the impact of persecution and martyrdom, the possibility began to be mooted that this language might have a more literal reference."[36] In his extensive work, Powys tracks the changing nature of Israel's post-mortem hope during the Old Testament period, claiming there were six different forms of hope expressed during this period, with most of them persisting in the first century CE.[37] He finds a further form of hope, a seventh form, emerging in the Greek and Hasmonean periods, expressed

---

31. Lunde, "Heaven and Hell," 310.

32. Kreitzer, "Eschatology," 261.

33. Fudge, *Fire That Consumes*, 209.

34. Caird, *Language and Imagery*, 244.

35. Powys identifies four passages: Job 19:25–27; Isa 25:8; Dan 12:1–4; and Isa 26:19. Powys, *"Hell,"* 86–87. Polkinghorne considers only Isa 26:19 and Dan 12:2 point to a positive destiny beyond death. Polkinghorne, *God of Hope*, 56.

36. Caird, *Language and Imagery*, 246.

37. Powys, *"Hell,"* 65–106. A diagram of this progression of hope is provided on page 89.

in Dan 12:2–3,[38] thought to have its origins in Isa 26:19.[39] It anticipates both post-mortem reward and punishment, although, as N. T. Wright argues, there is "little doubt" from the context that this is limited to just the martyrs and their torturers/murderers.[40] Powys argues this develops into an eighth form of hope during the early years of the Roman era, which he labels as "individual post-mortem compensation."[41] He demonstrates that by the time of Jesus, most of these different forms of hope were still prevalent in Second Temple Judaism, including Old Testament beliefs of a restored nation, a blessed life, reward after death, deliverance in the end time, vindication of the righteous and humiliation of the wicked after death.[42] It is not only the emerging eschatological beliefs of the intertestamental period that provide the backdrop of post-mortem hope in Second Temple Judaism, but the Old Testament plays a significant role.

Tools for Interpretation: The Apocrypha and Pseudepigrapha from the Greek, Hasmonean, and Early Roman Eras

Jewish thinking about the fate of the unrighteous expanded considerably in the intertestamental period.[43] "The conception of *Gehenna* within Judaism . . . was far from uniform . . . and spawned a range of views from the first-century CE onwards."[44] There was "no single Jewish view of hell,"[45] and, "as for the final state of the wicked, there is no consistent teaching."[46] According to Lusthaus,

---

38. Powys, *"Hell,"* 107–61.

39. Which in turn Mason argues is rooted in Hos 6:1–2; 13:14. Mason, "Life before and after," 73.

40. Wright, *Resurrection*, 110.

41. Powys, *"Hell,"* 162–210.

42. This is illustrated diagrammatically in Powys, *"Hell,"* 195.

43. See ACUTE, *Nature of Hell*, 40; and Scharen, "Hell Part 1," 329.

44. Lusthaus, "History," 180.

45. Pinnock, "Conditional View," 138.

46. Scharen, "Hell Part 1," 327, citing T. Francis Glasson. Bauckham also writes, "A particular view of the fate of the wicked after death (i.e., the active

the idea of eternal punishment appears to have formed during the intertestamental period.⁴⁷ Despite Parry's claim that "*all* the early Jewish texts outside the New Testament that mention Gehenna were written *after the destruction of Jerusalem in AD 70*,"⁴⁸ this does not mean there was no understanding of the term in Jesus' day. Lusthaus explains that although the author of 1 Enoch does not employ the term *géenna* (hell), possibly because it was written from the perspective of Enoch (Noah's great-grandfather) long before Jerusalem was founded, he "makes clear references to it."⁴⁹ This is significant because the book of 1 Enoch, according to Powys, "provided the conceptual resources for much New Testament and early Rabbinic thought."⁵⁰ Furthermore, Powys's analysis of Palestinian targumim indicates that *géenna* (hell) imagery was widely used in Palestinian synagogues in Second Temple Judaism.⁵¹

Analyzing both the Apocryphal texts and Pseudepigrapha for the use of *géenna* (hell) imagery during the intertestamental period is an enormous and complex task. Fudge attempts this and makes some progress. He concludes that "on the fate of the wicked, this literature [i.e., the Apocrypha] overwhelmingly reflects the teaching of the Old Testament" and that "Judith contains the single explicit reference to conscious everlasting pain."⁵² In a similar vein he contends that "it is also absolutely clear that the Pseudepigraphal literature thoroughly documents the older view of the sinner's total extinction as one Jewish opinion current during the period 200 BCE to 11 CE." He surmises, "We must categorically deny the common assumption that Jesus' hearers all held to everlasting torment."⁵³ However, his analysis has been questioned, with Har-

---

punishment of the wicked begins at death) was far from universally held in the first-century CE." Bauckham, "Early Visions," 357.

47. Lusthaus, "History," 183.
48. Parry, "Universalist View," 118.
49. Lusthaus, "History," 183.
50. Powys, "Hell," 129.
51. Powys, "Hell," 171–84.
52. Fudge, *Fire That Consumes*, 132.
53. Fudge, *Fire That Consumes*, 154.

mon criticizing his "inadequate use of intertestamental literature in interpreting the terms and words used in the New Testament."[54]

A more thorough exegesis of the Apocrypha and the Pseudepigrapha appears to be carried out by Powys. Like Fudge, he finds there is "little evidence (Judith 16:17 being the exception) of an expectation of endless torment for the unrighteous in Greek and Hasmonean Eras"[55] and that the expected punishment for the unrighteous was either shameful death or shameful destruction beyond death.[56] His analysis of the Pseudepigrapha during the early years of Roman rule has led him to conclude that "the ultimate fate of the unrighteous continued to be understood predominantly in terms of destruction."[57] He claims that Palestinian targumim "reflect the regular *theological diet* of ordinary Palestinian Jews as they participated week by week in synagogue services," and discovers four phrases used repeatedly in the targumim that are relevant to this study: *The World to Come, Reward and Punishment, Hell and Gan Eden,* and *Judgment.* He argues that from the middle of the first century BCE the dominant hope of Palestinian Judaism had moved from a hope for the nation (for Zion and a political solution) to a hope based on individual piety and individual destiny.[58] He further suggests this is challenged by Jesus and supplanted by a new form of hope which he terms *New Testament Hope,*[59] defined to be a theocentric hope founded on the anticipation of the full establishment of the kingdom of God by Christ at the parousia, one aspect of which is the resurrection of believers to immortal life.[60]

It is difficult to assess the value of Powys's contribution, particularly in relation to his work on the Pseudepigrapha and Palestinian targumim as the area is specialized and I have found no

---

54. This is Gray's summary of Harmon's criticism. Gray, "Destroyed Forever," 17.
55. Powys, *"Hell,"* 142.
56. Powys, *"Hell,"* 141.
57. Powys, *"Hell,"* 171.
58. Powys, *"Hell,"* 195.
59. Powys, *"Hell,"* 211–70.
60. Powys, *"Hell,"* 256.

reviews. Thiselton utilizes Powys's work extensively in a chapter on hell in *Life after Death*,[61] Powys is quoted several times in ACUTE, and Gray writes that "Powys's material may in fact be the most able defense of annihilationism thus far," although he feels that "even his extensive investigation leaves questions unanswered concerning the interpretation of specific texts."[62] Nonetheless, there appears enough evidence in his work to verify that *géenna* (hell) imagery was not used consistently to depict eternal conscious suffering at the time of Jesus.

Tools for Interpretation: The New Testament

As mentioned earlier, *géenna* (hell) imagery appears almost exclusively within the Synoptic Gospels in the New Testament. Johannine writings, except Revelation, do not use it. As ACUTE observes, "John's gospel and letters differ noticeably from the Synoptic gospels in that they contain no reference to *géenna* (hell), Hades, torment, fire, etc. Instead, they portray the fate of unbelievers in terms of *perishing, death* and *condemnation/judgement*."[63] Similarly, in the book of Acts, divine judgment is sometimes mentioned, but no detail is given.[64] "Resurrection and salvation are central to the apostles' preaching, but not *géenna* (hell)."[65] Neither does *géenna* (hell) make an appearance in the Pauline corpus. Paul talks often of the coming *krima* (judgment), of God's *orgē* (wrath), and describes those bound for *katakrima* (condemnation) as *apollumi* (perishing) and headed for *apóleia* (destruction). I shall look at this language later, but it is sufficient at this point to note, as Duke writes, "Paul never speaks of eternal torment."[66] Hebrews refers to

---

61. Thiselton, *Life After*, 145–65. However, he does not refer to Powys's work on the Pseudepigrapha and targumim.

62. Gray, "Destroyed Forever," 17.

63. ACUTE, *Nature of Hell*, 47.

64. E.g., Acts 2:24; 10:42; 11:18; and 24:25.

65. ACUTE, *Nature of Hell*, 48.

66. Duke, "Eternal Torment," 239.

Understanding Géenna (Hell) Imagery

the fate of those who fall away from Christ as destruction,[67] but Heb 10:27 states that for those who deliberately keep on sinning there is only a "fearful expectation of judgement and of raging fire that will consume the enemies of God." This mention of *fire* is a rare appearance of *géenna* (hell) imagery outside the Synoptics and Revelation. Another appearance occurs in Jude 7 where Sodom and Gomorrah are described as "an example of those who suffer the punishment [*diké*] of eternal fire," which I shall consider later. Jude closes his letter by returning to the image as he talks about how we must "save others by snatching them from the fire."[68] A final use of *géenna* (hell) imagery is found in Jas 3:6, which says of the tongue that "it corrupts the whole body, sets the whole course of one's life on fire, and is itself set on fire by hell." There are no further references to *géenna* (hell) imagery in James. Instead, he talks about *apollumi* (perishing)[69] and *thanatos* (death).[70]

While there are lots of images in 2 Peter about the coming judgment of the wicked, including talk of *kolazó* (punishing),[71] *apóleia* (destruction),[72] *apollumi* (perishing),[73] and the phrase *blackest darkness is reserved for them*,[74] *géenna* (hell) imagery is not employed. Likewise, there is no mention in 1 Peter, but there is a warning that pagans "will have to give account to him who is ready to judge the living and the dead."[75]

In contrast, Revelation employs the idea of fire for judgment. Anyone whose name is not written in the book of life is thrown into "the lake of fire,"[76] which the author explains is the second

---

67. Heb 6:4–8. This compares believers to unproductive land that "in the end will be burned."
68. Jude 23.
69. Jas 4:12.
70. Jas 1:15.
71. 2 Pet 2:9. This verb has the same root as the noun in Matt 25:46.
72. 2 Pet 3:7.
73. 2 Pet 3:9.
74. 2 Pet 2:17.
75. 1 Pet 4:5.
76. Rev 20:14.

thanatos (death). The destiny of sinners is "the fiery lake of burning sulfur."[77] Other imagery is used alongside *géenna* (hell) imagery to designate the eternal fate of the wicked. "The second death"[78] is the most common, while *diaphtheiró* (destroy)[79] and the idea of being excluded by being "outside"[80] are also mentioned and shall be discussed later. The presence of such varied images in the same book warns against the danger of over-pressing a literal interpretation of any single metaphor since some are mutually exclusive (such as "being in the fiery lake" and "being destroyed").

The lack of *géenna* (hell) imagery in large parts of the New Testament means that either the message it conveyed was not felt relevant to other communities,[81] or that authors found alternative language to express the ideas being conveyed through the metaphor.[82] I suspect the latter is true. Following Duke, it seems most sensible to interpret the more metaphorical and symbolic language of *géenna* (hell) imagery in the Synoptics in the light of plain-language terms used to describe the fate of the unrighteous found elsewhere, rather than the other way around.[83]

Tools for Interpretation: The Early Church Fathers

According to Shogren, "If the extant literature is any indication, then an overwhelming majority within the ancient church were persuaded that damnation leads to everlasting, conscious suffering."[84] Crockett concurs with Shogren and concludes, "The testimony in the first half of the second-century CE is consistent concerning the testimony of the wicked. During the time of the

---

77. Rev 21:8.
78. Rev 2:11; 20:6, 14; 21:8.
79. Rev 11:18.
80. Rev 22:15.
81. Such as N. T. Wright's interpretation.
82. Fudge observes that Paul uses stock words from philosophers and others of his day. Fudge, *Fire That Consumes*, 267–68.
83. Duke, "Eternal Torment," 238.
84. Shogren, "Hell, Abyss," 461.

Understanding Géenna (Hell) Imagery

early apostolic fathers, Christians believed hell would be a place of eternal, conscious punishment."[85] However, a careful analysis of the six texts used by Crockett to illustrate his argument demonstrates it is not as clear cut as he suggests.

His first example is from Ignatius of Antioch's *Letter to the Ephesians* 16:2, which reads, "Such a one shall go in his foulness to the unquenchable fire."[86] "The unquenchable fire" merely repeats *géenna* (hell) imagery found in the Synoptics[87] and there is no reason to presume this is more than a reiteration of Jesus' teaching.

Secondly, he quotes Ignatius's Epistle to Diognetus 10:7–8: "when you fear the death which is real, which is kept for those that shall be condemned to the everlasting fire, which shall punish up to the end those that were delivered to it. Then you will marvel at those who endure for the sake of righteousness the fire which is for a season."[88] The language again echoes Jesus' *géenna* (hell) imagery. I shall discuss the meaning of *aiōnios* (everlasting) later. The use of *kolazó* (punish) along with *aiōnios* (everlasting) strongly resembles Matt 25:46.

His third example from 2 Clement 6:7 reads, "Nothing shall rescue us from eternal punishment, if we neglect his commandments."[89] This uses the term *aiōnios kolasis* (eternal punishment) which again echoes Jesus' words in Matt 25:46.

Crockett's fourth example, from 2 Clement 17:7, provides the strongest evidence in support of his argument: "when they see those who have done amiss, and denied Jesus by word or deed, are punished with terrible torture in unquenchable fire . . . ."[90] Clement supplements the *géenna* (hell) image of unquenchable fire by adding they will be "punished with terrible torture." Here, fire's purpose is to inflict torture. I shall argue later this image was one of a range of its symbolic meanings at the time of Jesus. The

---

85. Crockett, "Metaphorical View," 65.
86. As cited in Crockett, "Metaphorical View," 65.
87. Mark 9:43.
88. As cited in Crockett, "Metaphorical View," 65.
89. As cited in Crockett, "Metaphorical View," 65.
90. As cited in Crockett, "Metaphorical View," 65.

How Real Is Hell?

noun *basanos* (torture) is used only three times in the New Testament, once for the physical afflictions of sick people healed by Jesus (Matt 4:24), and twice for the suffering of the rich man in the story of the rich man and Lazarus (Luke 16:23, 28) where the torment is caused by fire. Its associated verb *basanizó* and noun *basanismos* are used several times each in Revelation,[91] but not to describe everlasting punishment for the unrighteous, rather the everlasting fate of the devil, the beast, and the false prophet.[92] It is unclear whether Clement is clarifying or extending *géenna* (hell) imagery. It is also noted that he says nothing about the duration of this punishment.

Crockett's fifth and sixth examples both come from the Martyrdom of Polycarp. Chapter 2:3 reads, "And the fire of their cruel torturers had no heat for them, for they set before their eyes an escape from the fire which is everlasting and is never quenched."[93] The use of "fire which is everlasting and is never quenched" again reflects language used by Jesus, without elaboration. Chapter 11:2 says, "You threaten with the fire that burns for a time, and is quickly quenched, for you do not know the fire which awaits the wicked in the judgement to come and in everlasting punishment."[94] The "fire which awaits" the ungodly is described once again in terms identical to those used by Jesus: *krisis* (judgment) and *aiōnios kolasis* (eternal punishment).

With the possible exception of 2 Clement 17:7, it appears from Crockett's examples that the apostolic fathers merely reiterate Jesus' use of *géenna* (hell) imagery without adding to it. They only support Crockett's conclusion if Jesus uses *géenna* (hell) imagery and the term *aiōnios kolasis* (eternal punishment) to convey eternal conscious suffering. Second Clement 17:7 appears to go

---

91. The verb *basanizó* is used in Rev 9:5; 11:10; 12:2; 14:10; 20:10. The noun *basanismos* is used in Rev 9:5 (twice); 14:11; 18:7, 10, 15. See Verbrugge, *Theological Dictionary*, 207–8.

92. Rev 20:10.

93. As cited in Crockett, "Metaphorical View," 65.

94. As cited in Crockett, "Metaphorical View," 65–66.

further and may indicate an idea of ongoing, though not necessarily everlasting, pain.

A similar argument can be levied against Shogren. The texts he uses in support of the traditional view (Epistle of Barnabas 10:1; Ignatius *To the Ephesians* 16:1-2; 2 Clement 5:4; Epistle to Diognetus 10:7; Martyrdom of Polycarp 11:2 and 2:3; Hermas: Visions 3.7.2; Hermas: Parables 6.2.4 and 9.31.2)[95] also use language replicating the teachings of Jesus. On the whole, the apostolic fathers do not extend or elaborate on the biblical imagery, despite the fact that by the late first century into the second century CE, Jewish apocalyptic literature has moved in this direction and often contains vivid descriptions of the everlasting torments of the wicked.[96]

According to ACUTE, "One of the earliest surviving accounts of the view that unbelievers will suffer eternal conscious punishment in hell can be found in the writings of the North African Church father Tertullian (around 160 to 220 CE)."[97] Tertullian argues against the idea of annihilation and insists that "the fire of hell is eternal—expressly announced as an everlasting penalty."[98] Evidence of similar teaching is found in Lactantius (around 240-320 CE), Basil of Caesarea (around 330-379 CE), Jerome (around 342-420 CE), Cyril of Jerusalem (around 315-386 CE), John Chrysostom (around 347-407 CE), and most significant of all, Augustine of Hippo (354-430 CE).[99] Justin Martyr (around 100-165

---

95. Shogren, "Hell, Abyss," 460-61. Shogren also quotes Ignatius to the Philadelphians 3:3, but this reference did not seem correct, and Shepherd Parables 9.31.2, which is in Latin.

96. E.g., 2 Enoch 10:1-6; 40:12; 4 Macc 9:9; 10:12; 13:15; 4 Ezra 7:36 and 38. Fourth Ezra describes the "pit of torment" (v. 36) and the "fire of torments" (v. 38). Stone dates 4 Ezra after the destruction of Jerusalem. Stone, *Fourth Ezra*, 10. See Bauckham, "Early Visions," for discussion as to the development of imagery around the fate of the unrighteous in the Jewish cosmic tours of hell from third century BCE to fourth century CE. Fudge also recounts some of the imagery around the eternal conscious suffering of the wicked employed in Jewish literature in the first and second centuries CE. Fudge, *Fire That Consumes*, 145-53.

97. ACUTE, *Nature of Hell*, 53.

98. ACUTE, *Nature of Hell*, 53.

99. ACUTE, *Nature of Hell*, 54-56.

CE) is also cited as an early advocate for the traditional view,[100] and some of his writings appear to indicate this.[101] However, elsewhere, he appears to support the idea of conditional immortality.[102]

From this brief survey it appears that a systematic belief in eternal conscious suffering began to emerge by the late second century CE, although it is possible that it was present in the middle second century CE. Before this, the apostolic fathers conveyed ideas related to the fate of the unrighteous in terms very close to the New Testament and regularly employed similar *géenna* (hell) imagery to Jesus. I suggest Shogren's conclusion, that "[the] canon of Scripture refrained from the elaborate descriptions of hell found in other literature,"[103] is also true of the apostolic fathers and the earliest church fathers. Overwhelmingly, their message is a reiteration of the message of Jesus and the rest of the New Testament.

Platonism, with its belief in the immortality of the soul, is cited by conditionalists to explain the emergence of understanding *géenna* (hell) as a place of everlasting punishment.[104] ACUTE says, "The precise extent of Platonic influence on the church fathers continues to be debated. Even so, most traditionalists have been willing to concede that some did indeed co-opt Platonic anthropology."[105]

I have found there appears to be little evidence from the writings of the early church fathers that such influence was present

---

100. Shogren, "Hell, Abyss," 461.

101. In Justin Martyr's *First Apology* 52, the punishment and sensation of the wicked is linked with "their worm shall not rest and their fire shall not be quenched."

102. In Justin Martyr's *Dialogue with Trypho* 5:1 he says the wicked are duly "punished" and must then "die." For further details see ACUTE, *Nature of Hell*, 61; Fudge, *Fire That Consumes*, 322–27.

103. Shogren, "Hell, Abyss," 459.

104. E.g., Stott pertains to this in Edwards and Stott, *Essentials*, 316.

105. ACUTE, *Nature of Hell*, 98. Bauckham questions whether the Jewish tours of hell developed because of Greek influence as is widely assumed. He thinks the development of the literature may be rooted in Jewish apocalyptic literature. Could it be that Jewish apocalyptic literature influenced the early church fathers? Bauckham, "Early Visions," 376.

Understanding Géenna (Hell) Imagery

before the mid to late second century CE, and therefore later Platonic influence seems to provide a plausible explanation.

Fire and Worm Imagery

The text that employs the starkest fire and worm imagery is Mark 9:48: "The worm that eats them do not die, and the fire is not quenched."[106] For some, this verse is convincing evidence of eternal conscious punishment,[107] and ACUTE claims this is a *key* text that conditionalists need to explain.[108]

In order to understand this text I shall first analyze the range of meaning of *pur* (fire) imagery. In his liberal-evangelical dialogue with Edwards thirty years ago, Stott argues, "It is doubtless because we have all had experience of the acute pain of being burned, that fire is associated in our minds with *conscious torment*. But the main function of fire is not to cause pain, but to secure destruction, as all the world's incinerators bear witness."[109] In contrast, Peterson claims, "The abundant scriptural testimony [is] that hellfire speaks of the pain of the wicked, not their consumption."[110] How is the word used in other parts of Scripture and the intertestamental literature?

The word *pur* (fire) and its cognates are used 350 times in the LXX (Septuagint) with a variety of purposes.[111] Fire destroys (e.g., Deut 13:16; Judg 20:48), sometimes in order to purify the community (e.g., Lev 13:52, 55; Num 31:23). It is regularly associated with divine judgment (e.g., Lev 10:2; Num 11:1; Mal 4:1), although it is difficult, perhaps with the exception of Isa 66:24 which I will

---

106. Several translations use "their worm," such as ESV, NKJV, NASB, and ERV.

107. E.g., Carson, Hoekema, Blanchard, and Head in ACUTE, *Nature of Hell*, 78; Shogren, "Hell, Abyss," 461; Lunde, "Heaven and Hell," 311; Burk, "Eternal Conscious Punishment," 24.

108. ACUTE, *Nature of Hell*, 78.

109. Edwards and Stott, *Essentials*, 316.

110. Peterson, *Hell on Trial*, 167.

111. Verbrugge, *Theological Dictionary*, 1121–22.

consider below, to find support for the idea that destruction could involve ongoing conscious suffering. More positively, fire is used as a sign to indicate Yahweh's grace and acceptance (e.g., Lev 9:23–24; 1 Chr 21:26), and to depict Yahweh's holiness and glory (e.g., Exod 19:18; Ezek 1:27–28). It is also used on at least one occasion as a metaphor for refining (Isa 6:6). In the intertestamental literature, there appears to be some evidence, although it is far from extensive, that fire was a means of inflicting punishment. Judith 16:17 and 4 Ezra 7:38 are the clearest passages suggesting this, although some claim support from 1 Enoch 91:9 and 100:9.

This leads me to conclude that by the first century CE, although fire could depict ongoing punishment, this was just one of a wide range of meanings, and there is little evidence this was the primary understanding of the metaphor. Fernando's claim that "the Jewish writers of the intertestamental period used fire in the sense of torment when referring to punishment"[112] fails to acknowledge this is just one of many meanings of fire imagery, and there are only a few occasions in the Old Testament and intertestamental literature where it is used to depict torment.[113] It is too much to claim that Second Temple Judaism would have assumed this interpretation.

The New Testament literature employs fire imagery in a similar way. It is closely related to divine judgment (e.g., Matt 3:10; John 15:6; Jude 7) but is also used as an indication of God's presence or glory (e.g., Acts 2:3; Rev 1:14). Universalists find support in 1 Pet 1:7 for the idea of fire as a means of purification, although this metaphor is not used widely in the New Testament. Traditionalists, arguing that fire imagery is routinely employed to represent eternal conscious suffering for the unrighteous, find support in Luke 16:23–24, Rev 14:10 and 20:10, all of which will be discussed later. Finally, to complete the picture, fire imagery is also used for sexual desire (1 Cor 7:9) and indignation over another's hurt (2 Cor 11:29).[114]

112. Fernando, *Crucial Questions*, 39.
113. Fernando cites only one such example: Judith 16:17.
114. Verbrugge, *Theological Dictionary*, 1122–23.

Understanding Géenna (Hell) Imagery

As with the Old Testament and intertestamental literature, there are not many texts in the New Testament that link fire with torment. Likewise, fire is only linked to purification in both the Old and New Testaments on rare occasions. I shall continue to examine the use of this imagery in Scripture, particularly the New Testament, but for now I conclude that Peterson's claim that "fire speaks of the pain of the wicked, not their consumption" is far from established,[115] as is the universalist idea that fire in *géenna* (hell) imagery predominantly signifies purification.

Secondly, I want to consider the use of *skólex* (worm) imagery. Blanchard suggests that the use of "their" to modify "worm" in Mark 9:44–48 refers to the sinner's conscience[116] and concludes the verse indicates eternal conscious punishment. Burk concurs but concedes the original idea behind worm imagery in Isa 66:24 was to convey disgrace. The corpses of those destroyed would be left exposed after their defeat and thus humiliated.[117] Others follow this line of thought and conclude its purpose is to indicate a shaming of God's enemies, and not an idea of ongoing punishment.[118] The worm is everlasting, but the punishment is not. Several suggest that the image from Isaiah refers to a worm which devours what is already dead,[119] such as Stackhouse, who writes, "They are consuming corpses, not zombies,"[120] and Duke, who argues, "First-century CE Jewish and Christian audiences . . . recognized *géenna* (hell) as a final judgement image of a place where bodies would be left to decay unburied."[121]

---

115. Peterson, *Hell on Trial*, 167.

116. Gray, "Destroyed Forever," 15, citing John Blanchard. The word *their* is used in several translations such as ESV, NKJV, NASB, and ERV.

117. Burk, "Eternal Conscious Punishment," 22–24.

118. Argued by Stott in Edwards and Stott, *Essentials*, 317; Fudge, *Fire That Consumes*, 185; Stackhouse, "Terminal Punishment," 46; Pinnock, "Conditional View," 155; Duke, "Eternal Torment," 255.

119. E.g., Fudge, *Fire That Consumes*, 185; Pinnock, "Conditional View," 155.

120. Stackhouse, "Terminal Punishment," 46.

121. Duke, "Eternal Torment," 255.

I have found no evidence offered by traditionalists to support their claim that the meaning of *skólēx* (worm) had changed by the time of Second Temple Judaism from its use in Isaiah. Therefore, I feel it is safest to assume the term is employed in Mark 9:44–48 to indicate the shame and contempt on the unrighteous that will accompany the coming judgment. Further, I concur with ACUTE's note of caution that this verse (along with the other *géenna* [hell] verses) does not "specifically mention" the duration of *géenna* (hell).

Weeping and Gnashing of Teeth

Alongside *géenna* (hell) imagery, the phrase *weeping and gnashing of teeth* is used regularly by Jesus in the Synoptics, particularly in Matthew. Erdey and Smith's survey reveals that although repeated in the same form seven times in the New Testament,[122] there are no other examples of its use in ancient literature.[123] While they analyze the words individually, they contend it is more significant to consider the phrase as a whole,[124] noting that both *klauthmos* (weeping) and *brugmos* (gnashing) are noisy words used to depict "the severity of judgement in extremely sobering language."[125] They say that the words convey both emotional and physical pain[126] and argue that even if the unrighteous are annihilated, "the process is torture and excruciating."[127] Fernando, Packer, Grudem, and Burk argue the term indicates conscious suffering.[128] However, Duke contends that the texts "never identify the recipients of judgement as the ones wailing,"[129] which leads him to suggest it may be a

122. Matt 8:12; 13:42, 50; 22:13; 24:51; 25:30; and Luke 13:28.
123. Erdey and Smith, "'Weeping and Gnashing,'" 142.
124. Erdey and Smith, "'Weeping and Gnashing,'" 143–44.
125. Erdey and Smith, "'Weeping and Gnashing,'" 165.
126. Erdey and Smith, "'Weeping and Gnashing,'" 169.
127. Erdey and Smith, "'Weeping and Gnashing,'" 159.
128. Fernando, *Crucial Questions*, 32; Packer, "Evangelical Annihilationism," 5; Grudem, *Systematic Theology*, 1149; Burk, "Eternal Conscious Punishment," 39.
129. Duke, "Eternal Torment," 256.

Understanding Géenna (Hell) Imagery

"formulaic funerary expression," which would serve as "a cultural signal of death." As he is unable to offer any supporting external evidence, this is an interesting but unproven hypothesis.[130] Similar to *géenna* (hell) imagery, we should proceed with caution in forcing literal interpretations of this metaphorical phrase, and Thiselton's suggestion it is "a powerful image of remorse"[131] is possibly as much as is appropriate to conclude.

Different Hells?

Finally in this section, I want to consider an issue of synthesis. Milikowsky questions whether Matthew's *géenna* (hell) is different from Luke's. Whereas Matthew depicts a corporeal *géenna* (hell) following a general resurrection and judgment, Luke has an immediate post-mortem *géenna* (hell), with only the righteous experiencing resurrection.[132] However, such differences in doctrinal matters do not sit well with evangelicals, and it is unsurprising to see Scharen's response, who declares, "There is not much evidence" for the hypothesis.[133] He does not expound his reasons, but I can see weaknesses to Milikowsky's argument. Milikowsky bases his hypothesis on the difference in the parallel passages of Matt 10:28 and Luke 12:5.[134] Two supporting arguments he uses are from further passages in Luke: the story of the rich man and Lazarus in Luke 16:19–31 and Jesus' declaration to the dying thief in Luke 23:43, "Today you will be with me in Paradise."[135] His conflation of Hades with *géenna* (hell) in Luke 16:19–31 is contested,[136] as is

---

130. Duke, "Eternal Torment," 256–57.

131. Thiselton, *Life After*, 152–53.

132. Milikowsky, "Retribution," 238–44. Lusthaus concurs. Lusthaus, "History," 176–77.

133. Scharen, "Hell Part 2," 463.

134. Milikowsky, "Retribution," 242.

135. Milikowsky, "Retribution," 242–43.

136. See also Nolland, *Luke 9:21—18:34*, 557 and 829; Green, *Gospel of Luke*, 607; Morris, *Luke*, 270.

the idea the word *paradise* refers to the man's eternal destiny.[137] If Milikowsky's reading of these two supporting passages is wrong, his argument that Matthew's *géenna* (hell) is different from Luke's is considerably weakened, and it may be safer to account for the differences in Matt 10:28 and Luke 12:5 by the fact that Luke writes to a predominantly gentile audience whereas Matthew addresses a predominantly Jewish audience.

Some Conclusions about the Metaphor of *Géenna* (Hell) and Associated Imagery

The evidence found to support an interpretation of *géenna* (hell) imagery in terms of eternal conscious suffering is slight. I have argued that hyperbole and overstatement are common in Semitic languages, and that images often conflict with each other. Their purpose is rhetorical, and it is wise not to press the imagery too literally.

Understanding *géenna* (hell) imagery can be aided by careful consideration of how it is used elsewhere. Alongside the Apocrypha, Pseudepigrapha and Palestinian targumim, the Old Testament should not be discounted and is central in understanding New Testament eschatological expectations. It has far more to contribute than just isolated *resurrection* texts. *Géenna* (hell) imagery appears to be rooted in Isa 66:24. I have found little reason to move away from Old Testament usage of *skóléx* (worm) to depict shame and dishonor. The purpose of *pur* (fire) in Isa 66:24 is to destroy, although there is some evidence that *pur* (fire) imagery was known as a symbol of ongoing punishment in Second Temple Judaism. However, *pur* (fire) imagery was used regularly to depict several different ideas, including destruction and cleansing. Further, there is minimal evidence from contemporary literature to

---

137. Powys argues that the term is used metaphorically to suggest the man would be part of God's coming kingdom. Powys, *"Hell,"* 257. Nolland says it refers to "[a] pleasant resting place of some of the privileged dead prior to the great day of resurrection." Nolland, *Luke 18:35—24:53*, 1153.

suggest people would have been strongly predisposed to interpret *géenna* (hell) imagery in terms of eternal conscious suffering.

Géenna (hell) imagery is largely found in the Synoptics and Revelation.[138] Notably, it is absent from many New Testament books including Pauline and other Johannine writings. I suggest these books convey the same message as *géenna* (hell) imagery, but do so in different, seemingly more straightforward terms, and, following Duke, I am inclined to interpret the metaphorical language of *géenna* (hell) imagery in the light of more plain teaching, and not vice versa.

The early church fathers up until the mid- and possibly late second century CE rarely go beyond the words used by Jesus and the apostles in teaching about the fate of the unrighteous, despite the increase in graphic portrayals of eternal torments of the wicked in Jewish writings of the time, particularly after the destruction of Jerusalem. It is not until the end of the second century CE that we see the emergence of a systemized belief in eternal conscious suffering of the unrighteous among the church fathers.

---

138. With the only other references in Hebrews (once) and Jude (twice).

CHAPTER 2

Eternal Punishment and the Age to Come

THERE IS MUCH DEBATE as to the meaning of the adjective *aiōnios* (eternal) used to modify *kolasis* (punishment) at the end of the parable of the sheep and goats (Matt 25:46): "Then they will go away to eternal punishment, but the righteous to eternal life." Scharen claims, "There is little doubt that contextually *aiōnios* means eternal, endless or forever."[1] Other traditionalists contend, "Since it is clear that Jesus offers genuinely everlasting, unending life to those who follow him, surely the logic goes, he must be warning of a retribution which will be correspondingly everlasting and unending for those who refuse him."[2] In contrast, conditionalists argue it refers to eternal consequences rather than eternal duration and suggest it is a statement of irreversibility.[3] Universalists, who see it as a punishment of the *age to come*, argue that it does not tell us

---

1. Scharen, "Hell Part 1," 336. This appears to be the standard traditionalist view (e.g., Lunde, "Heaven and Hell," 311; Burk, "Eternal Conscious Punishment," 28; Fernando, *Crucial Questions*, 47).

2. ACUTE, *Nature of Hell*, 79.

3. E.g., Cho, "Doctrine," 18, citing John Wenham; Fudge, *Fire That Consumes*, 194–96, 198; Gray, "Destroyed Forever," 15, citing Stephen Travis; Powys, "Hell," 291–93.

that the punishment will last forever[4] and understand the purpose of *kolasis* (punishment) is to purify us from our sin.[5]

First, I shall consider areas where there is common ground. It is widely accepted that much of the New Testament works within a framework of history that is divided into two ages: the *present age* and *an age to come*.[6] This is in agreement with much Jewish apocalyptic literature.[7] While details vary across the New Testament writings, Matthew is thought to operate very strongly within this framework.[8]

There is also some consensus around the idea that *eternal life* is primarily about the quality of life, and not just the quantity.[9] Verbrugge claims that *eternal life* should be understood in the Old Testament "primarily as life that belongs to God," and that from the time of Daniel onward it is "an expression of the longed-for eschatological blessings of salvation."[10] Martin-Achard claims that "for all of them (i.e., the great people of faith among the Israelites), the heart of the matter is not so much the question of everlasting life, as that of life with God."[11] Similarly, Pawson, speaking about the parable, says helpfully, "it is not just where the two groups ended up but who they ended up with that is the more important feature."[12] Pawson adds that, "at the very least, this means that the verdicts are final, without appeal or parole for the guilty and without change or cancellation for the acquitted," a statement

---

4. MacDonald, *Evangelical Universalist*, 148.

5. Bird, "Evaluating," 91, citing Thomas Talbott.

6. E.g., Packer, "Evangelical Annihilationism," 4; Kreitzer, "Eschatology," 255; Fudge, *Fire That Consumes*, 180; Travis, *Christian Hope*, 47.

7. See Verbrugge, *Theological Dictionary*, 73; Caird, *Language and Imagery*, 244; Scharen, "Hell Part 1," 336, citing Hermann Sasse.

8. See Travis, *Christian Hope*, 47, citing James D. G. Dunn; Verbrugge, *Theological Dictionary*, 74.

9. Conditionalists Stackhouse and Fudge, and traditionalist Fernando, say it does. See Stackhouse, "Terminal Punishment," 67; Fudge, *Fire That Consumes*, 49; and Fernando, *Crucial Questions*, 45–46.

10. Verbrugge, *Theological Dictionary*, 75.

11. Mason, "Life before and After," 81, citing Robert Martin-Achard.

12. Pawson, *Road to Hell*, 113.

with which many conditionalists agree. However, he concludes the verse refers to everlasting punishment, not because of what it says itself, but on the basis of Rev 20:10.[13] Fernando reaches a similar conclusion to Pawson, but argues that *aiōnios* (eternal) is referring to quantity here, and not quality as it does elsewhere, largely because it should parallel everlasting life in duration.[14] Hughes dismisses this argument, saying that "because *life* and *death* are radically antithetical to each other, the qualifying adjective *eternal* or *everlasting* [*aiōnios*] needs to be understood in a manner appropriate to each respectively. Everlasting life is existence that continues without end, and everlasting death is destruction without end, that is, destruction without recall, the destruction of obliteration."[15]

A further idea is proposed by N. T. Wright, who feels there are several passages "which appear to speak unambiguously of a continuing state for those who have rejected the worship of the true God and the way of humanness which follows it."[16] His solution, which he acknowledges is speculative, is to suggest the unrighteous continue in existence, but in an ex-human state, no longer reflecting the image of God.[17] He vehemently rejects the idea of "an everlasting torture chamber."[18]

There are two further arguments that are worth discussing before drawing this section to a close. First, several conditionalists point out that *aiōnios* (eternal) modifies several other concepts in the Bible, some of which are about eternal consequences rather than eternal duration.[19] Examples given include *aiōnios hamartéma* (eternal sin) in Mark 3:29; *aiōnios krimatos* (eternal judgment) in Heb 6:2 which Fudge says should be interpreted as a judgment

---

13. Pawson, *Road to Hell*, 114.
14. Fernando, *Crucial Questions*, 46.
15. Hughes, *True Image*, 405, italics original.
16. Wright, *Surprised*, 194.
17. Wright, *Surprised*, 195.
18. Wright, *Surprised*, 194.
19. Fudge, *Fire That Consumes*, 45–47, 274; Stackhouse, "Terminal Punishment," 68; Morgan, "Application," 30, citing John Wenham.

Eternal Punishment and the Age to Come

that belongs to the age to come;[20] *aiōnios lutrósis* (eternal redemption) in Heb 9:12 which, it is argued by Fudge, cannot be ongoing because redemption is once for all through the work of Christ;[21] and *aiōnios olethros* (eternal destruction) in 2 Thess 1:9, although this argument is rejected by traditionalists who argue that destruction can be ongoing. The word *kolasis* (punishment) in Matt 25:46, is a *sis* noun, which means it is about process, making the noun happen. *Kolasis* (punishment) is most naturally understood as the process of being punished. This contrasts with most of the other *eternal* examples given above, none of which are *sis* nouns except for *lutrósis* (redemption), which should also be thought of as the process of being redeemed. This appears to favor an interpretation of ongoing punishment, or even the idea of ongoing correction.

Secondly, some scholars question the use of the term *punishment* for *kolasis*. Rob Bell writes, "The word *kolazó* is a term from horticulture . . . it refers to the pruning and trimming of the branches of a plant so it can flourish."[22] This is strongly rejected by Burk, who says that Bell's argument is "completely undermined by the fact that *kolasis* (punishment) never means *correction* or *pruning* anywhere else in the New Testament . . . and in intertestamental literature . . . it often refers to the penalty imposed for wrongdoing (2 Maccabees 4:38; 3 Maccabees 1:3; 7:10; 4 Maccabees 8:9), but never to correction."[23] *Kolazó* (punishment) and its cognates only occur four times in the New Testament, which weakens Burk's argument, as does the fact that its classical roots lie in the idea of checking growth, pruning, or a formative process through harsher means.[24] The context of most of the references cited by Burk appear to be about retributive punishment rather than corrective punishment, but a couple of verses allow for a corrective purpose. I suggest, therefore, there is a possibility that *kolasis* (punishment) contains the idea of correction, as proposed

20. Fudge, *Fire That Consumes*, 274.
21. Fudge, *Fire That Consumes*, 45.
22. Bell, *Love Wins*, 91–92.
23. Burk, "Eternal Conscious Punishment," 30–31.
24. Liddell and Scott, *Lexicon*, 825.

by universalists, although this is not its usual meaning in Second Temple Judaism.

Some Conclusions about Eternal Punishment and the Age to Come

It is difficult to reach firm conclusions from this section. I have found some support that *kolasis* (punishment) is ongoing, although not necessarily everlasting. The idea that *aiōnios* (eternal) could be understood primarily in terms of quality rather than quantity, as *the age to come*, is appealing, particularly given Matthew's repeated use of two ages. However, the possibility of *kolasis* (punishment) being corrective also has support. None of these exegetical findings are conclusive, and as a result I feel this analysis does not firmly discount traditional, conditional, or universal interpretations, although the traditional interpretation appears to be strongest.

Finally, a note of caution. This verse is the concluding line of a parable and not a discourse on the fate of the wicked. Parables are rhetorical devices whose purpose is to motivate. The thrust of the message is that there is a coming judgment to be avoided at all costs. Remembering Caird's words about the possibility of "literalist misinterpretation" and following Duke's approach to interpret metaphors in the light of more straightforward teaching, I suggest it is best not to rely too heavily on this verse to determine an understanding of the fate of the unrighteous.[25]

---

25. A further example of this is found in Matt 24:45–51 where the parable talks about the master cutting the unfaithful servant to pieces. It is hard to believe this is to be understood literally.

CHAPTER 3

The Language of Destruction, Perishing, and Death

STOTT WRITES, "IT WOULD seem strange, therefore, if people who are said to suffer destruction are in fact not destroyed . . . it is difficult to imagine a perpetually inconclusive process of perishing."[1] Stackhouse expresses a similar sentiment, writing, "The Bible is replete with passages—literally dozens and dozens—that speak of the destiny of the lost as termination, end, disappearance, eradication, annihilation, and vanishing."[2] Similarly, Pinnock argues that "The impression Jesus leaves us with is a strong one: The impenitent wicked can expect to be destroyed by the wrath of God."[3] He continues by claiming, "The apostle Paul creates the same impression." This is the heart of the conditionalist hypothesis, and if we find conditionalists on the defensive in the exegesis of some of the passages we have looked at so far, here we find them very much on the front foot. There is not much variance in the conditional message at this point—terms that talk about destruction and death should be interpreted as meaning destruction and death. The onus lies on traditionalists and universalists to demonstrate otherwise.

---

1. Edwards and Stott, *Essentials*, 316.
2. Stackhouse, "Terminal Punishment," 69.
3. Pinnock, "Conditional View," 146.

How Real Is Hell?

In order to look at the language of death, destruction, and perishing, I shall examine the meaning and use of four words, as well as the New Testament portrayal of Sodom and Gomorrah as an example of the coming judgment.

The verb *apollumi* (perish) and its cognate *apóleia* (destruction) are common words in the New Testament, with the verb occurring ninety times and the noun appearing on eighteen occasions. The verb in the active and transitive means "to kill," whereas in the middle and passive form it usually means "to perish,"[4] although, as Fernando correctly points out, it can also depict "being lost" (Luke uses it eight times in his chapter on "lost" things in Luke 15).[5] Grudem adds that the noun is even used to describe the "waste" of the costly ointment in the anointing at Bethany (Matt 26:8).[6] While the ideas of lostness and waste are within the semantic range of the range of *apollumi* and *apóleia*, these are not regular uses of the terms. Most often the terms convey the idea of irrecoverable lostness or destruction. Surveying all their uses in the New Testament, I have found only a limited number of occurrences (most of which are in Matthew and Luke) where the word seems to refer to anything other than complete loss.[7] This corresponds to Verbrugge, who states, "Usually *apollumi* means ruin, destruction, though occasionally it means waste, squandering."[8] Additionally, he says that their uses by the apostles John and Paul "mean definite destruction for all eternity."[9] Further, I see that the LXX (Septuagint) deploys *apollumi* to describe the cutting off by stoning of those who make child sacrifices to Molech and sorcerers (Lev 20:3, 5, 6). It is also used regularly in intertestamental Jewish

---

4. Verbrugge, 166; Stott in Edwards and Stott, *Essentials*, 315.

5. Luke 15:4, 4, 6, 8, 9, 17, 24, and 32. See Fernando, *Crucial Questions*, 41.

6. Grudem, *Systematic Theology*, 1150.

7. The only verses I found which could be best understood as not referring to something that is completely lost or destroyed are Matt 10:6, 39; 15:24; 18:11; 26:8; Mark 14:4; Luke 15:4, 4, 6, 8, 9, 17, 24, 32; Rom 14:15; 1 Cor 8:11; 2 Pet 3:9; and Rev 18:14. The idea of *destruction* fits better with the other ninety verses.

8. Verbrugge, *Theological Dictionary*, 166.

9. Verbrugge, *Theological Dictionary*, 167.

apocalyptic literature for the eschatological destruction of the world.[10]

Packer's contention that, along with *olethros* (also translated "destruction"), the natural meaning of *apollumi* and *apóleia* is "wrecking,"[11] appears unsupported from both its common Greek usage and from its classical roots.[12]

On the basis of the above analysis, it is difficult to agree with Scharen, who claims there "is no lexicographical evidence it means to annihilate or to pass into non-existence."[13] The historical usage of these terms, as well as the contextual usage, suggests they are normally employed to describe utter destruction or complete loss, and only on rare occasions are they used for lostness or waste.[14] Further, it is noted that, as Thiselton states, "there appears to be no hint of eternal torment, only of destruction."[15]

The word *olethros* (destruction), and its cognates, occur seven times in the New Testament.[16] In contrast to *apollumi* (perishing) and *apóleia* (destruction), Verbrugge states it is only ever used for the destruction of persons.[17] Burk contends that it means completely ruined or a ruinous loss rather than something ceasing to exist.[18] However, this argument does not seem consistent with the way it is used in some passages. For example, 1 Cor 10:10 says, "Do not complain as some of them did, and were destroyed by the destroyer." According to Fee, this refers either to the banning of the Israelites from entering the promised land in Num

---

10. Verbrugge, *Theological Dictionary*, 166.

11. Packer, "Evangelical Annihilationism," 6.

12. Classical Greek meanings include "destroy utterly," "demolish," "lay waste," and "lose utterly." Liddell and Scott, *Lexicon*, 188.

13. Scharen, "Hell Part 2," 460.

14. It appears to me Luke 15 uses these terms to exaggerate the utter lostness of the things, and that recovering them is miraculous.

15. Thiselton, *Life after Death*, 153.

16. Acts 3:23; 1 Cor 5:5; 10:10; 2 Thess 1:9; 5:3; 1 Tim 6:9; and Heb 11:28.

17. Verbrugge, *Theological Dictionary*, 903.

18. Burk, "Eternal Conscious Punishment," 35.

14 or the plague following Korah's rebellion in Num 16.[19] Both accounts depict the destruction of the guilty, not just their ruin. They no longer existed. Furthermore, Heb 11:28 reads, "So that the destroyer of the firstborn would not touch the firstborn of Israel." Once again, it seems improbable to think the firstborn continued to exist in a state of ruinous loss, but rather "the destroyer" had completely destroyed them. From these examples, it appears *olethros* (destruction) is stronger than "ruin" or "ruinous loss," as Burk contends, and can even infer complete and utter destruction, involving a cessation of existence.

As mentioned above, there is little support for Packer's claim that *olethros* (destruction) means "wrecking."[20] It is further noted that, as with *apollumi* (perishing) and *apóleia* (destruction), it does not appear to carry an idea of eternal conscious punishment. I would agree with Burk's conclusion that *olethros* (destruction) provides no hope of restoration,[21] but I suggest this is because the word implies the finality of judgment rather than an idea of eternal conscious suffering.

One significant use of *olethros* (destruction) is found in 2 Thess 1:9: "They will be punished with everlasting destruction [*olethros*] and separated from [*apo*] the presence of the Lord and from the glory of his might." The word *and* between *olethros* (destruction) and *apo* (separated from) in the NIV translation is not in the Greek text but is added by the NIV translators to provide clarification. However, there is discussion as to whether *apo* should be understood as *separated from* (i.e., the punishment involves being *separated from* the Lord) or *coming from* (i.e., the punishment issues from the presence of the Lord). It seems perfectly plausible to translate *apo* as "coming from," as Fudge suggests.[22] Therefore,

---

19. Fee, *1 Corinthians*, 457–58.

20. Classical meanings include "ruin," "destruction," and "death." Liddell and Scott, *Lexicon*, 1040. Verbrugge concurs and says that, in the LXX (Septuagint), "words of this group often carry the meaning of eschatological destruction." Verbrugge, *Theological Dictionary*, 904.

21. Burk, "Eternal Conscious Punishment," 35.

22. For further discussion see Fudge, *Fire That Consumes*, 246–47.

The Language of Destruction, Perishing, and Death

Packer's argument that *apo* should be translated as "shut out from" and his strong conclusion that "by affirming exclusion, rules out the idea that destruction meant extinction"[23] places too heavy a demand on the simple preposition *apo*.

The verse is difficult for universalists, as Parry admits. In agreement with Fudge, he prefers to translate *apo* as "coming from," thus avoiding permanent conscious separation from the Lord.[24] He suggests *aiōnios olethros* (eternal destruction) could be translated "ruin of the coming age" and understands this in a similar vein as "the punishment of the coming age" in Matt 25:46. However, it seems to me that punishment and ruin are quite different ideas, and it is difficult to comprehend what "ruin of the coming age" might encompass without understanding ruin in terms that downplay the severity intrinsic to *olethros* (destruction).

The third word to consider is *phtheirō* and its cognates. The verb means to "destroy, ruin, corrupt, spoil"[25] and occurs nine times, as does its associated noun. The adjective, *phthartos*, meaning "perishable or corruptible," according to Fudge, "is used in a specific contrast between something that passes away (perishes or decays) and something that endures."[26] However, while this may be the case in its six occurrences in the New Testament,[27] we should be cautious about subsequently deducing the verb *phtheirō* suggests annihilation, because the verbal form has a wide range of meanings and does not always convey the idea of destruction, let alone utter destruction.[28] Even the intensified form, *diaphtheirō*, which can mean to destroy utterly, may also mean no more than to thoroughly spoil or corrupt.[29] This word brings less clarity to the debate than *apollumi* (perishing), *apóleia* (destruction), and

---

23. Packer, "Evangelical Annihilationism," 5–6.
24. MacDonald, *Evangelical Universalist*, 152.
25. Verbrugge, *Theological Dictionary*, 1301.
26. Fudge, *Fire That Consumes*, 258.
27. Rom 1:23; 1 Cor 9:25; 15:43, 54; and 1 Pet 1:18, 23.
28. Verbrugge, *Theological Dictionary*, 1301–3.
29. See Bible Hub, "diaphthora." Acts 2:31 says Jesus' body did not see *diaphthora* (decay).

olethros (destruction). At times it indicates a complete destruction, at others an ongoing process of deterioration.

Fourthly, the verb *apothnēskō* (die) occurs 112 times in the New Testament, and the noun *thanatos* (death) 120 times. Conditionalists argue that the plain meaning of this term, particularly as used in passages such as Rom 6:23, "the wages of sin is death," is the cessation of existence. In contrast, Fernando argues the term is "used often in a metaphorical sense," usually for spiritual death, and that people who are physically alive are "described as being dead."[30] While Fernando is correct that *apothnēskō* (die) and *thanatos* (death) can be used in a metaphorical sense, his further contention that death represents "an existence devoid of the blessings of the age to come" lacks justification.

A reasonable starting point for understanding the terms *apothnēskō* (die) and *thanatos* (death) appears to be the framework provided by the Old Testament. Fudge produces a detailed analysis of many Old Testament texts about the fate of the wicked.[31] He concludes, "These books reassure the godly again and again that those who trust will be vindicated, they will endure forever, they will inherit the earth. The wicked, however proud their boasts today, will one day not be found. Their place will be empty. They will vanish like a slug as it moves along. They will disappear like smoke."[32] Similarly, Stackhouse argues,

> Psalm after psalm and proverb after proverb reiterate the same biblical teaching (e.g., Ps. 1:4-6; Prov. 1:18-19). The wicked eventually and inevitably come to the same end: They will vanish from the face of the earth. Psalm 37 is just one of these many examples as it speaks of the wicked withering and dying like plants, disappearing so that they cannot be found, dissipating like smoke, being "cut off" so as to leave no trace (vv. 9, 22), and, finally,

---

30. Fernando, *Crucial Questions*, 42. He quotes several examples such as Eph 2:1, 5, and 1 Tim 5:6.
31. Fudge, *Fire That Consumes*, 90–117.
32. Fudge, *Fire That Consumes*, 116.

being simply "destroyed" (v. 38) .... They are not off somewhere else being punished.[33]

Burk dismisses Stackhouse's examples, claiming they teach about temporal judgment, temporal destruction, and temporal death.[34] However, this is not obvious from the text.

Fudge's and Stackhouse's approach of using the Old Testament as a starting point for understanding the New Testament terms *apothnéskó* (die) and *thanatos* (death) is endorsed by Verbrugge, who states, "The New Testament view of death is in direct continuity with the old Jewish view. Humans are *thnétos* (mortal); they live in the shadow of death."[35] Although *apothnéskó* (die) and *thanatos* (death) are routinely used metaphorically in the New Testament, there does not seem to be a strong argument to suggest that when they are used in a literal sense, they should be understood as anything other than ceasing to exist. Given the Jewish background of these terms, it is the task of traditionalists and universalists to prove otherwise, and I have not seen evidence to demonstrate this.

Finally, there is the example of Sodom and Gomorrah. Jude 7 and 2 Pet 2:6–10 both use the destruction of Sodom and Gomorrah as an example of fiery judgment.[36] Conditionalists argue that as Sodom and Gomorrah were utterly destroyed with nothing left, they serve as an example of the extinction that awaits the unrighteous.[37] In contrast, Parry observes that Jesus talks about how Sodom and Gomorrah would be treated on the day of judgment, arguing they have not been extinguished forever. He quotes Ezek 16:53 that promises the restoration of Sodom and contends, "If Sodom really is the core biblical paradigm of final punishment, and it is—then why can it not also be a biblical basis for hope beyond final destruction."[38] Although an intriguing argument, it

---

33. Stackhouse, "Terminal Punishment," 70.

34. Burk, "Eternal Conscious Punishment," 86–87.

35. Verbrugge, *Theological Dictionary*, 534.

36. Shogren, "Hell, Abyss," 459.

37. E.g., Stackhouse, "Terminal Punishment," 71; Pinnock, "Conditional View," 146.

38. Parry, "Universalist View," 92–93.

is helpful to consider the purpose Sodom and Gomorrah serve in their contexts in 2 Peter and Jude, which are both about the severity of judgment awaiting the wicked. In Jude 7, we are told that Sodom and Gomorrah "serve as an example by undergoing a punishment of eternal fire." Second Peter is even more explicit: "having reduced the cities of Sodom and Gomorrah to ashes, he condemned them to destruction." Their purpose appears to provide an example of utter destruction, emphasized by the word *tephroó* (being reduced to ashes).[39] Nothing more remains, such is God's judgment. Second Peter explains that Sodom and Gomorrah were made "an example of what is coming to the ungodly."[40] As Bauckham writes, "Undoubtedly the author sees the judgement of Sodom and Gomorrah by fire as a pattern for the fiery judgement of the ungodly at the Parousia. This conclusion is strengthened by the words *mellontōn asebesin* (what is going to happen to the ungodly)."[41] What happens to Sodom and Gomorrah on the Day of Judgment appears to be irrelevant to the example they serve in these verses. The purpose they serve is to warn of the destruction that awaits the wicked.

Some Conclusions about the Language of Destruction, Perishing, and Death

In this section, I have sought to find evidence that terms translated as "destruction," "perishing," and "death" do not refer to complete destruction and a cessation of being. I have found little. While *apollumi* (perishing) and *apóleia* (destruction) can sometimes be understood in terms of lostness and waste, their most common meaning conveys destruction, and this appears to be how they are used routinely in the New Testament. *Olethros* (destruction), used rarely in comparison, although sometimes referring to ruinous

---

39. Some translations (e.g., NRSV) use *extinction* for *katastrophé*. However, Strong's *Dictionary* suggests the word has a variety of meanings such as "overthrowing" or "destruction." Bible Hub, "katastrophé."

40. 2 Pet 2:6.

41. Bauckham, *Jude, 2 Peter*, 252.

The Language of Destruction, Perishing, and Death

loss, can also refer to destruction. *Phtheiró* (ruin/corrupt) has a wide range of meanings which vary from complete destruction to a process of destruction and is the only word of those considered that gives some weight to the idea of ongoing punishment. There seems little reason to understand the terms *apothnéskó* (die) and *thanatos* (death) in a way that differs from a traditional Jewish understanding of death as ceasing to exist. Finally, I have found scant evidence to reject the example of Sodom and Gomorrah's demise as an indication of utter destruction awaiting the wicked on the Day of Judgment.

I find the traditional and universalist arguments wanting in this section and agree with Fudge's conclusion: "There is no good reason, therefore, not to take Paul's primary words in their most ordinary and common senses. He says the wicked will 'perish,' 'die,' be 'corrupted,' or be 'destroyed.'"[42]

---

42. Fudge, *Fire That Consumes*, 257.

CHAPTER 4

The Relevance of the Story of the Rich Man and Lazarus

THE STORY OF THE rich man and Lazarus in Luke 16:19–31 has often been promoted in defense of the traditional view.[1] The rich man experiences *basanos* (torment) having been consigned to Hades, and is fully aware of his suffering, which is both psychological and physical.[2] While it is widely accepted that it is based on a well-established Near Eastern folk tale, which was used in rabbinical teachings of the time,[3] there appears to be little other consensus about how the story should be interpreted.

First, there is debate as to whether the parable is referring to the intermediate state or the final state of the wicked. Traditionalists argue that the rich man's location is hell,[4] with some citing the reference to Lazarus's finger and the rich man's tongue as indicative of the resurrected state.[5] Conversely, conditionalists point to the continued existence of the man's house and family, Abraham's concluding statement "they will not be convinced even if someone rises from the dead," and the location as Hades, as evidence this

1. E.g., Pawson, *Road to Hell*, 121–29; and Peterson, *Hell on Trial*, 65–68.
2. ACUTE, *Nature of Hell*, 81.
3. See Powys, "Hell," 218; ACUTE, *Nature of Hell*, 81.
4. E.g., Grudem, *Systematic Theology*, 1149; Fernando, *Crucial Questions*, 32, 48; and Pawson, *Road to Hell*, 127–29.
5. E.g., Pawson, *Road to Hell*, 128–29.

cannot refer to the final state of the person.[6] The identification of *géenna* (hell) with Hades in the Synoptics is contested. Boyd and Lunde suggest they are synonymous terms on the lips of Jesus.[7] Jeremias, Lusthaus, Duke, Powys, and Clayton reject this,[8] and their contention that Hades usually refers to the place of the dead, whereas *géenna* (hell) is the abode of the wicked, is convincing. As Duke observes, "[The] two different conceptual images of Hades and Gehenna have popularly, but wrongly, been conflated into a composite image of 'hell.'"[9] It therefore appears this is unlikely to be a description of the rich man's state after the final judgment.[10]

There is also debate about the purpose of the parable. Gray suggests the "two main thrusts of the story are the reversal of fortunes and the irreversibility of the two states."[11] Fudge argues from the context in Luke 16, where Jesus has been preaching on covetousness and stewardship, that the story's purpose is to warn against greed and neglecting the poor.[12] A similar conclusion is reached by N. T. Wright, who claims the story is "not to teach about what happens after death but to insist on justice and mercy within the present life."[13] This is supported by Grobel's analysis that the parable is focused around the rich man, with his speech accounting for 244 words, Abraham speaks 69, and Lazarus utters none.[14] The central figure is the rich man, and the story is told about him. Powys goes further, citing the parable as "a chilling rhetorical attack on Pharisaic piety and hope, rather than as a window on the

---

6. ACUTE, *Nature of Hell*, 82.

7. Boyd, "Hell," 12; Lunde, "Heaven and Hell," 311.

8. Jeremias, "γέεννα," 658; Lusthaus, "History," 179; Duke, "Eternal Torment," 255; Powys, "*Hell*," 276; Clayton, "*Hell*," 42.

9. Duke, "Eternal Torment," 255.

10. As also argued by Stott in Edwards and Stott, *Essentials*, 317; Pinnock, "Conditional View," 157; Fudge, *Fire That Consumes*, 205–8; Duke, "Eternal Torment," 251–52; and MacDonald, *Evangelical Universalist*, 145–47.

11. Gray, "Destroyed Forever," 15.

12. Fudge, *Fire That Consumes*, 203–8.

13. Wright, *Surprised*, 189.

14. Grobel, "Whose Name," 373.

afterlife."[15] This seems plausible, and it is unlikely the purpose of the story was to teach about the eternal fate of the wicked. If so, there are significant difficulties in reconciling the order of events in this story, which assumes no general resurrection, with Jesus' teaching elsewhere in Luke.[16]

Finally, Powys helpfully identifies the uniqueness of the story.[17] There are many elements that set it apart from Jesus' parables and other teachings that may account for so many different interpretations of the story. However, packed with so much imagery, and lacking parallels elsewhere in the Synoptics, I am inclined to follow Stott, who urges caution.[18] As Travis concludes, "Jesus is here making use of a popular Jewish tale, and so we would be rash to press the details of the story."[19] This also means we should be wary of pressing the idea of a fixed chasm. If conditionalists argue traditionalists cannot press the detail of the story, then conditionalists must not fall into the same error by arguing against universalism for a fixed chasm based on this story.

Some Conclusions about the Relevance of the Story of the Rich Man and Lazarus

The evidence examined above leans toward understanding the story as describing the intermediate state, rather than the final state of the wicked, although this is not beyond challenge. If true, this renders the story irrelevant to our discussions. Furthermore, the story's primary purpose is not to teach about the fate of the wicked. Together with its unique imagery, it seems sensible to be cautious about formulating strong ideas from this parable about the nature of hell, heeding Duke's advice that more interpretive

---

15. Powys, "Hell," 218.

16. Jesus talks about the resurrection of the righteous in Luke 14:14 and the general resurrection in Luke 20:27–40.

17. Powys, "Hell," 222–25.

18. Edwards and Stott, *Essentials*, 317.

19. Gray, "Destroyed Forever," 15, citing Stephen Travis.

weight needs to be given to "the plain sense of well-known biblical texts"[20] than the more metaphorical ones.

20. Duke, "Eternal Torment," 237–38.

CHAPTER 5

Sulfur, Smoke, Torment, and Second Death

TWO PASSAGES THAT FEATURE at the heart of many traditional arguments are Rev 14:9–11 and Rev 20:10, 14–15.[1] Discussing Rev 14, Wenham describes it "as the most difficult passage that the conditionalist has to deal with" and that, "on the face of it, having no rest day or night with smoke of torment going up forever and ever, sounds like everlasting torment."[2] Conditionalists and universalists both warn against pressing the imagery of these passages too far, with Nigel Wright arguing that "to insist on taking its words literally at this point would be inconsistent with the way the book is understood at most other points."[3] Likewise, Stackhouse contends that because the language of the apocalyptic is "typically extravagant, poetical and allusive, we ought not to press the language of everlasting torment into a metaphysical construction of an actual state of affairs."[4]

First, I shall consider Rev 14:9–11. "If anyone worships the beast and its image," they will "drink the wine of God's fury which has been poured full strength." As Fudge points out, the idea of

1. Burk cites these passages as two of his ten *foundational* passages. Burk, "Eternal Conscious Punishment," 39–41.

2. ACUTE, *Nature of Hell*, 82, citing John Wenham.

3. Wright, *Radical Evangelical*, 91.

4. Stackhouse, "Terminal Punishment," 74.

Sulfur, Smoke, Torment, and Second Death

the *cup of God's fury* is rooted in the Old Testament.[5] The passage continues, "they will be tormented with burning sulfur." The verb *basanizó* (torment) and its associated noun *basanismos* (torment) are strong words which, although they can refer to the buffeting of the boat in Matt 14:24 and the straining at the oars by the disciples in Mark 6:48, have moved in common Greek usage beyond their classical roots of testing and, according to Verbrugge, should be understood as "torture" or "torment" in the New Testament.[6] They will be tormented by "burning sulfur," probably a reference to the destruction of Sodom and Gomorrah, and "the smoke of their torment will rise for ever and ever." Traditionalists see this as an indication the suffering of the wicked will be eternal,[7] whereas conditionalists point out it does not say they are tormented for ever, only that the smoke will rise for ever.[8] Blanchard argues the personal pronoun *their* is an indication of the everlasting nature of the torment.[9] I will return to this image in a moment, but the following statement "There is no rest day or night" causes additional challenges for conditionalists, with Peterson claiming it proves "Stott is wrong."[10] Fudge, following Guillebaud, counters this by contesting that "day and night" take the genitive form and therefore can be understood as continuous suffering, which need not be everlasting.[11]

The second passage is Rev 20:10, 14–15. Verse 10 tells us the devil will join the beast and false prophet in "the lake of burning sulfur." Most commentators agree the beast represents the

---

5. Fudge, *Fire That Consumes*, 295. See Job 21:20; Pss 60:3; 75:8; Isa 51:17, 22; Obad 16; particularly Jer 25:13–38.

6. Verbrugge, *Theological Dictionary*, 207–8. Strong's *Dictionary* concurs. Bible Hub, "basanizó."

7. E.g., Fernando, *Crucial Questions*, 38; Peterson, *Hell on Trial*, 169; Burk, "Eternal Conscious Punishment," 40.

8. E.g., Stott in Edwards and Stott, *Essentials*, 318; Pinnock, "Conditional View," 157.

9. Gray, "Destroyed Forever," 15, citing John Blanchard.

10. Peterson, *Hell on Trial*, 169.

11. Fudge, *Fire That Consumes*, 299–301. ACUTE, *Nature of Hell*, 84, citing H. E. Guillebaud.

How Real Is Hell?

persecuting imperial power (i.e., Rome)[12] and the false prophet represents those insisting on worship of this imperial power.[13] We are told, "They will be tormented day and night for ever and ever." Stott observes this as the only time *basanizó* (torment) is described as lasting "for ever and ever" and is significantly applied "not to individual people but symbols of the world in its varied hostility to God."[14] In verse 14, we read that "death and Hades were thrown into the lake of fire." According to Shogren, *the lake of fire* was not an uncommon phrase in apocalyptic literature and belonged to *géenna* (hell) imagery.[15] Duke adds that the term was commonly understood as "fire imprisonment for fallen angels."[16] The subsequent sentence offers an interpretation for "the lake of fire," saying, "The lake of fire is the second death." Peterson argues, "The lake of burning sulfur" in verse 10 explains what is involved in "the second death."[17] However, following Fudge and Guillebaud, the use of *houtos* (this) in the Greek text seems clear in suggesting "the second death" interprets "the lake of fire" and not vice versa.[18] The "lake of fire" constitutes "death." The final verse, which reads, "anyone whose name was not found written in the book of life was thrown into the lake of fire," defines death in terms of absence of life. Traditionalists understand this as saying the wicked will experience the same fate as the devil, the beast, and the false prophet, and "they will be tormented *for ever and ever* as in verse

---

12. See Wright, *Revelation*, 99–100; Bauckham, *Book of Revelation*, 89; Beasley-Murray, *Book of Revelation*, 210–11; Mounce, *Book of Revelation*, 246; Keener, *Revelation*, 335.

13. For further discussion and variances in understandings see Wright, *Revelation*, 120; Bauckham, *Book of Revelation*, 89–90; Beasley-Murray, *Book of Revelation*, 216–17; Mounce, *Book of Revelation*, 244; Keener, *Revelation*, 350–52.

14. Edwards and Stott, *Essentials*, 318.

15. Shogren, "Hell, Abyss," 460.

16. Duke, "Eternal Torment," 244. He says it is used this way in 1 Enoch 10:13; 18:14–15; 21:1–10; and 2 Pet 2:4.

17. Peterson, *Hell on Trial*, 169.

18. Fudge, *Fire That Consumes*, 306; Peterson, *Hell on Trial*, 169, citing H. E. Guillebaud.

20:10."[19] Burk even goes so far as to suggest the unrighteous will be given a body "supernaturally fit to endure the same torment as the devil and his minions."[20] Conditionalists deny this, with Fudge claiming that "the lake of fire stands for utter, absolute, irreversible annihilation."[21] Michael Green further suggests that this isolated verse is not enough on which to build what he refers to as "the savage doctrine of eternal suffering."[22]

Some Conclusions about Sulfur, Smoke, Torment, and Second Death

In assessing these arguments, I suggest it is helpful to apply three approaches mentioned earlier. First, following Duke, to prioritize the more plain-speaking passages over and above the passages that are full of imagery.[23] Secondly, following Caird, to recognize that "hyperbole and overstatement are common in Semitic language"[24] and allow for some "literalist misinterpretation,"[25] and therefore not to press images, particularly apocalyptic ones, too far. Thirdly, following Fudge, to recognize that the Old Testament can play a significant role in helping us to correctly interpret metaphorical language.[26]

Jenkins believes that many Christians have difficulty in understanding Revelation because "they lack an awareness of the use of the Old Testament which permeates the book."[27] The Old Testament helps us to understand the meaning of smoke in Rev 14:9–11. This imagery finds its roots in Gen 19:23–28, the account

---

19. E.g., Beasley-Murray, *Book of Revelation*, 304. He argues Rev 20:10 implies the lake of fire cannot be annihilation.
20. Burk, "Eternal Conscious Punishment," 41.
21. Fudge, *Fire That Consumes*, 304.
22. Gray, "Destroyed Forever," 15, citing Michael Green.
23. Duke, "Eternal Torment," 238.
24. Caird, *Language and Imagery*, 110.
25. Caird, *Language and Imagery*, 256.
26. Fudge, *Fire That Consumes*, 122.
27. Fudge, *Fire That Consumes*, 293, citing Ferrell Jenkins.

of Sodom and Gomorrah, which describes "dense smoke rising from the land, like the smoke from a furnace." Isaiah 34:9-10 applies this to the forthcoming destruction of Edom, whose "dust [will be turned] into burning sulfur,"[28] and "it will not be quenched night and day; its smoke will rise forever. From generation to generation it will lie desolate; no one will ever pass through it again."[29]

The similarity between the language of Rev 14:9-11 and Isa 34:9-10 is striking, and it seems reasonable to assume the author of Revelation is recalling Isa 34. Isaiah 34 is about utter destruction, not ongoing punishment, and while the sulfur "will not be quenched night and day" and "its smoke will rise forever," in context this indicates the irreversibility of God's judgment and his utter triumph over his enemies. As Stackhouse claims, the smoke ascending is a sign that God's enemies "are well and truly dead, with only smoke to mark the spot."[30]

Applying these three approaches to these two passages central to the traditional case, I find the argument to be seriously undermined. The Old Testament provides a strong interpretive key to understand what is meant by "their smoke will rise for ever and ever. There will be no rest day or night . . . ." The language is highly figurative and must not be pressed too literally. Once again it seems safer to interpret such apocalyptic texts in the light of plain-speaking texts, rather than the other way around.

A Universalist Approach to These Texts

A very different approach is taken by Parry. He argues that universal postscripts follow both passages. Revelation 15:2-4, following on from 14:9-11, contains the line "all nations will come and worship before you." He observes that this does not talk about people from all nations, but all nations, which he argues is a sign

---

28. Isa 34:9.
29. Isa 34:10. See Fudge, *Fire That Consumes*, 29.
30. Stackhouse, "Terminal Punishment," 72.

of universal hope.[31] Likewise, Rev 21:9—22:17 is a postscript to 20:10, 14–15, and 21:6–7. The passage describes the new Jerusalem with its walls and gates. He argues the walls separate the redeemed from the ungodly, and the passage continues in 22:15 that "Outside are the dogs, those who practice magic arts, the sexually immoral, the murderers, the idolaters and everyone who loves and practices falsehood." However, the gates remain open, as it says in 21:25–26.[32] Parry claims this is an indication of the hope that those outside will one day enter into God's kingdom. He does not claim to have disproved the traditional interpretation of these passages, nor to have demonstrated the truth of his suggestions, but merely to propose "a range of possible interpretations that are both compatible with universalism and with the text of Revelation."[33] His reference to Rev 22:15 where the ungodly continue to remain outside the city is problematic for conditionalists. Powys navigates round this by suggesting if they do remain, it is not for long, which accords with Pinnock's and Brow's picture of the impenitent wicked "dwindling out of existence."[34] This again reminds us of the challenges of interpreting the apocalyptic language of Revelation and its multitude of conflicting metaphors.

---

31. MacDonald, *Evangelical Universalist*, 109–14.

32. MacDonald, *Evangelical Universalist*, 114–20.

33. MacDonald, *Evangelical Universalist*, 131.

34. ACUTE, *Nature of Hell*, 86, citing David J. Powys, Clarke Pinnock, and Robert Brow.

CHAPTER 6

All Things Reconciled

Up to this point I have considered passages that are used to defend traditional or conditional positions. I want now to briefly consider some passages championed by universalists. Parry argues one of the common features within any doctrinal position is the prioritizing of some passages over and above others, and that all positions have to live with "some awkward texts."[1] I have mentioned above the universalist responses to the two Revelation passages, the phrase *eternal punishment* in Matt 25:26, and an explanation of 2 Thess 1:9, which Parry says is the "biggest problem for universalism."[2] These have proved to be the "awkward texts" for universalists. Parry suggests such texts should be interpreted in the light of universal teachings of other passages,[3] and so I shall now consider four of the main passages Parry argues should take priority.

First, Parry draws our attention to Col 1:20: "through him to reconcile to himself all things, whether things on earth or things in heaven, by making peace through his blood, shed on the cross."[4] Set in the context of a hymn,[5] Parry observes the passage indicates

---

1. MacDonald, *Evangelical Universalist*, 37.
2. Parry, "Universalist View," 336.
3. Bird, "Evaluating," 78, citing Robin A. Parry.
4. MacDonald, *Evangelical Universalist*, 41–42.
5. O'Brien, *Colossians, Philemon*, 32; Bruce, *Colossians, Philemon*, 55.

reconciliation has already taken place.⁶ This speaks of a cosmic salvation,⁷ with Dunn commenting, "What is being claimed is quite simply and profoundly that the divine purpose in the act of reconciliation and peace-making was to restore the harmony of the original creation, to bring into renewed oneness and wholeness *all things, whether things on earth or things in the heavens.*"⁸

Parry contends the *all things* that are reconciled in verse 20 are, "without doubt, the same *all things* that are created in verse 16."⁹ He says there is no evidence in the text this will involve coercion, contra Powys and O'Brien.¹⁰ Parry further suggests the church is a forerunner of reconciliation, finding support for this idea in Lincoln,¹¹ and can agree with Marshall that reconciliation is conditional on faith (as vv. 21–23 suggest), believing people will be saved as they turn to Christ in the end.¹² The weakness of this argument is the lack of evidence elsewhere in Scripture for the idea of post-mortem salvation.¹³

The second passage is Rom 5:18–19, which reads, "Consequently, just as one trespass resulted in condemnation for all people, so also one righteous act resulted in justification and life for all people. For just as through the disobedience of the one man the many were made sinners, so also through the obedience of the one man the many will be made righteous." The issue is who to include in the *all*. Some contend *all* refers to those who are in Christ, although this is not made explicit within the text. Parry suggests it refers to every human being and feels *all* who were condemned in the first part of the verse should be understood as the *all* who

---

6. MacDonald, *Evangelical Universalist*, 46. See also O'Brien, *Colossians, Philemon*, 53.

7. See Bruce, *Colossians, Philemon*, 74; O'Brien, *Colossians, Philemon*, 55–56.

8. MacDonald, *Evangelical Universalist*, 45, citing James D. G. Dunn.

9. MacDonald, *Evangelical Universalist*, 45.

10. Powys, "Hell," 337; O'Brien, *Colossians, Philemon*, 57.

11. MacDonald, *Evangelical Universalist*, 51.

12. MacDonald, *Evangelical Universalist*, 47.

13. Burk, "Eternal Conscious Punishment," 129.

are justified and have life in the second part of the verse. Richard Bell argues this points back to Rom 3:23–24: "For all have sinned and fall short of the glory of God; and all are justified freely by his grace through the redemption that came by Christ Jesus."[14] This seems reasonable. However, I am also persuaded by N. T. Wright's contention that *all* in Rom 3:23–24 is not so much about every individual but about Jews and gentiles alike,[15] and therefore feel Rom 5:18–19 does not champion a universalist cause but refers to salvation for Jews and gentiles together.

A similar argument can be employed against Parry's third passage, Rom 11, which says in verse 26: "In this way all Israel will be saved," and in verse 32, "For God has bound everyone over to disobedience so that he may have mercy on them all." Parry rejects the idea Paul could have been referring to different things when using the term *Israel* in Rom 9–11.[16] While such consistency has some appeal, I do not feel it necessary, particularly given the wider context of the message of Romans. In chapters 9–11 Paul argues that God's purposes are being worked out through the hardening of the majority of Jews, which will enable the gospel to be spread worldwide. Chapter 11 serves to remind the gentiles they must not believe they are superior to the Jews, and Paul anticipates a large scale turning of the Jews to God through Christ as they are provoked to jealousy: "In this way all Israel will be saved." As argued above, it seems unlikely *all* refers to every human being, but rather to the whole of God's people, Jews and gentiles together, who will be saved. A similar reading follows in verse 32 where *all* refers to Jew and gentile alike.[17] Once again, such a reading undermines the universalist case.

The fourth and final passage is Phil 2:10–11: "That at the name of Jesus every knee should bend, in heaven and on earth and under the earth, and every tongue acknowledge that Jesus Christ is Lord, to the glory of God the Father." These concluding verses

14. MacDonald, *Evangelical Universalist*, 79, citing Richard Bell.
15. Wright, "Towards a Biblical View," 56.
16. MacDonald, *Evangelical Universalist*, 95.
17. Wright, "Towards a Biblical View," 56.

of what is widely thought to be a hymn[18] are taken directly from Isa 45:23. We see the similarities in language between Phil 2:10–11 and the LXX translation of Isa 45:23, which reads: "Every knee will bow, and every tongue will swear."[19] Isaiah 45 "strongly emphasizes the sole authority of God"[20] and is applied by Paul to the name of Jesus. Parry points out that Isa 45 is a "vision of universal salvation," which envisages all nations that survive destruction as coming to worship Yahweh.[21] Paul extends the scope of those bringing worship to include those "in heaven and on earth and under the earth," which Hawthorne says makes clear "the universality of this homage," with the neuter forms implying "the totality of creation."[22] Others suggest not all who bow will do so willingly.[23] However, Parry challenges this on the basis of Isa 45 where there is no forced subjection,[24] but rather a willing response to Yahweh's call to the nations to turn to him and be saved. The subsequent verse in the passage is a statement of trust: "They will say of me, 'In the Lord alone are deliverance and strength.'"[25] Although the passage states, "all who have raged against him will come to him and be put to shame,"[26] Parry suggests this can be understood in terms of recognizing their error. Marshall's contention that Paul is writing "a phrase of purpose and we are not told whether or not it will be fulfilled," which avoids the need to rely on Isaiah

---

18. Hawthorne, *Philippians*, 76. Fee, though, "has considerable doubts." Fee, *Philippians*, 192–93.

19. According to Fee, there is "[a] considerable textual variant" in the LXX (Septuagint) with *omeitai* (to swear) used in place of *exomologeó* (to confess) in some manuscripts. Fee states that ὀμεῖται was a later correction, "almost certainly created by Origen." Fee, *Philippians*, 223.

20. Hawthorne, *Philippians*, 92.

21. MacDonald, *Evangelical Universalist*, 98–99.

22. Hawthorne, *Philippians*, 93.

23. E.g., Fee, *Philippians*, 224.

24. Oswalt observes the verse allows for both possibilities that "bowing down" may be the act of *a condemned criminal* or *a pardoned worshiper*. Oswalt, *Isaiah 40–66*, 224.

25. Isa 45:24a.

26. Isa 45:24b.

to understand Phil 2:10–11, feels unsatisfactory as it renders the double use of the word *pas* (every) redundant. New Testament authors regularly quote parts of Old Testament passages to invoke the whole. Parry's suggestion that Phil 2:10–11 carries the message of Isa 45 is an interesting idea. However, in Rom 14:11–12 Paul quotes again from Isa 45:23 to teach that all will be called to give an account to God for all we have done ("It is written: 'As surely as I live,' says the Lord, 'every knee will bow before me; every tongue will acknowledge God.' So then, each of us will give an account of ourselves to God."). This swings the argument for me against Parry's interpretation of Phil 2:10–11.

Some Conclusions Relating to the Universalist Key Texts

Having examined four texts, I have seen there are strong arguments to dismiss a universal interpretation of two of them (Rom 5:18–19 and Rom 11:26), a strong case in favor of a universal interpretation for one (Col 1:20), and sufficient reason to reject a universal interpretation for the other (Phil 2:10–11). Given the difficulties encountered with some other texts, particularly around the language of destruction, and the many texts that teach the final division of lost and saved, as well as the lack of any clear evidence of post-mortem salvation, I feel the universal case is far from convincing. I am inclined to agree with Stackhouse, who says, "For universalism, therefore, only deductive arguments can be seriously mounted, not strong exegetical ones."[27] From the evidence I have found, he may be correct in concluding that universalism is "the triumph of hope over exegesis."[28]

---

27. Stackhouse, "Terminal Punishment," 136.
28. Stackhouse, "Terminal Punishment," 134.

CHAPTER 7

Conclusion to the Descriptive and Synthetic Tasks

As I EMBARKED UPON this study of the biblical texts, I expected to find strong evidence to challenge my theological shift toward conditionalism. I was also expecting very little from the universalist case. However, I have found more support for conditionalism than I envisaged. Conversely, the traditional case does not appear to be as strong as I believed. Further, the universalist argument has brought some interesting and helpful perspectives, and although it still appears to me to fall exegetically short in some areas, it offers insight into others and raises questions which both traditionalists and conditionalists need to address.

I have relied heavily on three principles to aid my exegesis. First, I have placed a high interpretative value on the Old Testament, in line with Fudge and Powys. This has informed my conclusions on several of the sections surveyed including interpreting *géenna* (hell) imagery; the language of destruction, perishing, and death; sulfur, smoke, and second death; and all things reconciled. Traditionalists place a lot of weight on a few verses in the Apocrypha and Pseudepigrapha that mention the eternal suffering of the wicked, but it appears to me they give undue weight to these and do not pay sufficient attention to the Old Testament. On close analysis, I find the arguments appealing to the apostolic fathers unconvincing as, with just one exception in 2 Clement, the apostolic

How Real Is Hell?

fathers merely repeat biblical phraseology and resist contemporary ideas that were growing in Judaism detailing the horrors of eternal suffering the wicked would face. Only in the mid- to late second century CE is there evidence of a systemized belief in eternal conscious suffering by some of the church fathers. This development may be explained by creeping Platonic influence.

Secondly, I have followed Duke's argument that we should interpret metaphorical texts in the light of the plain-speaking ones. This seems a sensible and justifiable approach and has resulted in giving greater priority to verses that talk about destruction, perishing, and death, and has promoted caution against being too dogmatic in interpreting *géenna* (hell) imagery, the meaning of *weeping and gnashing of teeth*, the story of the rich man and Lazarus, the meaning of *aiōnios* (eternal) in *aiōnios kolasis* (eternal punishment), and the interpretation of contentious passages in Revelation. Hays's synthetic task demands an explanation as to why the Synoptic Gospels employ *géenna* (hell) imagery when both Paul and John, except in Revelation, use very different language. In broad terms, traditionalists interpret Pauline and Johannine terminology using the framework of *géenna* (hell) imagery, whereas conditionalists interpret *géenna* (hell) imagery from the framework of terms used by Paul and John. Following Duke, I feel the conditionalist approach is preferable, particularly because there is no clear evidence Second Temple Judaism interpreted *géenna* (hell) imagery consistently or predominantly as eternal conscious suffering.

The third idea I have relied on is Caird's contention that Semitic language tends to be full of hyperbole and exaggeration, and there is much room for "literalist misinterpretation."[1] Therefore, I have avoided pressing apocalyptic and metaphoric imagery too hard such as in Revelation, the story of the rich man and Lazarus, the functioning of *pur* (fire) and *skóléx* (worm) in *géenna* (hell) imagery, and the meaning of the phrase *klauthmos* (weeping) *and brugmos* (gnashing) *of teeth*.

---

1. Caird, *Language and Imagery*, 256.

Conclusion to the Descriptive and Synthetic Tasks

However, there remain a few hermeneutical challenges to the conditional position. First, it is not clear cut *aiōnios kolasis* (eternal punishment) means "punishment of the age to come," and both the traditional and universal readings of that phrase seem more convincing. Secondly, the verse about the ungodly remaining outside the city in Rev 22:15 does not sit well with a conditional understanding. The best argument put forward by conditionalists is to appeal to their metaphoric and apocalyptic context, but this does not thoroughly explain it. Thirdly, it seems clear there is some evidence *géenna* (hell) imagery was used in Second Temple Judaism in terms of everlasting conscious suffering, although the case is regularly overstated by traditionalists. Fourthly and finally, conditional (and traditional) arguments against the universal reading of all things being reconciled to Christ in Col 1:20 are not entirely convincing.

CHAPTER 8

So What?

The Hermeneutical Task and Discussion with Conversation Partners—Relating the Text to Our Situation

ALTHOUGH LIMITED BY ITS bias, my survey presents evidence of change over the last ten years within UK evangelicalism about beliefs concerning the nature of hell. I have found that positions have become more polarized, with a greater proportion of evangelicals now willing to reject the traditional view, particularly among ministers. This might be due to the continued trickle-down effect of the views of prominent evangelicals such as Stott and Wenham and the subsequent debates that took place in the evangelical world largely in the 1990s. Whereas questioning the traditional view of hell within UK evangelicalism in former times "would have been regarded as not just wrong, but positively dangerous,"[1] it has become "increasingly acceptable."[2] Further, the emergence of a more robust theological defense of evangelical universalism has raised additional questions that need addressing.

Before embarking upon this study, theological arguments had persuaded me the conditional view was preferable to the traditional understanding of hell, although I suspected the textual

---

1. Holmes, "Evangelical Theology," 26.
2. Holmes, "Evangelical Theology," 26.

support for the traditional view was stronger. However, in light of the textual analysis above, the traditional view appears to have severe exegetical challenges. I find the traditional position wanting in terms of exegetical evidence and the conditional case to be the most exegetically sound, although not without difficulties.

Research by Pryce and Stoddart explores espoused beliefs about the doctrine of hell and the application of the doctrine by Scottish ministers to pastoral situations. Do ministers warn people who are dying and have not trusted in Christ about the dangers of hell? At funerals, do they offer false hope rather than staying true to their own beliefs? Their research reveals that aversion to raising the topic of hell in pastoral contexts will be greater the more *inclusive*[3] the minister's doctrine.[4] They also find that pastors who are more sensitive about the idea of hell more readily embrace *loopholes*.[5] Further, they conclude that an applied-theology model of ministry, by which they mean applying a doctrine to a pastoral situation, is problematic as it fails to encourage reflection and can result in pastoral practitioners abdicating responsibility for the message—they are "just passing it on."[6] They commend a praxis-reflection model, similar to the one attempted in this book, in which I have attempted to grapple with the biblical texts in response to a pastoral situation. These texts are interpreted differently by the three positions on hell we have considered, and each of these interpretations leads to different pastoral challenges.

Following Pryce and Stoddart, it is important that pastoral theological guidance is offered from a place of conviction rather than *passing on* an inherited doctrine. Because I believe there is strong exegetical support against the traditional view, the guidance

---

3. They define *exclusive* as those who believe only a limited subset of humanity would be saved, and *inclusive* for those who believe many groups will be part of God's eternal kingdom. The most *inclusive* would be those believing in universal salvation. Pryce and Stoddart, "Observed Aversion," 133–34.

4. Pryce and Stoddart, "Observed Aversion," 134.

5. They define *loopholes* as "doctrinal beliefs which allow them to avoid raising the subject in pastoral contexts." Pryce and Stoddart, "Observed Aversion," 134.

6. Pryce and Stoddart, "Observed Aversion," 131, 133–34.

How Real Is Hell?

I would offer primarily involves countering a belief in eternal conscious suffering. For those who remain convinced by the traditional view, their guidance would need to offer a theological and exegetical defense of the doctrine. In either situation, the evangelical context dictates that advice needs to be grounded in careful biblical exegesis.

However, although my textual analysis has led me to reject the traditional view, it has not led me to reject the idea of judgment. In fact, it has strengthened my conviction that the Bible warns of a coming judgment that will be fearful for those who are on the wrong side of it. As Smith observes in his book on death and bereavement, "If the idea of hell had never been on Jesus' lips but could be attributed to other thinkers, we might have avoided reference to the subject. But it is Jesus who warns frequently of the reality of hell."[7]

The graphic *géenna* (hell) imagery used by Jesus is consistent with the Jewish expectation of the Day of the Lord where God will judge "the living and the dead."[8] Jesus regularly warns people to avoid falling on the wrong side of this judgment, and the *géenna* (hell) imagery portrays: "it is a dreadful thing to fall into the hands of the living God."[9] Alongside Paul's warnings of God's coming wrath[10] and the mention of *basanismos* (torment) in Rev 14:9–11, there is no gentle passing into non-existence at the moment of death for the unsaved, but first a calling to account for all wrongdoing. The imagery used to depict the nature of this punishment is best understood as metaphorical, and although this does not discount the possibility of physical pain alongside psychological distress, we should be mindful of Caird's advice not to press Semitic metaphor too literally. Further, I wonder if the related biblical concept that all things will be brought into light

---

7. Smith, *Gateway to Life*, 77.

8. This is taught throughout the canon of the New Testament e.g., Matt 25:31–46; John 12:48; Acts 10:42; 1 Thess 5:1–3; Heb 12:23; 1 Pet 4:5; 2 Tim 4:1.

9. Heb 10:31.

10. E.g., Rom 2:5.

on that day indicates that the nature of judgment will involve a full realization of the effect of the things we have done upon God, upon others, and upon ourselves, and that such realization may alone cause such distress that it warrants the use of the vivid imagery and warnings given in the New Testament, even accounting for their hyperbole. While this remains a speculative suggestion, my textual analysis has highlighted that judgment is regularly depicted in severe and graphic terms.

Therefore, it seems to me that an evangelical conditionalist position needs to incorporate an understanding of judgment that is consistent with the employment of the graphic imagery used by Jesus and the New Testament writers. Pawson's criticism that "those who no longer preach hell are usually strangely mute about future judgement"[11] needs to be addressed. Kerrigan reminds us of the solemnity of future judgment when he writes, "However we struggle with the details of post-death existence and events, it seems irrefutable that outside of Christ is a precarious state in which to die."[12] This means that pastoral theological guidance may not totally remove the sense of disturbance the person feels.

The Pragmatic Task—Living the Text

Finally, let me return to the scenario I introduced at the start of this book: offering pastoral support to a person disturbed by the doctrine of eternal conscious suffering. There are various possible causes of their disturbance, including concern about the fate of one of their relatives; a struggle with what such a doctrine indicates about the severity and fairness of God; or a questioning whether they still want to follow a God who does this to people. For some, issues around fairness are more important than feelings; for others feelings and gut-instinct play a larger part. Any pastoral response needs to begin by seeking to ascertain why the person is troubled by the doctrine.

---

11. Pawson, *Road to Hell*, 79.
12. Kerrigan, "What Does the Bible Say," 8.

How Real Is Hell?

All pastoral responses need to acknowledge the disturbance felt by the person. In his dialogue with Edwards, Stott expresses similar disturbance: "emotionally I find the concept [of hell torment] intolerable and do not know how people can live with it without either cauterising their feelings or cracking under the strain."[13] However, he moves quickly to dismiss the inadequacy of emotion as a guide for our understanding of God: "As a committed evangelical, my question must be—and is—not what does my heart tell me, but what does God's word say?"[14] Schaeffer, when once asked for a theological exposition of the doctrine of hell, remained silent and wept.[15] While Stott may be correct about the unreliability of our emotions, they still have a place to encourage investigation, and disturbance can play a helpful role in encouraging a pursuit of God.

Even for conditionalists though, the biblical warnings about the horror of coming judgment and belief that many, if not most, will be lost may mean the sense of disturbance is not assuaged by a conviction that judgment does not involve eternal conscious suffering. Evangelicals have long utilized this disturbance as a catalyst for mission, though as Nigel Wright argues,

> The motives for mission are far greater and richer than this. We engage in mission because the Christian gospel is true, it enables human beings to find liberation and fulfil their destiny, because through it people receive the Spirit of the messianic age and come themselves to participate in his mission of redemption, and because through the gospel people learn how to give glory to God, Father, Son and Holy Spirit. This seems to be enough motivation to be going on with.[16]

While agreeing with Wright that mission should not be restricted to the *rescue of souls*, the minister may feel it appropriate to utilize

---

13. Edwards and Stott, *Essentials*, 314.
14. Edwards and Stott, *Essentials*, 315.
15. See ACUTE, *Nature of Hell*, 112.
16. Wright, *Radical Evangelical*, 100.

the disturbance positively for increased prayer, more committed discipleship, and greater witness.

Nearly forty years ago, Dowsett wrote a pastoral book to respond to a hypothetical situation where a young Christian was distressed by the traditional view of hell.[17] His approach was to encourage the young person to take the Bible seriously, to argue that what God says is more important than anything else, to defend the doctrine as fair and just, and to allow the lostness of others to motivate us to share the gospel. The book was written when evangelicals overwhelmingly accepted the traditionalist position. In the book there is no encouragement for dialogue, nor any suggestion the doctrine could be challenged.

One of Dowsett's encouragements to the young Christian was to read the Bible. Peppiatt observes that, "despite claims about the centrality and authority of Scripture, the amount of engagement with the Bible for normal evangelical Christians is, in fact, minimal."[18] However, EAUK's survey in 2010 provides a more encouraging picture with eight out of ten UK evangelicals claiming to read the Bible a few times a week.[19] In the evangelical context envisaged in this book, the pastoral response needs to encourage theological reflection and engagement with Scripture. However, as has been demonstrated in the textual analysis above, this is far from straightforward. Goodliff contends that one of the key roles of a minister is that of *theological guide*.[20] He states that one of the essential ministerial tasks is "to discern the essentials from that which might be negotiated, the ground of faith from its cultural superstructure."[21] Since evangelicalism prioritizes Scripture as the means of establishing doctrine, it is appropriate to question concepts about the nature of hell that are the consequence of cultural infiltration. For me this would include challenging some notions of eternal conscious suffering, which owe more to Dante than the

17. Dowsett, *That's Not Fair!*
18. Peppiatt, "Response," 38.
19. EAUK, *21st Century Evangelicals*.
20. Goodliff, *Shaped for Service*, 210–18.
21. Goodliff, *Shaped for Service*, 217.

How Real Is Hell?

Bible, as well as Platonic influence such as the immortality of the soul.

Further, it would be appropriate for the minister to explain that the traditional view is one of several held by evangelicals and to outline the different views and the biblical and theological reasons underpinning these views. Conversely, it would be dishonest for a minister to infer a single view to which all evangelicals subscribe. It may be helpful to discuss exegetical issues as outlined above depending on the ability and interest of the person to engage with such analysis, and to allow room for further exploration. It is not always easy to have a genuine two-sided conversation since, as Litchfield identifies, "it can be hard to challenge someone who appears to have greater theological knowledge."[22] She also warns against the abuse of power in the pastoral relationship, stating that "spiritual abuse includes using religious power and authority and the concept of Christian obedience to coerce others into behavior or matters of belief which they would not freely choose for themselves."[23]

The evidence of the second and third centuries CE ranges from gruesome accounts of never-ending punishment to Origen's belief in the ultimate restoration of all people, suggesting that the earliest reception history of these texts was far from clear and unambiguous. Therefore, it is perhaps unsurprising that today there are a range of views held by sincere and respected evangelicals as to how to interpret the biblical text, both among ministers and lay members as well as theologians. Exploring these together could help the person understand they are not alone in the disturbance they feel, alongside enabling them to glean wisdom from evangelicals of different positions, and to find a way to utilize their disturbance positively.

---

22. Litchfield, *Tend My Flock*, 49.
23. Litchfield, *Tend My Flock*, 50.

So What?

Conclusion

Some years ago, aware of a disparity between my beliefs and my pastoral experience, I began to question the evidence for a belief in the traditional view of hell. My exploration has continued in this book, as I have sought to bring my own beliefs, ideas, and feelings; an analysis of the contemporary situation; and the biblical text into conversation. This study has led me to a stronger embrace of the conditional position. It has also enabled me to be more aware of the strengths and weaknesses of the traditionalist, conditionalist, and universalist evangelical positions on hell, and I hope better equipped to offer theological guidance to a person disturbed by the doctrine of eternal conscious suffering.

For the person disturbed by the traditional view I have suggested the minister needs to enter into genuine dialogue with them, acknowledging their disturbance and seeking to help find appropriate ways forward largely through examining biblical texts together. Within the evangelical context this approach seems necessary. Further, I have suggested the minister needs to share openly from their own convictions. They also need to help the person see there are a range of sincerely held views among evangelicals and encourage them to explore which are consistent with the whole sweep of Scripture. However, such guidance, no matter how carefully given, may not eradicate all feelings of disturbance, even if the person is persuaded to adopt conditionalist beliefs. This may be why universalist ideas have such persistent appeal.

Appendix: Survey

The purpose of the survey was two-fold:

i. To explore whether there is a difference between UK evangelicals today compared to 2010 regarding belief in hell as a place where the condemned will suffer eternal conscious suffering.[1]

ii. To explore whether there is a difference between ministers and lay members in UK evangelical churches in beliefs about hell as a place where the condemned will suffer eternal conscious suffering.

Design

In order to compare data from the survey with the EAUK 2010 survey I asked the same question using the same five-point Likert scale. I offered a further option to respondents, which was "rather not answer," but no one chose this response. The survey was deliberately short (it consisted of one main question and took less than five minutes to complete) so as to encourage broad participation. It began by asking people to state whether they were a minister or not. I allowed people to self-designate because of the complexities of defining what a minister is across different denominations. The questions can be seen in the results section below.

---

1. This was one of the questions asked in EAUK's 2010 survey.

APPENDIX: SURVEY

Distribution

By using an online survey, I was able to promise confidentiality. I felt this was important to help people to answer honestly, particularly those of my own congregation. The survey was limited to over eighteens to avoid the additional demands of surveying children. It was distributed via an email request in two ways:

i. To ministers local to me. I sent the request to all ministers but invited only those who consider their church to be evangelical to complete the survey and to distribute it to their congregations for participation.

ii. To ministers whom I know personally, expecting they would be likely to engage with the request. Again, while sending the request to all ministers I know personally, I invited only those who consider their church to be evangelical to complete the survey and to distribute it to their congregations.

Possible Bias

Due to time limitations, I was unable to conduct a survey that avoided the possibility of bias. I am aware bias may have occurred because the majority of ministers I contacted in group (ii) belong to my denomination. Furthermore, bias may have been introduced because the area within which the local ministers live may not be representative of nationwide UK evangelicalism. An inner-city locality may have yielded different results than the town where I am based. With this in mind, the results should be interpreted with caution, and a further survey is required to establish whether this snapshot is truly reflective of the current situation among UK evangelicals.

APPENDIX: SURVEY

Results

1. Eighty-four people began the survey, but two of these were under eighteen and so only eighty-two answered the question about their understanding of the nature of hell.

2. Seventeen people considered themselves to be a minister or pastor, and their views as to how much they agree with the statement "Hell is place where the condemned will suffer eternal conscious suffering" are shown in chart 1 below:

CHART 1: RESULTS FOR MINISTERS/PASTORS

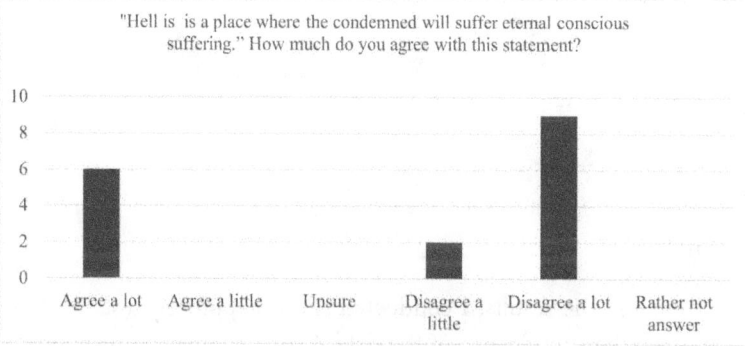

3. Sixty-five people did not regard themselves as a minister, and their views are shown in chart 2 below.

CHART 2: RESULTS FOR THOSE WHO ARE NOT MINISTERS/PASTORS

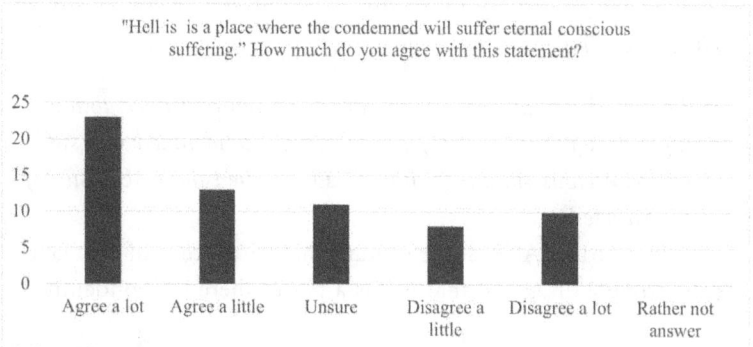

APPENDIX: SURVEY

4. Combining the results for all eighty-two respondents gives the results as shown in chart 3 below:

CHART 3: COMBINED RESULTS FOR ALL SURVEY PARTICIPANTS (MINISTERS AND NON-MINISTERS)

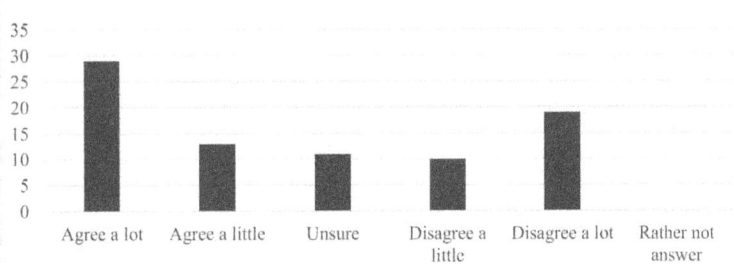

Analysis

To analyze the results, I conducted seven hypothesis tests to determine the significance of the data. When comparing responses in my survey with 2010 responses I used the results of the EAUK 2010 survey to provide population estimates for my hypothesis tests. When comparing responses of ministers with those of lay members, I used the combined results to provide population estimates for the hypothesis tests.

Hypothesis Test 1

Is there evidence that UK evangelicals are more inclined today to strongly disagree "Hell is a place where the condemned will suffer eternal conscious suffering" than in 2010 (when the EAUK survey was conducted)?

The 2010 EAUK survey found that 11 percent of evangelicals strongly disagreed that hell is a place where the condemned

Appendix: Survey

will suffer eternal conscious pain.[2] My survey found that nineteen out of eighty-two participants (23 percent) responded in this way. However, my survey included a high proportion of ministers, which biased the results, and so I tested the hypothesis with the ministers' results removed. Ten out of sixty-five lay members (15 percent) strongly disagreed with the statement.

After excluding the ministers' data, a simple hypothesis test reveals there is no significant evidence (even at the 20 percent level) to suggest that UK evangelicals are more inclined today to strongly disagree that "Hell is a place where the condemned will suffer eternal conscious suffering" than in 2010.

Hypothesis Test 2

Is there evidence UK evangelicals are less inclined today to strongly agree "Hell is a place where the condemned will suffer eternal conscious suffering" than in 2010 (when the EAUK survey was conducted)?

The 2010 EAUK survey found that 37 percent of evangelicals strongly agreed that hell is a place where the condemned will suffer eternal conscious pain.[3] My survey found that twenty-nine out of eighty-two participants (35 percent) responded in this way. However, it is noted again that because the survey included a high proportion of ministers, the results were biased, and so I tested the hypothesis with the ministers' results removed. Twenty-three out of sixty-five lay members (35 percent) strongly agreed with the statement.

A simple hypothesis test reveals no evidence to suggest that UK evangelicals are less inclined today to strongly agree "Hell is a place where the condemned will suffer eternal conscious suffering" than in 2010.

---

2. EAUK, *21st Century Evangelicals*.
3. EAUK, *21st Century Evangelicals*.

APPENDIX: SURVEY

Hypothesis Test 3

Is there evidence UK evangelicals are less inclined to say they are unsure whether "Hell is a place where the condemned will suffer eternal conscious suffering" than in 2010 (when the EAUK survey was conducted)?

The 2010 EAUK survey found that 31 percent of evangelicals were unsure whether hell is a place where the condemned will suffer eternal conscious pain.[4] My survey found that eleven out of eighty-two participants (13 percent) responded in this way. As above, I removed the ministers' results because of the potential bias. Eleven out of sixty-five lay members (17 percent) responded by saying they were "unsure."

A simple hypothesis test reveals there is very strong evidence (at the 1 percent level) to suggest that UK evangelicals are less inclined today to say they are unsure whether "Hell is a place where the condemned will suffer eternal conscious suffering" than in 2010. Although this conclusion is limited by the possibility of sampling bias, the strength of evidence indicates a greater confidence in people's beliefs about hell. Some are more certain it is about eternal conscious suffering, others more certain it is not. Fewer sit in the place of uncertainty.

Hypothesis Test 4

Is there evidence ministers in UK evangelical churches today are more inclined to disagree (either slightly or strongly) that "Hell is a place where the condemned will suffer eternal conscious suffering" than UK evangelicals in 2010 (when the EAUK survey was conducted)?

The 2010 EAUK survey found that 19 percent of evangelicals disagreed (slightly or strongly) that hell is a place where the condemned will suffer eternal conscious pain.[5] My survey found that eleven out of seventeen ministers (65 percent) responded in this way.

4. EAUK, *21st Century Evangelicals*.
5. EAUK, *21st Century Evangelicals*.

Appendix: Survey

A simple hypothesis test reveals there is extremely strong evidence to suggest that ministers in UK evangelical churches are more inclined today to disagree (slightly or strongly) "Hell is a place where the condemned will suffer eternal conscious suffering" than UK evangelicals in 2010.

Hypothesis Test 5

Is there evidence ministers in UK evangelical churches today are less inclined to agree (either slightly or strongly) "Hell is a place where the condemned will suffer eternal conscious suffering" than UK evangelicals in 2010 (when the EAUK survey was conducted)?

The 2010 EAUK survey found that 50 percent of evangelicals agreed (slightly or strongly) that hell is a place where the condemned will suffer eternal conscious pain.[6] My survey found that six out of seventeen ministers (35 percent) responded in this way.

A simple hypothesis test reveals there is insufficient evidence (even at the 10 percent level) to suggest ministers in UK evangelical churches are less inclined today to slightly or strongly agree "Hell is a place where the condemned will suffer eternal conscious suffering" than UK evangelicals in 2010.

Hypothesis Test 6

Is there evidence ministers in UK evangelical churches today are more inclined to disagree (either slightly or strongly) "Hell is a place where the condemned will suffer eternal conscious suffering" than lay members?

My survey found that eleven out of seventeen ministers (65 percent) responded in this way, compared to eighteen out of sixty-five lay members (28 percent).

A simple hypothesis test reveals there is strong evidence (at a 1.31 percent level) to suggest ministers in UK evangelical churches are more inclined today to disagree (slightly or strongly) "Hell is

---

6. EAUK, *21st Century Evangelicals*.

APPENDIX: SURVEY

a place where the condemned will suffer eternal conscious suffering" than lay members.

Hypothesis Test 7

Is there evidence ministers in UK evangelical churches today are less inclined to agree (either slightly or strongly) "Hell is a place where the condemned will suffer eternal conscious suffering" than lay members?

My survey found that six out of seventeen ministers (35 percent) responded in this way, compared to thirty out of sixty-five people (46 percent) who are lay members.

A simple hypothesis test reveals there is insufficient evidence to suggest that ministers in UK evangelical churches are less inclined today to agree (slightly or strongly) "Hell is a place where the condemned will suffer eternal conscious suffering" than lay members.

Bibliography

ACUTE (Evangelical Alliance Commission on Unity and Truth Among Evangelicals). *The Nature of Hell*. London: Acute, 2000.
Allison, Dale C. *The End of the Ages Has Come: An Early Interpretation of the Passion and Resurrection of Jesus*. Edinburgh: T. & T. Clark, 1985.
———. "Eschatology." In *Dictionary of Jesus and the Gospels*, edited by Joel B. Green et al., 206–9. Leicester: InterVarsity, 1992.
———. "Jesus and Hell." In *Testimony and Interpretation: Early Christology in Its Judeo-Hellenistic Milieu: Studies in Honour of Petr Pokorný*, edited by J. Mrazek and J. Roskovec, 114–24. London: T. & T. Clark International, 2004.
Badham, Paul. *Christian Beliefs about Life after Death*. London: MacMillan, 1976.
Barker, Margaret. *The Revelation of Jesus Christ*. Edinburgh: T. & T. Clark, 2000.
Bauckham, Richard. "Early Visions of Hell." *Journal of Theological Studies* 41 (1990) 355–85.
———. *The Theology of the Book of Revelation*. Cambridge: Cambridge University Press, 1993.
———. "Universalism: A Historical Survey." *Themelios* 4.2 (1978) 47–54.
———. *Jude, 2 Peter*. Word Biblical Commentary 50. Waco, TX: Word, 1983.
Beasley-Murray, G. R. *The Book of Revelation*. New Century Bible. London: Oliphants, 1974.
Bebbington, D. W. *Evangelicalism in Modern Britain*. London: Routledge, 1993.
Beker, Johan Christiaan. *Paul the Apostle: The Triumph of God in Life and Thought*. Edinburgh: T. & T. Clark, 1980.
Bell, Rob. *Love Wins: At the Heart of Life's Big Questions*. London: Collins, 2011.
Bible Hub. "basanizó. 928." https://biblehub.com/greek/928.htm.
———. "diaphthora. 1312." https://biblehub.com/greek/1312.htm.
———. "katastrophé. 2692." https://biblehub.com/greek/2692.htm.
Bird, Aaron. "Evaluating the Newest Evangelical Answer for the Dark Doctrine of Hell." PhD diss., Trinity Evangelical Divinity School, 2013.
Bock, Darrell L. *Luke*. The NIV Application Commentary. Grand Rapids: Zondervan, 1996.

BIBLIOGRAPHY

Borchert, Gerald L. "Wrath." In *Dictionary of Paul and His Letters*, edited by Gerald F. Hawthorne et al., 991–93. Leicester: InterVarsity, 1993.

Boyd, W. "Hell according to J. Jeremias." In *Studia Biblica 1978*: Vol. 2, *Papers on the Gospels*, edited by Elizabeth A. Livingstone, 9–12. Sheffield: JSOT, 1980.

Bruce, F. F. *The Epistle to the Colossians, to Philemon, and to the Ephesians*. The New International Commentary on the New Testament. Grand Rapids: Eerdmans, 1984.

Burk, Denny. "Eternal Conscious Punishment." In *Four Views on Hell*, edited by Stanley N. Gundry and Preston M. Sprinkle, 17–43, 82–88, 128–33, 174–78. Grand Rapids: Zondervan, 2016.

Caird, G. B. *The Language and the Imagery of the Bible*. London: Duckworth, 1980.

Cameron, Helen, et al. *Talking about God in Practice*. London: SCM, 2010.

Cameron, Helen, and Catherine Duce. *Ministry and Mission—A Companion*. London: SCM, 2013.

Cho, Dong. "The Doctrine of Eternal Punishment: The Biblical and Theological Rationales of Augustine." PhD diss., Southwestern Baptist Theological Seminary, 2008.

Clayton, David. *"Hell"—Fact or Fiction? Explorations in Human Destiny*. London: Athena, 2006.

Collins, Gary R. *Christian Counselling*. Waco, TX: Word, 1987.

Cotterell, Peter. *Dealing with Death: A Christian Perspective*. London: Scripture Union, 1994.

Crockett, William V. "The Metaphorical View." In *Four Views on Hell*, edited by Stanley N. Gundry and William V. Crockett, 43–76. Grand Rapids: Zondervan, 1996.

Date, Christopher M., et al. *Rethinking Hell: Readings in Evangelical Conditionalism*. Eugene, OR: Cascade, 2014.

Derrett, J. Duncan M. "Judgment and 1 Corinthians 6." *New Testament Studies* 37 (1991) 22–36.

Dowsett, Dick. *God, That's Not Fair!* Bromley: STL, 1982.

Duke, Rodney Kent. "Eternal Torment or Destruction? Interpreting Final Judgment Texts." *Evangelical Quarterly* 88.3 (2016) 237–58.

Dunn, James D. G. *Romans 1–8*. Word Biblical Commentary 38A. Dallas, TX: Word, 1988.

———. *Romans 9–16*. Word Biblical Commentary 38B. Dallas, TX: Word, 1988.

EAUK (Evangelical Alliance UK). *21st Century Evangelicals*. 2011. https://www.eauk.org/church/resources/snapshot/upload/21st-Century-Evangelicals.pdf.

Edwards, David L., and John Stott. *Essentials: A Liberal-Evangelical Dialogue*. London: Hodder & Stoughton, 1988.

Egan, Harvey D. "Hell: The Mystery of Eternal Love and Eternal Obduracy." *Theological Studies* 75 (2014) 52–73.

BIBLIOGRAPHY

Erdey, Zoltan L. E., and Kevin G. Smith. "'Weeping and Gnashing of Teeth'— The Nature of the Suffering of the Wicked in Matthew." *Conspectus: The Journal of the South African Theological Seminary* 15 (2013) 141–73.

Fee, Gordon D. *1 Corinthians*. The New International Commentary on the New Testament. Grand Rapids: Eerdmans, 1987.

———. *Paul's Letter to the Philippians*. The New International Commentary on the New Testament. Grand Rapids: Eerdmans, 1995.

Fernando, Ajith. *Crucial Questions about Hell*. Eastbourne: Kingsway, 1991.

Fitzmyer, Joseph A. *The Gospel according to Luke X–XXIV*. London: Doubleday, 1985.

Fudge, Edward William. *The Fire That Consumes: A Biblical and Historical Study of the Doctrine of Final Punishment*. Eugene, OR: Cascade, 2011.

Goodliff, Paul. *Shaped for Service*. Eugene, OR: Pickwick, 2017.

Graham, Elaine, et al. *Theological Reflection: Methods*. London: SCM, 2005.

———. *Theological Reflection: Sources*. London: SCM, 2007.

Gray, Tony. "Destroyed Forever: An Examination of the Debates Concerning Annihilation and Conditional Immortality." *Themelios* 21 (1996) 14–17.

Grobel, K. ". . . Whose Name Was Neves." *New Testament Studies* 10 (1963) 373–82.

Green, Joel B. *The Gospel of Luke*. The New International Commentary on the New Testament. Grand Rapids: Eerdmans, 1997.

Green, Laurie. *Let's Do Theology*. London: Mowbray, 1990.

Grudem, Wayne. *Systematic Theology: An Introduction to Biblical Doctrine*. Nottingham: InterVarsity, 1994.

Gundry, Stanley N., and William V. Crockett, eds. *Four Views on Hell*. Grand Rapids: Zondervan, 1996.

Gundry, Stanley N., and Preston M. Sprinkle, eds. *Four Views on Hell*. Grand Rapids: Zondervan, 2016.

Hawthorne, Gerald F. *Philippians*. Word Biblical Commentary 43. Waco, TX: Word, 1983.

Hays, Richard B. *The Moral Vision of the New Testament: A Contemporary Introduction to New Testament Ethics*. Edinburgh: T. & T. Clark, 1996.

Hick, John. *Death and Eternal Life*. Louisville, KY: Westminster/John Knox, 1994.

Hock, Ronald F. "Lazarus and Micyllus: Greco-Roman Backgrounds to Luke 16:19–31." *Journal of Biblical Literature* 106 (1987) 447–63.

Holmes, Stephen R. "Evangelical Theology and Identity." In *21st Century Evangelicals: Reflections on Research by the Evangelical Alliance*, edited by Greg Smith, 23–36. Watford: Instant Apostle, 2015.

Holmes, Stephen, and Russell Rook, eds. *What Are We Waiting For? Christian Hope and Contemporary Culture*. Milton Keynes: Paternoster, 2008.

Hughes, Philip Edgcumbe. *The True Image: The Origin and Destiny of Man in Christ*. Eugene, OR: Wipf & Stock, 1999.

Jeremias, Joachim. "ᾅδης." In *Theological Dictionary of the New Testament*, edited by G. W. Bromiley et al., 146–49. Grand Rapids: Eerdmans, 1964.

BIBLIOGRAPHY

———. "γέεννα." In *Theological Dictionary of the New Testament*, edited by G. W. Bromiley et al., 657–58. Grand Rapids: Eerdmans, 1964.

Keener, Craig S. *Revelation*. The New Application Commentary. Grand Rapids: Zondervan, 2000.

Kerrigan, David. "What Does the Bible Say about Death and Its Implications for Theology and Pastoral Care." *Mission Catalyst* 1 (2013) 6–8.

Kirk, Alexander N. "Reflections on the Hereafter." *Expository Times* 124 (2013) 384–86.

Kreitzer, Larry J. "Eschatology." In *Dictionary of Paul and His Letters*, edited by Gerald F. Hawthorne et al., 253–69. Leicester: InterVarsity, 1993.

Kvanvig, Jonathan L. *The Problem of Hell*. New York: Oxford University Press, 1993.

Lewis, C. S. *The Great Divorce*. San Francisco: HarperCollins 2001.

Liddell, Henry, and Robert Scott. *A Greek-English Lexicon*. 1901. https://archive.org/details/greekenglishlexoolidduoft/mode/2up.

Litchfield, Kate. *Tend My Flock: Sustaining Good Pastoral Care*. Norwich: Canterbury, 2006.

Lunde, Jonathan. "Heaven and Hell." In *Dictionary of Jesus and the Gospels* edited by Joel B. Green et al., 307–12. Leicester: InterVarsity, 1992.

Lusthaus, Jonathan. "A History of Hell: The Jewish Origins of the Idea of Hell in the Synoptic Gospels." *Journal for the Academic Study of Religion* 21 (2008) 175–87.

MacDonald, Gregory [Robin A. Parry]. *The Evangelical Universalist*. London: SPCK, 2012.

Mason, Rex. "Life before and after Death in the Old Testament." In *Called to One Hope: Perspectives on Life to Come*, edited by John Colwell, 67–82. Carlisle: Paternoster, 2000.

Milikowsky, Chaim. "Retribution and Eschatology." *New Testament Studies* 34 (1988) 238–49.

Moore, E. "Hell." In *New Dictionary of Christian Apologetics*, edited by Walter Campbell et al., 301–4. Leicester: InterVarsity, 2006.

Morgan, Christopher William. "The Application of Jonathan Edwards's Theological Method to Annihilationism in Contemporary Evangelicalism." PhD diss., Mid-America Baptist Theological Seminary, 1999.

Morris, Leon. *Luke*. Tyndale New Testament Commentaries 3. Nottingham: InterVarsity, 1988.

Mounce, Robert H. *The Book of Revelation*. The New International Commentary on the New Testament. Grand Rapids: Eerdmans, 1998.

Nickelsburg, George W. E. "Resurrection, Immortality, and Eternal Life in Intertestamental Judaism and Early Christianity." *Harvard Theological Studies* 56 (2006) 168–78.

Nolland, John. *Luke 9:21—18:34*. Word Biblical Commentary 35B. Dallas, TX: Word, 1993.

———. *Luke 18:35—24:53*. Word Biblical Commentary 35C. Dallas, TX: Word, 1993.

BIBLIOGRAPHY

O'Brien, Peter T. *Colossians, Philemon.* Word Biblical Commentary 44. Waco, TX: Word, 1982.

Oswalt, John N. *The Book of Isaiah Chapters 1–39.* The New International Commentary on the Old Testament. Grand Rapids: Eerdmans, 1986.

———. *The Book of Isaiah Chapters 40–66.* The New International Commentary on the Old Testament. Grand Rapids: Eerdmans, 1998.

Packer, James I. "Evangelical Annihilationism in Review." *Reformation and Revival* 6.2 (Spring 1997). http://www.the-highway.com/annihilationism_Packer.html.

Parry, Robin A. "A Universalist View." In *Four Views on Hell*, edited by Stanley N. Gundry and Preston M. Sprinkle, 48–54, 89–94, 101–27, 184–90. Grand Rapids: Zondervan, 2016.

Pawson, David. *Road to Hell.* London: Hodder & Stoughton, 1992.

———. *Unlocking the New Testament: A Commentary on the Book of Revelation.* Ashford: Anchor Recordings, 2013.

Peppiatt, Lucy. "Response to Stephen Holmes' Evangelical Theology and Identity." In *21st Century Evangelicals: Reflections on Research by the Evangelical Alliance*, edited by Greg Smith, 37–38. Watford: Instant Apostle, 2015.

Peterson, Robert A. *Hell on Trial: The Case for Eternal Punishment.* Philadelphia: Presbyterian and Reformed, 2012.

Pinnock, Clarke. "The Conditional View." In *Four Views on Hell*, edited by Stanley N. Gundry and William V. Crockett, 135–66. Grand Rapids: Zondervan, 1996.

Polkinghorne, John. *The God of Hope and the End of the World.* London: SPCK, 2002.

Powys, David J. *"Hell": A Hard Look at a Hard Question: The Fate of the Unrighteous in the New Testament.* Carlisle: Paternoster, 1998.

Pryce, Gwilym, and Eric Stoddart. "Observed Aversion to Raising Hell in Pastoral Care: The Conflict between Doctrine and Practice." *Journal of Empirical Theology* 18 (2005) 129–53.

Reiser, Marius. *Jesus and Judgment: The Eschatological Proclamation in Its Jewish Context.* Minneapolis: Fortress, 1997.

Scharen, Hans. "Hell in the Synoptics, Part 1." *Bibliotheca Sacra* 149 (1992) 324–37.

———. "Hell in the Synoptics, Part 2." *Bibliotheca Sacra* 149 (1992) 454–70.

Schürer, Emil. *A History of the Jewish People in the Time of Jesus Christ.* Edinburgh: T. & T. Clark, 1885–90.

Shogren, Gary S. "Hell, Abyss, Eternal Punishment." In *Dictionary of the Later New Testament and Its Developments*, edited by Ralph P. Martin and Peter H. Davids, 459–62. Leicester: InterVarsity, 1997.

Smith, Anthony M. *Gateway to Life: Death and Bereavement: Help and Hope on the Journey.* Leicester: InterVarsity, 1994.

Spiegel, James S. "Annihilation, Everlasting Torment and Divine Justice." *International Journal of Philosophy and Theology* 76 (2015) 241–48.

Bibliography

Sprinkle, Preston M. "Conclusion." In *Four Views on Hell*, edited by Stanley N. Gundry and Preston M. Sprinkle, 191–206. Grand Rapids: Zondervan, 2016.

———. "Introduction." In *Four Views on Hell*, edited by Stanley N. Gundry and Preston M. Sprinkle, 9–16. Grand Rapids: Zondervan, 2016.

Stackhouse, John G., Jr. "Terminal Punishment." In *Four Views on Hell*, edited by Stanley N. Gundry and Preston M. Sprinkle, 44–47, 61–81, 134–39, 179–183. Grand Rapids: Zondervan, 2016.

Stone, Michael. *Fourth Ezra: A Commentary on the Book of Fourth Ezra*. Minneapolis: Fortress, 1990.

Thiselton, Anthony C. *Life after Death: A New Approach to the Last Things*. Grand Rapids: Eerdmans, 2012.

Tidball, Derek J. *Who Are the Evangelicals?* London: Marshall Pickering, 1994.

Travis, Stephen H. *Christian Hope and the Future of Man*. Leicester: InterVarsity, 1980.

———. "Eschatology." In *New Dictionary of Theology*, edited by Sinclair B. Ferguson et al., 228–31. Leicester: InterVarsity, 1988.

Trench, Richard Chenevix. *Synonyms of the New Testament*. London: Keegan Paul, Trench, Trübner, 1894.

Verbrugge, Verlyn D. *The NIV Theological Dictionary of New Testament Words*. Grand Rapids: Zondervan, 2000.

Woodward, James, et al. *The Blackwell Reader in Pastoral and Practical Theology*. Oxford: Blackwell, 2000.

Wright, Nigel. *The Radical Evangelical: Seeking a Place to Stand*. London: SPCK, 1996.

Wright, N. T. *Jesus and the Victory of God*. London: SPCK, 1996.

———. *The New Testament and the People of God*. London: SPCK, 1992.

———. *The Resurrection of the Son of God*. London: SPCK, 2003.

———. "Towards a Biblical View of Universalism." *Themelios* 4 (1979) 54–58.

Wright, Tom. *Paul for Everyone*. London: SPCK, 2004.

———. "Q & A." *Mission Catalyst* (2013) 4–5.

———. *Revelation for Everyone*. London: SPCK, 2014.

———. *Surprised by Hope*. London: SPCK, 2011.

www.ingramcontent.com/pod-product-compliance
Lightning Source LLC
Chambersburg PA
CBHW071743090426
42738CB00011B/2547

ENDORSEMENTS

Dr. Andrew Jackson has done us a great service by pulling together the story of the life of Jesus, directly from the Bible, and presenting it in an accessible, chronological book. Combining his academic prowess and his writing ability, Dr. Jackson has given us a magnificent presentation of the greatest story ever told - and it's all true!

—*Len Munsil, President, Arizona Christian University.*

Jesus Christ is a fresh retelling of the gospel story, merging together the narrative accounts of the four Gospels. Dr. Andrew Jackson is an experienced writer with a knack for telling the story in a clear, concise, and engaging manner. Although *Jesus Christ* is not a commentary, Dr. Jackson weaves insights, cultural details, and interpretive observations into the narrative. This is an outstanding synopsis of the life of Christ.

— *Dr. Mark Fairchild, Professor of Bible at Huntington University, Indiana.*

Jesus Christ is truly a great book. It is very easy to read. Dr. Andrew Jackson has done a masterful job of weaving the Gospels into a single narrative. He puts all of the pieces in the story of Jesus into a readable format and uses just the right amount of historical data, geographical information, and creative license. The Church needs a resource like this! *Jesus Christ* is a great launching point for deep conversations about Jesus for those who do not yet know him. I am sharing *Jesus Christ* with my unchurched friends, and our church will use it in our city outreaches.

—*Tim Armstrong, Senior Pastor of The Chapel Church, Ohio.*

In *Jesus Christ*, Dr. Andrew Jackson does a great job of taking the good news of the four Gospels and blending them into a storyteller's format. It is very readable. I am sure that *Jesus Christ* will be translated into many other languages and bring the eternal hope of Jesus to many other nations around the world.

—*Al Gregory, Commercial Airline Captain.*

Reading the Bible can intimidate readers, but Dr. Andrew Jackson's *Jesus Christ* presents the Gospels in an easily accessible novel format. Presentation matters in our understanding of God. This chronological harmony will allow both new and experienced Bible readers to better appreciate God's good news."

—*Joshua Claybourn, Attorney, Historian, Author.*

I am asking all of my friends who lead and train others to not only read *Jesus Christ* for themselves, but to use it as an important tool in the disciple-making process.

—*David Hinman. Disciple Making Movement Catalyst for New Generations and North America, and Vineyard USA Missions Representative to Africa.*

Reading the story of Jesus in a chronological format helps bring insight, clarity, and understanding to his life and teaching. *Jesus Christ* will challenge and provoke you in the best possible ways. You will discover Jesus who is continually trying to connect with people's hearts and possibly you will discover him connecting with your heart.

—*Adam Haynes, Landscaping Business Owner, Oregon.*

I loved reading about the life of Jesus in this single narrative format. Dr. Andrew Jackson presents the stories of Jesus' life and ministry in chronological order, brings them to life with clear pictures of Israel's geography and Jesus' travel itineraries, and includes the text of verses from the Old Testament that makes clear to the reader the fulfillment of prophecy. I've read the Gospels numerous times, but I have learned more from this book about the details of Jesus' life, and also explanations of words, customs, and people of the time. Whether you are a long-time Christian or just beginning to explore the person of Jesus, *Jesus Christ* is a must-read.

—*Dr. Jennifer Prior, Professor Emeritus, Northern Arizona University.*

In *Jesus Christ* Dr. Andrew Jackson weaves together the four Gospels in a way that gives new life to the familiar stories of the life of Jesus. He references Old Testament passages within the stories that show the unity of the Old and New Testaments, and his expertise in biblical geography really adds contextual depth. I highly recommend *Jesus Christ* to both Christians and non-Christians.

—*Paul Haroutunian, Associate Director of Evangelicals for Social Action and Love, California.*

Jesus Christ's chronological narrative of the Gospels is a very effective way of helping linear thinkers like me keep track of the life and teaching of Jesus. *Jesus Christ is* one of the most readable book formats I have seen. The background information in each story brings depth to our understanding of Jesus' life and ministry. I recommend this book to any first-time reader of the Gospels or life-long students of God's Word.

—*Clayton Ritter, Senior Pastor of Seashore Church, Virginia.*

Jesus Christ weaves the four Gospels together to give us the life of Jesus in one story. It introduces us to the Jesus who has real power over darkness, gives lasting peace, and can really change people's life! This is the same Jesus that changes the lives of the girls who are rescued from the darkness of human sex trafficking in Tanzania. When we follow Jesus and his ways, nothing is impossible, and no one is hopeless!

—*Pastor Joel and Stephanie Midthun, Executive Directors of Courage House, Tanzania, Africa.*

As a pastor, one of the most challenging aspects of helping people find and follow Jesus is helping them see more of a "whole picture" of his life and teaching in the four Gospels. Dr. Andrew Jackson's novel approach in *Jesus Christ* captures readers right from the beginning and paints a masterpiece that compels them from start to finish and leaves them with an unmistakable portrait of Jesus. Start the journey through the pages of this book. You'll be so glad you did. For Jesus the Jesus Christ specializes in real life change.

—*David Wright, Lead Pastor of Life Link Church, Arizona.*

With Bible literacy on a steep decline, *Jesus Christ* is a welcome resource. This novel format will be a great tool for those who are new to the truths of the gospel, but also refreshing for those who want to reread the greatest story every told! Dr. Andrew Jackson does a superb job bringing the details of Jesus' story to light and connecting them to the larger narrative. Read and enjoy!

—*Steve Weber, Missionary to the Slavic World.*

Jesus Christ is a great help in understanding the life and ministry of Jesus. God has used it to increase my faith level and love for Jesus. I am sure that *Jesus Christ* will spread widely and be fruitful into many nations. I highly recommend it!

—*David Sanders, Missionary to Berlin, Germany.*

Dr. Andrew Jackson provides a chronological pictorial stream of the Gospels without the technical, and sometimes distracting, chapter and verse divisions that can be challenging to the newcomer of the Bible. Interwoven are topographical insights that aid the reader's narrative journey into a richer appreciation of the gospel message. A copy of *Jesus Christ* should be placed in the hands of every new believer as a valuable resource in learning about the life and teachings of Jesus. Also, *Jesus Christ* is insightful for the seasoned Christian as it immediately draws them into the fluidity of events of our Savior as he passionately ministered to fallen humanity.

—*Dr. Abel Aguilar, Dean of Students and Professor, THEOS Bible College.*

JESUS CHRIST

**THE STORY OF
HIS LIFE AND TEACHING**

ISBN
978-1-949503-14-2

Copyright
2023 by Andrew Jackson

All rights reserved. No part of this publication may be reproduced, stored in a retrieval system, or transmitted in any form by any means, electronic, mechanical, photocopy, recording, or otherwise, without the written permission of Dr. Andrew Jackson.

JESUS CHRIST
THE STORY OF HIS LIFE AND TEACHING

AUTHOR
Andrew Jackson

EDITOR
Jennifer Prior

COVER DESIGN/PAGE LAYOUT
Orlen Stauffer

BIBLE REFERENCES
The International English Bible ®

PUBLISHER
IEB Publishing

INTRODUCTION

Jesus is the most influential person in the history of the world. His early followers shaped Western Civilization, and over two billion people worship him around the world. However, today many people continue to entertain distorted portraits of Jesus that are repackaged and propagated over and over again in our modern, pop-culture world.

Jesus Christ provides you with the opportunity to discover the true life and teaching of Jesus. It is a popular and easily accessible novel presentation of a chronological harmony of the Gospels. There is nothing you read in *Jesus Christ* that is made-up or a creative invention. A chronological harmony of the Gospels is a single, merged narrative of the life and teaching of Jesus from the common and diverse material recorded in Matthew, Mark, Luke, and John. Although a harmony of the four Gospels cannot be created with absolute certainty, the *Jesus Christ* harmony is based on years of detailed research.

The pages of *Jesus Christ* reveal how the supernatural power of the kingdom of God invaded history in the person of Jesus. He is truly the light of the world! He demonstrated God's love by healing the sick, casting demons out of people, feeding the hungry, and mending broken hearts

Jesus continues to perform miraculous signs and wonders and impart spiritual transformation in the lives of millions of people. No matter who you are or what you have done, Jesus is the eternal Jesus Christ who can change your life and give you eternal hope. Today his wonderworking power is being experienced around the world.

Jesus Christ - His Life and Teaching

PART ONE

CHAPTER 1

King Herod the Great was a non-Jewish Edomite, who ruled Israel for the Romans from 37 to 4 BC. Under Caesar Augustus, the Romans appointed Herod the "King of the Jews." King Herod was a master-builder that gave him the title "the Great." His greatest building project was the rebuilding of the temple complex in Jerusalem. He doubled its size and surrounded it by massive walls with gates.

During the rule of King Herod the Great there lived a common temple priest named Zechariah. He belonged to the priestly division of Abijah. Israel had 24 divisions of priests—about 18,000 priests—that served at the temple. A temple priest served in Jerusalem for about two weeks each year. Unlike the elite chief priests, these common priests of the people had other occupations the rest of the year. Zechariah was probably a farmer or a craftsman. His wife Elizabeth was also a descendant of the priestly lineage of Aaron. Zechariah and Elizabeth were very old. They lived simple and righteous lives before God—blamelessly obeying all the Lord's commandments and regulations. But sadly, they had no children because Elizabeth could not conceive.

One day Zechariah's division was on temple duty, and so he went to Jerusalem to serve as a priest before God. According to the priestly custom, Zechariah was chosen by the throwing of dice to go into the temple sanctuary and burn incense on the altar in the Most Holy Place. The Most Holy Place was located in the center of the temple sanctuary and contained the altar of incense, the golden lamp stand, and the table of consecrated bread. Incense was offered in the Most Holy Place before the morning sacrifice and after the evening sacrifice. Incense—representing prayer—was kept burning continually before the Lord. Each day during the time of the burning of the incense, a large group of worshipers would gather together and pray outside the sanctuary.

While Zechariah was standing at the right side of the altar of incense in the Most Holy Place, the archangel Gabriel suddenly appeared to Zechariah. When Zechariah saw Gabriel, he was startled and gripped with fear. But Gabriel said to Zechariah, "Do not be afraid, for your prayer request has been heard by God. Your wife Elizabeth will give birth to a son, and you are to name him John. He will be a joy and delight to you, and many people will rejoice because of his birth. He will be great in the sight of the Lord. He will be filled with the Holy Spirit even before he is born. He will bring back many of the people of Israel to the Lord their God. And John will go before the Lord and fulfill what is written in *Malachi 4:5-6*, 'He will minister in the spirit and power of Elijah, to turn the hearts of the parents to their children, and the disobedient to the wisdom of the righteous—to make ready a people prepared for the Lord.'" With a puzzled look on his face, Zechariah asked Gabriel, "How do I know this will come true? For my wife and I are very old." Gabriel said to him, "I am the archangel Gabriel! I stand in God's presence, and he sent me to tell you this wonderful news. But because you have not believed my message, you will not be able to speak until John's birth. For my message will be fulfilled at the right time."

Meanwhile, the people praying outside the temple sanctuary were waiting anxiously for Zechariah to come out from the Most Holy Place. They were wondering why he stayed so long inside the temple. When Zechariah finally came out of the sanctuary, he looked confused and could not talk to the people praying for him. He was just making hand signs to them. Then all the people realized that Zechariah had seen a vision.

Startled by the appearance and promise of Gabriel, Zechariah returned to his home in the hill country of Judea, the southern region of Israel, after his temple service was finished. Soon after Zechariah returned home, Elizabeth became pregnant, and so she stayed secluded in her house for five months. Overwhelmed with joy, she declared, "The Lord has done this for me. In these days he has shown his grace to me and has taken away my shame from among the people."

In the sixth month of Elizabeth's pregnancy, God sent Gabriel to the small town of Nazareth in Galilee, to visit a young virgin girl named Mary. Gabriel appeared to her and said, "Greetings, you who have been greatly blessed! The Lord God is with you!" Mary was overwhelmed by Gabriel's words and wondered what kind of greeting this was. But Gabriel said to her, "Mary, do not be afraid, for you have found favor with God. You will conceive and give birth to a son. You are to give him the name Jesus, which means "the Lord saves." He will be great and will be called the Son of the Most High God! The Lord God will give Jesus the throne of his father David, and he will reign over Jacob's descendants forever. His kingdom will have no end."

Shaking with wonder, Mary asked Gabriel, "How can this happen, since I am a virgin?" Gabriel said to her, "The Holy Spirit will come on you, and the power of the Most High God will overshadow you. Therefore, the one born to you will be called the Son of God, the Messiah. Believe me, for even your relative Elizabeth is going to have a son in her old age. She is now six months pregnant. Nothing is impossible with God!" Then Mary said with confident faith, "I am the Lord's servant, so let your message to me be fulfilled." Then Gabriel left Mary.

As Gabriel had promised, Mary was soon found to be with child through the Holy Spirit. However, when Mary became pregnant, she was legally engaged to be married to a man named Joseph, a descendant of David. But because Joseph lived a righteous life and did not want to disgrace her in public, he decided to end his engagement with Mary in secret.

Finding herself pregnant, Mary immediately got ready and hurried to visit Zechariah and Elizabeth in a town in the hill country of Judea. When Mary arrived, she rushed into the house and greeted

Elizabeth with joy. When Elizabeth heard Mary's greeting, the baby leaped in her womb, and Elizabeth was filled with the Holy Spirit. Overflowing with the Holy Spirit, Elizabeth declared in a loud voice, "Blessed are you among women, and blessed is the son in your womb! Why am I so blessed that the mother of my Lord has come to visit me? As soon as I heard your greeting, the baby in my womb jumped for joy. Blessed are you for believing that the Lord would fulfill his promises!"

Then, overcome with wonder, Mary began to rejoice, "My soul magnifies the Lord! My spirit rejoices in God my Savior, for he has seen the humble heart of his servant. From now on all generations will call me blessed, for the Mighty One has done great things for me—holy is his name! His mercy goes out to all who fear him, from generation to generation. He has done mighty acts with his mighty arm. He has scattered those who are proud in their hearts. He has brought down rulers from their thrones, but has exalted the humble. He has filled the hungry with good things, but has sent the rich away empty. He has helped his servant Israel, remembering to be merciful to Abraham and his descendants forever, just as he promised our ancestors." Mary stayed with Elizabeth for about three months and then returned home to Nazareth.

God's promise to Elizabeth came true, and she gave birth to a son. Her relatives and neighbors heard that the Lord had shown her great mercy, and they rejoiced with her. Eight days after his birth, all the relatives and neighbors came together to celebrate the circumcision of the baby boy. They were about to name him Zechariah after his father, but Elizabeth quickly spoke up and said, "No! His name must be John." They were all surprised and said to her, "There is no one in your family who has the name John." And then they made hand signs to Zechariah, for they wanted to know what he wanted to name his son. Zechariah asked for a writing tablet, and to everyone's amazement he wrote, "His name is to be John."

Suddenly Zechariah was filled with the Holy Spirit and began praising God. He prophesied: "Blessed be the Lord, the God of Israel, for he has come and redeemed his people. He has raised up the king of salvation for us in the house of his servant David. As God said through the Old Testament prophets long ago, 'Salvation from our enemies and from all those who hate us—to show mercy to our ancestors and to remember his holy covenant, the oath of promise he swore to our father Abraham; to rescue us from the hand of our enemies, and to enable us to serve him without fear, in holiness and righteousness before him all our days. And you, my son John, will be called a prophet of the Most High God, for you will go before the Messiah to prepare the way for him. You will give his people the knowledge of salvation through the forgiveness of their sins. For the compassionate mercy of our God—by which the rising sun will come to us from heaven—will shine on those living in darkness and in the shadow of death, and will guide our feet into the path of peace."

All the relatives and neighbors were filled with amazement, and throughout the hill country of Judea people were talking about the birth. Everyone who heard what had happened was puzzled and asked each other, "Who is this boy going to be?" For they knew the Lord's hand was with him. John grew up in the strength of the Holy Spirit, and he lived in the Wilderness of Judea until he started his public ministry to the people of Israel.

Now back in Nazareth, when Joseph was still thinking about how to end his engagement with Mary, an angel of the Lord appeared to him in a dream and said, "Joseph, son of David, do not be afraid to take Mary home as your wife, for the baby in her womb is from the Holy Spirit. Mary's first child will be a son, and you are to name him Jesus, for he will save his people from their sins." All this took place to fulfill what is written in *Isaiah 7:14*, "The virgin will conceive and give birth to a son, and they will call him Immanuel," which means God with us. When Joseph woke up from his sleep, he did what the angel of the Lord had told him. He married Mary and took her home as his wife, but he did not have sexual intercourse with her before she gave birth to a son.

CHAPTER 2

During the ninth month of the pregnancy of Mary, the Roman Emperor Caesar Augustus gave an order that a population census must be taken of the entire Roman Empire. He commanded that all people travel to their home towns to register their names. So Joseph and Mary traveled from Nazareth in Galilee to Bethlehem in Judea to register, for he belonged to the lineage of David. While Joseph and Mary were in Bethlehem, Mary gave birth to her first baby, a son. She wrapped him in strips of cloth and laid him in a manger, an animal's feeding trough, for there was no place for them in the guest room.

At the time of Jesus' birth there were shepherds living in the fields near Bethlehem. Shepherds were among the lowest occupations in the first-century. They lived outside with their sheep during the warmer months of the year to keep guard over their flocks during the night. Suddenly, an angel of the Lord appeared to them, and the majestic glory of God's presence shone all around them. The shepherds were terrified, but the angel said to them, "Do not be afraid, for I bring you good news of great joy for all the people. Today in Bethlehem—the town of David—a Savior has been born to you; he is the Messiah, the Lord. This will be a sign to you: You will find a baby boy wrapped in cloths and lying in a manger." Then a great army of heavenly angels appeared, worshiping God and declaring, "Glory to God in heaven, and on earth peace to all people on whom his grace rests!"

After the angels went back to heaven, the shepherds said to one another, "Let's go to Bethlehem and see what the Lord has made known to us." So the shepherds hurried to Bethlehem and found Joseph, Mary, and Jesus. When the shepherds saw Jesus, they told Joseph and Mary what the angel had declared to them. Joseph and Mary were amazed at what they heard the shepherds tell them. Mary remembered everything the shepherds said, and she pondered them in her heart. Then the shepherds went back to watch over their sheep in the fields. And they glorified and praised God for all the things they had heard and seen. Everything happened just as they had been told by the angel.

Joseph and Mary circumcised their son eight days after his birth and named him Jesus. Forty days after Jesus' birth, it was the time for Mary's birth purification sacrifices required by the law of Moses, and also time to dedicate Jesus to the Lord. So Joseph and Mary took Jesus up to the Jerusalem temple to dedicate him to the Lord, as it is written by Moses in *Exodus 13:2*, "Every firstborn male is to be consecrated to the Lord." At the temple, Joseph and Mary offered a sacrifice for the birth purification of Mary. Their temple offering was according to *Leviticus 12:8*, "a pair of doves or two young pigeons," the sacrifice required for the lower class of society.

Now there was a man living in Jerusalem named Simeon who was waiting in prayer for the restoration of Israel. He lived a holy and righteous life before God and the Holy Spirit was upon him. The Holy Spirit had revealed to him that he would not die before he saw the coming of the Messiah. Then one day, the Holy Spirit led Simeon into the temple at the same time that Joseph and Mary brought Jesus to be dedicated to the Lord. After Simeon greeted them, he took Jesus in his arms and praised God saying, "Sovereign Lord, as you have promised; you can now dismiss your servant in peace, for my eyes have seen your salvation—a light for revelation to the nations and the glory of your people Israel." Joseph and Mary marveled at what Simeon said about Jesus. Then Simeon blessed them and said to Mary, "Jesus will cause the falling and rising of many people in Israel. The thoughts of many hearts will be revealed." Then Simeon said, "Mary, a sword will pierce your soul," in which he prophesied about the crucifixion of Jesus.

Chapter 2

At that time in Jerusalem there also lived a prophetess named Anna, who was the daughter of Phanuel, of the tribe of Asher located in the region of Galilee. Anna was 84 years old. She was married for seven years before her husband died, and then she remained a widow and consecrated herself to God. Every day she worshiped God from morning to evening through fasting and prayer in the temple Court of the Women. Coming up to Joseph and Mary in the temple, Anna gave thanks to God and told everyone who was looking for the redemption of Jerusalem about Jesus.

Some time after the birth of Jesus, wise men with their caravan traveled about 900 miles from the east in Babylon to Jerusalem. While in Jerusalem they were asking people, "Where is the one who has been born king of the Jews? We saw his guiding star rising in the east, and we have come to worship him."

When King Herod the Great heard about the arrival of the wise men and their caravan in Jerusalem, he was overcome with alarm and was greatly troubled along with all of Jerusalem. So King Herod quickly gathered together the Jewish religious leaders in his spacious palace and asked them where the Messiah was to be born. They told him, "In Bethlehem of Judea, for it is written in *Micah 5:2*, 'But you, Bethlehem, in the land of Judah, are by no means least among the rulers of Judah; for out of you will come a ruler who will shepherd my people Israel.'" Bethlehem was located around 5 miles south of Jerusalem.

King Herod met privately with the wise men at his palace and found out from them the exact time the guiding star had appeared to them. Then King Herod sent the wise men to Bethlehem saying, "Go and search for the child. And as soon as you find him, report back to me, so that I too can go and worship him."

As the wise men left Jerusalem the guiding star again appeared and led them to the house where Jesus was in Bethlehem. They went into the house and saw Jesus, and they bowed down and worshiped him. Then they opened their treasures and gave Jesus the gifts of gold and the sweet-smelling resins of myrrh and incense. After worshiping Jesus, the wise men were warned by God in a dream not to return to King Herod in Jerusalem, so they quietly went back to their own country in the east by another route.

After the wise men had left Bethlehem, an angel of the Lord appeared to Joseph in a dream and said, "Get up! Take Mary and Jesus and escape to Egypt, for King Herod will search for the child to kill him. Stay in Egypt until I tell you when to return to Israel." So Joseph immediately got ready and left that night with Mary and Jesus. They traveled about 300 miles to the Roman province of Egypt. They lived there until the death of King Herod, fulfilling what is written in *Hosea 11:1*, "Out of Egypt I called my son."

King Herod was known for his outbursts of murderous anger, and he was furious when he realized that the wise men had fooled him. Full of rage, he commanded his Roman soldiers to kill every boy in Bethlehem and its surrounding area. He ordered them to kill every boy two years old or younger, based on the time that he had learned from the wise men. This fulfilled what is written in *Jeremiah 31:15*, "A voice is heard in Ramah, weeping and great mourning, Rachel weeping for her children and refusing to be comforted, for they are no more." Ramah was about 5 miles northwest of Bethlehem and it was where Rachel, the wife of Jacob, had died.

After King Herod died a painful death from kidney disease that included the maggot-infested gangrene of the genitals, an angel of the Lord appeared in a dream to Joseph in Egypt and said, "Get up, take Mary and Jesus and go to the land of Israel, for King Herod is dead." So Joseph immediately got up, and took Mary and Jesus and traveled to the land of Israel. But when Joseph heard that Herod Archelaus was now ruling over Judea in the place of his father King Herod, he became afraid for Herod Archelaus was even more brutal than his father.

Having been warned from God in a dream, Joseph immediately traveled to the region of Galilee in northern Israel and lived in Nazareth. Nazareth was located about 12 miles southwest of Lake Galilee; it was a small village with a population of about 1000 people. So this fulfilled what was said through the prophets, that Jesus would be called a Nazarene. In Nazareth, Jesus grew and became strong; he was filled with wisdom and God's grace was on him. During the life of Jesus, the region of Galilee was governed by Herod Antipas, another of King Herod's sons.

Chapter 2

Every year Joseph and Mary went up to Jerusalem to celebrate the Passover Feast. The Passover was the Jewish festival that commemorated the deliverance of Israel from slavery in Egypt. So according to their practice, they went up to Jerusalem for Passover when Jesus was 12 years old.

When the Passover was over, Joseph and Mary returned to Nazareth, but they did not realize that Jesus had stayed behind in Jerusalem. They thought he was traveling with them in the Passover caravan of their family and friends. After a day's journey, they asked their family and friends if they knew where Jesus was. When they could not find him, Joseph and Mary hurried back to Jerusalem to look for Jesus. After searching frantically for Jesus over three days, they finally found him sitting among the religious teachers in the temple courts, listening to them and asking them questions. Everyone who heard Jesus was amazed at his understanding and his answers. Joseph and Mary were shocked when they found Jesus in the temple. Exhausted, Mary said to him, "Son, why have you scared us like this? We have been looking for you everywhere." Jesus said calmly, "Why were you searching for me? Didn't you know that it is necessary for me to be in my Father's house?" Joseph and Mary did not understand what Jesus was talking about, but Mary remembered all these things in her heart.

Then Jesus returned back to Nazareth with Joseph and Mary, and he was obedient to his parents. Jesus grew in wisdom, in years, and in favor with God and the people. Before his public ministry, Jesus' early life in Nazareth covers about 18 years, from when Jesus was 12 to when he was about 30. During these years, Jesus worked as a craftsman with his father Joseph.

CHAPTER 3

The word of God came to John the Baptist that launched his public ministry in the Wilderness of Judea. The public ministry of John was the beginning of the good news about Jesus the Messiah. Like the prophet Elijah, John lived a simple life. He wore clothes made of camel's hair with a leather belt around his waist, and ate locusts and wild honey

John began his ministry in Bethany on the east side of the Jordan River. But moved by the Holy Spirit, he went throughout the Wilderness of Judea declaring that the kingdom of God has arrived! He proclaimed that people must "Repent and turn to God!" He preached a water-baptism of repentance for the forgiveness of sins. His ministry fulfilled what is written in *Isaiah 40:3-5*, "A voice of one calling in the wilderness, 'Prepare the way for the Lord. Make straight paths for him. Every valley will be filled in. Every mountain and hill made low. The crooked roads will become straight. The rough ways will be made smooth. And all people will see the salvation of God.'"

John came as a witness to tell the people about the light, so that through him all people might believe. John was not the light, but he came only as a witness to the light. For the true light that gives light to everyone was coming into the world. And his name was Jesus. Jesus was in the world, and even though the world was created through him, the world did not know him. He came to his own people, but his own people did not receive him. But whoever did receive him—whoever believed in his name—he gave the right to become children of God—children spiritually born of God and not of human blood.

While John was ministering in the Wilderness of Judea, large crowds of people from Jerusalem, the region of Judea, and the Jordan River went out to him, confessing their sins and being water-baptized by him in the Jordan River. The crowds of people asked John, "What should we do?" John said, "Anyone who has two shirts should share with a person who does not have one, and anyone who has food should share with the person who has nothing to eat." Although Jewish tax collectors were despised for their partnership with the Romans, they also came to be water-baptized by John. They asked him, "Teacher, what should we do?" John told them, "Don't collect any more taxes than you are required to collect." Even Jewish soldiers came to be water-baptized by John. They asked John, "What should we do?" John said, "Don't take money by force and don't accuse people falsely—be content with what you are paid.

Many people of Israel thought John the Baptist might be the Messiah, and so they were waiting with great expectancy. But John said to them: "After me comes the one who is much greater and more powerful than me. I am not worthy to bow down and untie the straps and remove his sandals. I baptize you with water for repentance, but the one coming after me will baptize you with the Holy Spirit and with fire. His pitchfork is in his hand to clear his threshing floor and separate the wheat from the waste. He will gather the wheat into his barn, and the waste will be burned up with unending fire." And with many other words John exhorted the people and proclaimed the good news of God to them.

When John saw crowds of Jewish religious leaders from Jerusalem coming to be water-baptized, he shouted to them: "You are a generation of snakes! Who warned you to escape the coming wrath of God? You must turn to God and live a life that produces fruit worthy of repentance. You must live a life that shows that you have repented of your sins and stop saying that Abraham is your father. For I tell you the truth: God is able to raise up descendants of Abraham from the rocks on the ground. Even now the ax is ready to cut the root of the tree, for every tree that does not produce good fruit will be cut down and thrown into the fire.

The religious leaders sent temple priests from Jerusalem to ask him who he was. Without hesitating, John confessed openly, "I am not the Messiah." They asked him, "Are you Elijah?" John said, "No, I am not." They asked, "Are you the Prophet that Moses spoke of?" John said, "No." Finally they said, "Who are you? Tell us! We must give an answer to those who sent us. Tell us who you are." John answered them by quoting *Isaiah 40:3*, "I am the voice of one calling in the wilderness. Make straight the way of the Lord." Now the religious leaders who had been sent asked him, "Why then are you baptizing if you are not the Messiah, nor Elijah, nor the Prophet?" John said to them, "I baptize with water, but one is living among you that you do not know. He is the one coming after me, and I am not worthy to untie the straps of his sandals."

At that time when all the people were being water-baptized by John, Jesus walked from Nazareth in Galilee to be baptized by John in Bethany on the eastern side of the Jordan River. When Jesus arrived, John tried to stop him from being baptized. John said to Jesus, "Why do you come to me? I need to be baptized by you." Jesus said to him, "Let me be baptized, for it is good for us to fulfill all righteousness." Finally, John did as he was asked and baptized him in the Jordan River. As soon as Jesus came up out of the water, he began to pray and immediately John saw heaven open up, and the Holy Spirit came down upon Jesus in the form of a dove and remained on him. Then a voice came from heaven and said, "You are my Son, who I love; with you I am very pleased. Now Jesus was about 30 years old when he began his public ministry.

Jesus was full of the Holy Spirit after his water-baptism, and immediately the Holy Spirit sent him into an isolated place in the Wilderness of Judea to be tempted by the devil. Jesus fasted for about six weeks—40 days and nights. Because he did not eat the whole time, Jesus became very hungry. He lived with wild animals around him, and angels came and ministered to him.

First, the devil—the tempter—approached Jesus and said, "If you are the Messiah, the Son of God, tell these rocks to become bread." Jesus said, "It is written in *Deuteronomy 8:3*, 'Humans do not live on bread alone, but by every word that comes from the mouth of God.'"

Second, the devil led Jesus to the holy city of Jerusalem, and had him stand on the highest point of the temple complex. Satan said to Jesus, "If you are the Messiah, the Son of God, throw yourself down from here, for it is written in *Psalm 91:11-12*, 'God will command his angels to protect you. They will lift you up in their hands, and you will not strike your foot against a rock.'" Jesus said to Satan, "It is also written in *Deuteronomy 6:16*, 'Do not test the Lord your God.'"

And finally, the devil led Jesus to a very high mountain, and showed him the glory of all the kingdoms of this world. The devil said to him, "I will give you all the power and glory of the kingdoms of the world, for their authority has been given to me, and I can give it to anyone I want to. You can have it all! All you need to do is bow down and worship me." Jesus said, "Satan, away from me! For it is written in *Deuteronomy 6:13*, 'Worship the Lord your God and serve him only.'" After Satan had finished tempting Jesus, he left him until another opportune time. Then angels came and ministered to Jesus.

After being tempted in the wilderness, Jesus returned to Bethany east of the Jordan River where John was baptizing. The next day John saw Jesus walking toward him, and said to his disciples, "Look! It is Jesus the Lamb of God, who takes away the sin of the world! This is the one I told you about when I said, 'The one who comes after me is much greater than me because he existed before me.' I did not know him, but the reason I came baptizing with water was so that he would be revealed to Israel. I saw the Holy Spirit descend from heaven like a dove and remain on him. And I did not know him, but God who sent me to baptize with water told me, 'The one on whom you see the Holy Spirit descend from heaven and remain, this is the one who will baptize with the Holy Spirit.' I am an eyewitness to what has happened, and I tell you that Jesus is the Son of God, God's Chosen One!"

The next day John the Baptist and two of his disciples saw Jesus walking by them. John turned and said to his disciples, "Look! Jesus, the Lamb of God!" When the two disciples heard John say this, they followed Jesus. Then Jesus turned around and saw them following him and said, "What do you want?" They said to him, "Teacher, where are you staying?" Jesus said, "Come and you will see." So they went and saw where Jesus was staying, and they spent that day with him.

Andrew was one of the two disciples who heard what John had said and followed Jesus. The first thing Andrew did was to find his brother Peter and said to him, "We have found the Messiah." Andrew took him to meet Jesus. Jesus looked at him and said, "You are Simon, but now you will be called Cephas" (*in Aramaic*), which means Peter (*in Greek*). The names Cephas and Peter mean "rock."

The next day Jesus decided to walk back to Galilee in northern Israel. When he was about to leave, Jesus found Philip and said to him, "Follow me!" Then Philip found Nathanael and said to him, "We have found the one Moses wrote about in the law, and about whom the prophets also wrote—Jesus of Nazareth." Nathanael said to Philip, "Nazareth! Can anything good come from Nazareth?" Philip said to him, "Come and see for yourself." When Jesus saw Nathanael walking toward him, he said, "Look! Here is an Israelite with a clean heart!" Nathanael said to Jesus, "How do you know me?" Jesus said, "I saw you under a fig tree before Philip called you." Then Nathanael declared, "Teacher, you are the Son of God! You are the king of Israel!" Jesus said to him, "You believe in me because I told you I saw you under the fig tree? You will see greater acts of God than that. I tell you the truth: You will see heaven open, and God's angels ascending and descending on the Son of Man."

CHAPTER 4

Jesus and his new disciples walked to Galilee and were invited to attend a wedding in the town of Cana, which was located about eight miles north of Nazareth. Because it was an extended family wedding, Mary the mother of Jesus was also present. After several days of celebration Mary said to Jesus, "The wedding guests have no more wine!" Jesus said, "Mother, what does this have to do with me? For my time has not yet come." Mary said to the wedding servants, "Do whatever he tells you."

Now nearby there were six stone water jars that were used by the Jews for purification washings, each could hold about 20 to 30 gallons. Jesus told the servants, "Fill these jars with water." So they filled the jars. Then he told them, "Now take some of the water to the wedding master." So they took it to him. Although the servants knew where the water came from, the wedding master did not. After he tasted the water that had been turned into wine, he called the bridegroom aside and said to him, "Everyone serves the best wine first and then serves the cheaper wine. But you have saved the best wine until now!" Turning water into wine at Cana was the first miraculous sign through which Jesus revealed his glory; and his disciples believed in him.

After the wedding in Cana, Jesus, along with his mother, brothers, sisters, and disciples walked about 16 miles to the town of Capernaum located on the northwestern shore of Lake Galilee. And they stayed there for a few days.

Because it was time for the Jewish Passover, Jesus and his disciples left Capernaum and walked south to Jerusalem. When Jesus arrived in Jerusalem he went into the temple courts. In the temple he saw people selling cattle, sheep, and pigeons for sacrifices, and moneychangers sitting at tables exchanging money to make a profit. So Jesus made a whip out of rope and drove everyone out of that area of the temple courts, along with the sheep and oxen. And he turned over the tables of the moneychangers, scattering their coins onto the ground. Jesus shouted to the pigeon sellers, "Get out of here! Stop turning my Father's house into a public market!" Later on his disciples remembered that it is written in *Psalm 69:9*, "Zeal for your house will consume me."

After seeing Jesus clear out a section of the temple courts, some Jews said to him, "Show us a miracle to prove to us that you have the authority to do these things!" Jesus said to them, "Destroy this temple sanctuary, and I will raise it again in three days." The Jews were shocked and said, "It took 46 years to build our temple, how are you going to raise it up in three days?" But Jesus was talking about the temple of his body. After Jesus was raised from the dead, his disciples remembered that Jesus said this, and they believed God's word and all the things Jesus said.

Many people saw the miracles that he was doing during the Passover Feast and believed in his name. But Jesus would not entrust himself to them for he knew the condition of the hearts of all people. He did not need anyone to tell him about the human condition, for he knew what was in the heart of each person.

In Jerusalem there was a religious leader named Nicodemus, who was a member of the Jewish religious council. He came to Jesus under the darkness of night so he would not be seen and said, "Teacher, we know that you are a teacher who has come from God, for no one could do the miracles you are doing unless God was with him." Jesus said to him, "I tell you the truth: No one can see the kingdom of God unless they are born again from above." Nicodemus was puzzled and said to

Jesus, "It is impossible for an adult to reenter his mother's womb and be born again." Jesus said, "I tell you the truth: No one can enter the kingdom of God unless they are born of water and the Holy Spirit. Those born of the flesh are flesh, but those born of the Holy Spirit are spirit. You should not be surprised that I said, 'You must be born again.' For the wind blows wherever it wants and you hear its sound, but you do not know where it comes from or where it is going. So it is with everyone who is born by the Holy Spirit." Nicodemus asked Jesus, "How can this be possible?" Jesus said, "You are a teacher of Israel, and you do not understand my teaching? I tell you the truth: We speak about what we know and have seen, but still you do not believe my testimony. I have told you earthly things and you do not believe me, so how can you believe if I tell you heavenly things? No one has ever gone into heaven except the Son of Man who has come from heaven. Just as Moses lifted up the snake in the wilderness, so the Son of Man must be lifted up and everyone who believes in him will have eternal life." Jesus was speaking about his crucifixion on the cross.

Then Jesus said to the people gathering around him, "God so loved the world that he gave his one and only Son, so that whoever believes in him will not perish, but have eternal life. For God did not send his Son into the world to condemn the world, but to save the world through him. Whoever believes in him is not condemned. But whoever does not believe is condemned already, for he has not believed in the name of the one and only Son of God. The light has come into the world, but people love the world's darkness instead of God's light because their works are evil. For whoever does evil hates God's light, and will not come into the light for fear that their evil deeds will be exposed. But whoever lives a life of truth comes into God's light."

When the week-long Passover Feast was over, Jesus and his disciples left Jerusalem and walked to Aenon near Bethany on the Jordan River. John the Baptist was water-baptizing people here. Jesus stayed in Aenon with John the Baptist for some time.

While Jesus was in Aenon, an argument erupted between some of John the Baptist's disciples and a certain Jew over the issue of purification washings. John's disciples were upset and went to him and said, "Teacher, Jesus who was with you on the other side of the Jordan River—the one you testified about—look, he is baptizing and everyone is going to him." John said to them, "No one receives anything unless it is given to him from God in heaven. You know that I have already told you that I am not the Messiah, but I was sent to prepare the way for the coming of Jesus. The bride belongs to the bridegroom, but the friend of the bridegroom waits and listens for his coming, and is full of joy when he hears the bridegroom's voice. I tell you, my heart is full of joy, for the time has come. Jesus must increase; and I must decrease. He comes from heaven and is above all things. The one who is from the earth belongs to the earth, and speaks as one from the earth. Jesus tells us what he has seen and heard. Whoever believes his testimony confirms that God is true. For God sent Jesus into this world and he speaks the words of God, for he gives the Holy Spirit in all its fullness. The Father loves the Son and has placed all things under his authority. Whoever believes in Jesus has eternal life in the kingdom of God, but whoever rejects Jesus will not see eternal life, for the just wrath of God remains on them."

At that time Jesus learned that the religious leaders in Jerusalem had heard that he was gaining and baptizing more disciples than John the Baptist—although it was not Jesus who was baptizing but his disciples. The religious leaders were suspicious that Jesus was becoming too dangerously popular among the people, for they might think he was the Messiah. So Jesus and his disciples left Judea and began walking back to Galilee in northern Israel. On his way to Galilee, Jesus had to walk through the region of Samaria. The region of Samaria was between Judea in the south and Galilee in the north.

After Jesus had left Aenon, John the Baptist continued to exhort the people and proclaimed the good news of God to them. When Herod Antipas married Herodias, the wife of Herod's brother Philip, John declared to Antipas, "It is not lawful for you to marry your brother's wife." John had also condemned Antipas for all the other evil things that he had done. Herodias became very angry with John and wanted to have him killed, but she was not able to on her own. Although Antipas also wanted to kill John, he was afraid of the crowd of people who believed that he was a prophet of God. Antipas feared John, for he knew that he was a righteous and holy man. He enjoyed listening to John, even though he was greatly perplexed when he heard him speak. But in order to please his wife Herodias, Antipas gave orders to have John arrested, bound, and put in prison.

As Jesus and his disciples were walking toward Galilee, they entered the Samaritan town called Sychar. Sychar was about two miles northeast of Shechem near the field that Jacob had given to his son Joseph. It was about noon, and Jesus sat down at Jacob's well because it was hot and he was tired from his long journey.

As Jesus was sitting at Jacob's well, a Samaritan woman came to draw water from the well. Jesus said to her, "Can you give me a drink of water?" Jesus was alone because his disciples had gone into town to buy food. The Samaritan woman said to him, "You are a Jew and I am a Samaritan woman. Why do you ask me for a drink of water?" For Jews would not associate with Samaritans. Jesus said to her, "If you only knew the gift of God and who it is that asks you for a drink, you would have asked me and I would have given you living water." The woman said to him, "Sir, the well is deep, and you do not have a bucket to draw water. Where are you going to get this living water? Are you greater than our father Jacob, who gave us this well and drank from it himself, as did his sons and animals?" Jesus said to her, "Whoever drinks this water will be thirsty again, but whoever drinks the water that I will give them will never be thirsty. The water that I will give them will become a spring of water gushing up within them to eternal life." Then the woman said to Jesus, "Sir, give me this water so that I won't be thirsty, and I will not have to draw water from this well ever again." Jesus said to her, "Go and bring your husband to me." The woman was startled with guilt and said, "I don't have a husband." Jesus said to her, "You are right in saying 'I do not have a husband.' The truth is, you have had five husbands, and the man you now live with is not your husband." The woman said to him, "Sir, I can see that you are a prophet. Our Samaritan ancestors worshiped on this mountain Gerizim, but you Jews say that we must worship at the Jerusalem temple." Jesus said to her, "Woman, believe me, the time is coming when you will not worship the Father on your mountain nor in Jerusalem. You Samaritans worship what you do not know, but we worship what we know, for salvation is from the Jews. But the time is coming and has now come, when the true worshipers of God will worship the Father in the Holy Spirit and truth. The Father seeks these kind of worshipers. God is Spirit, and his worshipers must worship in the Holy Spirit and in truth." The woman said to him, "I know that the Messiah is coming. And when he comes, he will explain everything we need to know." Then Jesus said to her, "The one who is speaking to you is the Messiah—I am he!"

Just then Jesus' disciples returned from buying food, and they were amazed that he was talking with a Samaritan woman." Then the woman dropped her water jar and hurried into town and told the people, "Come with me, meet a man who told me everything I ever did. Do you think he could be the Messiah?" Many Samaritans rushed out of the town to meet Jesus.

Meanwhile, Jesus' disciples said to him, "Teacher, you need to eat something." But Jesus said to them, "I have food to eat that you do not know about." Then his disciples looked confused and said to each other, "Has someone given him food?" Jesus said, "My food is to do the will of of him who sent me into this world and to finish his work. You often say, 'There are still four months until the harvest.' Look! I tell you the truth: Lift up your eyes and see that the fields are already ripe for harvest. Many of the Samaritans from the town Sychar believed in Jesus because the woman said, "He told me everything I ever did."

So when the Samaritans came to Jesus, they asked him to stay with them, and he stayed there for two more days. And during that time, many more Samaritans believed in Jesus because of his teaching. They said to the woman, "We first believed because of what you told us, but now we have heard for ourselves, and we know that this man is truly the Savior of the world!" After spending two days in Samaria, Jesus left and walked north into Galilee.

PART TWO

CHAPTER 5

Jesus entered Galilee in the power of the Holy Spirit, and news about him spread throughout the whole region. The region of Galilee was 45 miles north-south and 25 miles east-west, with a population of about 300,000 living in about 200 villages and towns. All the people of Galilee welcomed Jesus, for they had seen the miracles that he had done at the Passover Feast in Jerusalem. Jesus taught in their synagogues and was praised by everyone. From that time on, Jesus proclaimed the good news of God, and that the kingdom of God has arrived! He declared that the time has been fulfilled and that the people must repent, turn to God, and believe the good news of God.

Once again, Jesus walked to Cana in Galilee, where he had turned water into wine. In Capernaum there lived a Roman military officer whose son was very sick. When this man heard that Jesus had returned to Galilee from Judea, he hurried to Cana to meet Jesus and begged him to come to Capernaum and heal his dying son. Jesus said to him, "Unless you people see miraculous signs and wonders you will never believe." The official said to him, "Sir, come down before my son dies." Jesus said, "Go, your son will live." The man believed what Jesus said and left for his home. While he was walking from Cana to Capernaum, his servants met him and said, "Your son is living!" The man asked them, "What time did he begin to get better?" They said, "Yesterday in the early afternoon." Then the father realized that it was the exact time that Jesus had said to him, "Your son will live." So, the official and his whole household believed in Jesus. This was the second miracle that Jesus did after coming from Judea to Galilee.

After the healing of the officer's son, Jesus walked from Cana to his hometown of Nazareth. On the Sabbath day Jesus went into the synagogue. When he stood up to read, he was given the scroll of the prophet Isaiah. Jesus unrolled the scroll and read *Isaiah 61:1-2* out loud, "The Spirit of the Lord has come upon me, for he has anointed me to proclaim the good news to the poor. The Lord has sent me to proclaim freedom for the prisoners and to give sight to the blind, to set free everyone who is oppressed, and to declare the year of the Lord's favor.'" Then Jesus rolled up the scroll, handed it back to the synagogue attendant and sat down. Everyone in the synagogue was staring at him. Then Jesus said to them, "Today, this passage in Isaiah is fulfilled in your hearing." All the people in Nazareth were saying good things about Jesus and were amazed at the gracious words that he spoke. They asked each other, "Isn't this Joseph's son?" Jesus said to them, "Surely you will tell me, 'Do the miracles here in Nazareth that we hear you did in Capernaum.' But I tell you the truth: No prophet is accepted by the people of his hometown. I assure you that there were many widows in Israel during the time of Elijah, when there was no rain for three and one half years and there was a severe famine throughout the land. Yet Elijah was not sent to any of the widows of Israel, but to a widow in the town of Zarephath in the non-Jewish region of Sidon. And many people in Israel had leprosy during the time of the prophet Elisha, but none of them were healed except Naaman the Syrian." When the people in the synagogue heard Jesus speak about God's favor on non-Jews, they became filled with anger. They got up, drove Jesus out of the town, and took him to the edge of the cliff on which Nazareth was built, so they could throw him over. But Jesus walked right through the crowd and went on his way.

After being rejected in Nazareth, Jesus went to live in the town of Capernaum. Capernaum was located on the north coast of Lake Galilee. It had a population of about 1,500. Jesus' permanent move to

Capernaum fulfilled what is written in *Isaiah 9:1-2*, "Land of Zebulun and land of Naphtali, the Way to the Sea, east of the Jordan River in Perea, Galilee of the non-Jews—the people living in darkness have seen a great light; on those living in the land of the shadow of death a light has risen.

One day Jesus left Capernaum and was walking along the northwest coast of Lake Galilee. As Jesus was walking along the shore, he saw the brothers Peter and Andrew. Peter and Andrew were fishermen, and they were throwing a fishing net into the lake. Jesus called out to them, "Come, follow me, and I will send you out to fish for people." Immediately they left their fishing nets and followed Jesus. Walking a little further along the shore, Jesus saw the brothers James and John in a fishing boat with their father, Zebedee, mending their fishing nets. Jesus called James and John to follow him. They immediately left their fishing boat, their father Zebedee, and the hired men, and followed Jesus.

Leaving the coast of Lake Galilee, Jesus, Peter, Andrew, James, and John walked back into Capernaum. On the Sabbath day, Jesus entered the synagogue and began to teach the people. Suddenly, a demon-possessed man screamed out in the synagogue, "Jesus of Nazareth, what do you want with us? Leave us alone! Have you come to destroy us? Go away, Jesus of Nazareth! Why are you bothering us? We know you are the Holy One of God!" Jesus spoke with God's authority and ordered the demon, "Be quiet! Come out of him!" The demon shook the man violently and threw him to the ground in front of everyone. Then the demon came out of the man with a loud shriek, but the demon did not hurt him.

After casting out the demon from the man, the people attending the synagogue were all amazed at what they saw and asked each other, "What is this? What kind of teaching is this? Is this a new teaching with authority? Jesus' message has God's authority and power to order demons to come out of people. He commands demons and they obey him. Jesus teaches with God's authority and not like our religious leaders." After Jesus set free the demon-possessed man in the Capernaum synagogue, news about Jesus spread throughout the whole surrounding region of Galilee.

With James and John, Jesus left the Capernaum synagogue and entered the house of Peter and Andrew which was nearby. When they arrived, Peter's mother-in-law was lying in bed suffering with a terrible fever. They told Jesus about her and asked him to help her. Jesus went and touched her hand, bent over her, and ordered the fever to leave her. And the fever left her. Then Jesus took her hand and helped her up from her bed. She immediately got up and began to serve them.

That evening—after sunset when the Sabbath was over—the people of Capernaum gathered outside the door of Peter's house. They brought to Jesus the people who suffered from various kinds of sickness—those who were sick and demon-possessed. Jesus healed the people of all kinds of diseases and all who were sick by placing his hands on them. He drove out the demons from people with a single command. Demons came out of many people shouting, "You are the Son of God!" But Jesus rebuked the demons and ordered them not to speak because for they knew that he was the Messiah. This fulfilled what is written in *Isaiah 53:4*, "He took up our infirmities and carried our diseases."

The next morning, Jesus got up just before daybreak. He left Peter's house in Capernaum and walked to an isolated place in the hills west of Lake Galilee where he could be alone and pray. Peter and many people left Capernaum and went out to search for Jesus. When they found him, they said, "Everyone in Capernaum is looking for you!" And they tried to stop Jesus from leaving them. But Jesus said to Peter and the crowd of people, "Let's leave here and walk through the nearby towns of Galilee, so that I can proclaim the good news of the kingdom of God there also, for this is the reason that I came into the world." So they walked throughout Galilee, preaching and teaching in their synagogues, proclaiming the message of the kingdom of God, casting demons out of people, and healing every kind of disease and sickness among the people. And Jesus kept on preaching in the synagogues of Galilee.

As a result of his ministry, news about Jesus spread throughout the whole region of Syria, a non-Jewish region north of Galilee between Damascus and the Mediterranean Sea. And people brought to Jesus all who were sick with various diseases, those suffering severe pain, those tormented by demons, those having seizures, and those who were paralyzed. Jesus healed them all! Large crowds of people from Galilee, the Decapolis, Jerusalem, Judea, and the region of Perea east of the Jordan River followed Jesus

One day as Jesus was standing on the northwest coast of Lake Galilee, a crowd of people pressed around him to listen to the word of God. Jesus saw two fishing boats at the shore that had been left there by some fishermen washing their nets. Jesus got into Peter's fishing boat, and asked him to push the boat out a short way from the shore. Then he sat down in the boat and taught the people.

When Jesus had finished teaching, he told Peter, "Row your boat into deep water, and let down your nets for a catch of fish." Peter said, "Master, we've fished all night and have not caught anything. But because you say so, I will let down my nets." When they did what Jesus had told them, they caught such a large number of fish that their nets began to tear. So Peter and Andrew called to their fishing partners James and John in the other boat to come and help them. They came and filled both boats with so many fish that they began to sink. When Peter saw this catch of fish, he fell at Jesus' feet and declared, "Lord! Go away from me, for I am a sinful man!" They were all amazed at their catch of fish. Then Jesus said to Peter, "Don't be afraid; from now on you will fish for people." So when they pulled their boats up onto the shore, they left everything and followed Jesus.

When Jesus was in one of the towns of Galilee, a man walked by who was covered with a severe skin disease. When he saw Jesus, he came and fell on his knees and then bowed with his face to the ground before him. The man begged Jesus saying, "Lord, if you are willing, you can heal me and make me clean." Jesus was filled with compassion and reached out his hand and touched the man saying, "I am willing. Be healed! Be clean!" Immediately his skin disease disappeared and he was healed. Then Jesus sent him away with a strong warning. He ordered the man, "Make sure you don't tell anyone that I healed you, but go to Jerusalem and show yourself to the temple priests and offer the sacrifices according to the law Moses commanded for your cleansing. For this will be a witness to them." But instead of going to the

Jerusalem temple, the man healed of a skin disease went out and told everyone about Jesus.

Because of Jesus' ministry, news about him spread even more, so that large crowds of people came to hear him teach and be healed of their sicknesses. Because of the growing crowds, Jesus could no longer walk into a town in Galilee openly. So he would often withdraw from the crowds of people and go out to stay in rural, isolated places, where he could be alone and pray. But people would still go out to see him from everywhere.

When the people heard that Jesus was in Capernaum, they went to Peter's house and gathered in such large numbers that there was no room left, not even outside the door. Jewish religious leaders were also sitting there from every village of Galilee and Judea and from Jerusalem. And Jesus taught them the word of God.

When God's power was with Jesus to heal the sick, four men carried a paralyzed man on a stretcher to him. They tried to take him into Peter's house and lay him before Jesus, but they could not get near him because of the large crowd of people. So the four men took stairs onto the roof, dug a hole in the roof, and lowered the paralyzed man on his stretcher through the tiles into the middle of the crowd—right in front of Jesus. When Jesus saw the faith of the four men who brought him, he said to the paralyzed man, "My friend, take heart; your sins are forgiven." Now when the religious leaders heard Jesus, they said to one another, "Why is he talking like this? He is blaspheming! Who can forgive sins, but God alone? He is making himself equal with God." Jesus knew in his spirit what the religious leaders were thinking in their hearts. He said to them, "Why are you thinking this way? Why do you allow evil thoughts to enter your hearts? What is easier for me to say, 'Your sins are forgiven,' or to say, 'Stand up, take your stretcher and walk'? I want you to know that the Son of Man has God's authority on earth to forgive sins." Then Jesus said to the paralyzed man, "Stand up, take your stretcher and go home." The paralyzed man was healed immediately. He stood up in front of everyone, took his stretcher, and walked out of the house for everyone to see. He walked home praising God. When the crowd of people saw that the paralyzed man was healed, they were amazed and praised God because he had given such authority to man. They were filled with awe and said, "We have never seen anything like this before! We have seen a miracle today!"

Jesus left Capernaum and once again walked along the northwest coast of Lake Galilee. At that time a large crowd of people gathered around Jesus, and he began to teach them. As Jesus was walking along the shore, he saw Matthew, a chief tax collector, sitting at his tax booth. Jesus called out to Matthew, "Follow me!" So Matthew immediately stood up, left his booth and everything else, and followed Jesus.

After becoming a disciple of Jesus, Matthew held a large banquet for him at his house in Capernaum. While Jesus was at Matthew's house, a large crowd of tax collectors and sinners were eating with Jesus and his disciples. Many of them were followers of Jesus. When the religious leaders saw Jesus eating with tax collectors and sinners, they complained and asked Jesus' disciples, "Why do you and your teacher eat and drink with tax collectors and sinners?" Eating with people—table fellowship—was an indication of friendship. The religious leaders would not eat with those they considered to be nonreligious sinners and social outcasts. In contrast, Jesus broke down these barriers by eating with all classes of people to show them the love of God. People who did not live a lifestyle according to God's law were called 'sinners'. They were religious outcasts. Jesus heard the religious leaders and said, "It is not the healthy who need a doctor, but the sick. I have not come into the world to call the righteous, but sinners to repent and turn to God. You need to go and learn the meaning of *Hosea 6:6*, 'I desire mercy, not sacrifice.'"

The disciples of John the Baptist and the Jewish religious leaders would often pray and fast. And so after seeing Jesus banqueting at Matthew's house, the disciples of John the Baptist came and asked Jesus, "Why do we fast and pray, but your disciples continue to eat and drink and do not fast?" Jesus said to them, "You cannot make the wedding guests of the bridegroom mourn and fast while he is still with them. But the time will come when the bridegroom will be taken away from them, and then my disciples will fast." Jesus used the example of a wedding celebration to respond to those asking why his disciples did not fast. As part of the wedding celebration, the bridegroom went out to receive his bride from her parents' home and bring her to his own. His friends and family participated in the joyful procession. After this bridegroom procession, they ate a marriage feast. Jesus identified himself as the bridegroom, and his disciples as the wedding guests. It would be after Jesus' ascension to heaven that his disciples would fast. Jesus was referring to his ascension into heaven when he said that the bridegroom will be taken away from them.

Then Jesus told them these stories of the old and the new: "No one takes a new cloth patch and sews it on an old garment. The new patch will shrink when the garment is washed, and the new patch will tear away from the old. The tear will be worse than it was at the beginning. The new patch will not match the old garment. Neither do people pour new wine into old wineskins, otherwise the new wine will expand and cause the old wineskins to break open. Then the new wine will pour out, and both the new wine and wineskins will be ruined and useless. Instead, pour new wine into new wineskins, and then both of them will be preserved. No one after drinking old wine wants to drink new wine, for they will say, 'The old wine is better.'" In saying this, Jesus emphasized that the new covenant with God was totally incompatible with rigid religious traditionalism and human rules. For in Jesus, the kingdom of God became a new present reality.

CHAPTER 6

Jesus left Galilee and walked up to Jerusalem to attend a Jewish feast. He entered Jerusalem through the Sheep Gate, where he passed a pool of water called Bethesda. The pool was surrounded with a large number of disabled people—blind, lame, and paralyzed—lying helplessly on the ground.

There was a man lying at the pool who had been disabled for 38 years. When Jesus saw him lying on the ground, and learned that he had been in this condition for a long time, he asked him, "Do you want to be healed?" The disabled man said, "Sir, I have no one to put me into the pool when the water stirs. And when I do try to get in, someone else goes down before me." At that time they believed that they would be healed if they got into the water when an angel stirred it. Then Jesus said to him, "Stand up! Pick up your mat and walk." Immediately, the man was healed, and he picked up his mat and walked away.

Now the healing of this disabled man took place on the Sabbath day, and some religious Jews said to the man who had been healed, "You are breaking the law of Moses by carrying your mat on the Sabbath." But the man said to them, "The man who healed me told me, 'Pick up your mat and walk.'" So the Jews asked him, "Tell us, who is this man who told you to pick up your mat and walk?" The man who was healed had no idea who he was, for Jesus had slipped away into the crowd of people.

Later Jesus found the man in the temple and said to him, "You are now healed! Stop sinning or something worse can happen to you." The man left and told the religious leaders that it was Jesus who had healed him. So the religious leaders began to persecute Jesus for healing on the Sabbath. But Jesus said to them, "My Father is always at his work to this very day, and I too am working." After Jesus said this, the religious leaders tried even more to kill him, not only because he was breaking the Sabbath law, but because he was also calling God his Father—making himself equal with God.

Jesus said to the religious leaders, "I tell you the truth: The Son can do nothing on his own; he can do only what he sees his Father doing, for whatever the Father does the Son also does. For the Father loves the Son and shows him all he does. Yes, and the Father will show him even greater works than these, so that you will be amazed. For just as the Father raises the dead and gives them life, even so the Son gives life to those he is pleased to give it. Moreover, the Father judges no one, but he has given all judgment to the Son, so that everyone will honor the Son just as they honor the Father. Whoever does not honor the Son does not honor the Father, who sent him into this world. I tell you the truth: Whoever hears my word and believes him who sent me has eternal life and will not be judged, but has crossed over from death to life. A time is coming and is now here, when the dead will hear the voice of the Son of God, and those who hear will live. For as the Father has life in himself, so he has also granted the Son to have life in himself. And the Father has given the Son authority to execute judgment because he is the Son of Man."

Then Jesus said, "Do not be surprised at my teaching, for a time is coming when the dead in their graves will hear the Father's voice and be raised to life—those who have done what is good will rise to life, but those who have done what is evil will rise to be condemned. I can do nothing on my own. I judge only what I hear, and my judgment is just, for I do not seek to please myself, but the will of the Father who sent me into this world. If I testify about myself, then my testimony is not true. But there is another one who testifies about me, and I know that his testimony is true. You religious leaders sent men to question John the Baptist, and he told you the truth. I don't need any human testimony, but I say this so that you will be saved. John was a burning lamp that shined forth light, and you chose for a while to enjoy his light. But I have a much greater testimony than that of John. For the works that the Father has given me to accomplish—the very works that I am doing—prove that the Father sent me into this world. And the Father who sent me testifies about me. You have never heard his voice nor seen his form, nor does his word live in you, for you do not believe in the one he sent. You study God's word zealously because you think that in it you have eternal life. However, these are the very Scriptures that testify about me, but you still refuse to come to me to receive eternal life. I know that you do not have the love of God in your hearts. I came in my Father's name, and you do not believe in me; but if someone else comes in his own name, you will embrace him. How can you believe when you accept praise from one another, but make no effort to seek the glory that comes from the only God? But do not think that I will accuse you before the Father. For Moses—the one you put your hope in—is the one who accuses you. For if you believed Moses, you would believe me, for he wrote about me. But since you do not believe in the writings of Moses, how will you believe my teaching?"

After returning from the Jewish feast in Jerusalem, Jesus and his disciples were walking through the grain fields in Galilee on the Sabbath day. His disciples were hungry and so they picked some heads of grain, rubbed them in their hands, and ate the kernels. When some of the Jewish religious leaders saw the disciples do this, they asked them, "Why are you doing work that is unlawful on the Sabbath?" Then they said to Jesus, "Look! Your disciples are doing work that is unlawful on the Sabbath." Jesus heard them and said, "Haven't you read *1 Samuel 21:1-6* when David and his men were in need and were hungry? In those days David went into God's temple and ate holy bread and gave some of it to his men to eat, which was unlawful because the holy bread was only for the priests to eat. Listen to me! The Sabbath was made for people, not people for the Sabbath. I tell you the truth: Someone greater than the temple is here. If you really knew the meaning of *Hosea 6:6*, 'I desire mercy, not sacrifice,' you would not have accused those who are innocent. For the Son of Man is the Lord of the Sabbath!"

Jesus walked away and entered the Capernaum synagogue to teach on the Sabbath day. In the synagogue was a man who had a shriveled right hand. Some Jewish religious leaders were looking for a reason to accuse Jesus of doing something wrong so they could bring charges against him. They watched him closely to see if he would heal the man on the Sabbath. Then the religious leaders asked Jesus, "Is it lawful to heal on the Sabbath?" Jesus said to them, "If any of you has a sheep and it falls into a hole on the Sabbath, will you not pull it out? How much more valuable are people to God than sheep! Therefore, it is lawful to do good on the Sabbath." Jesus knew what the religious leaders were thinking. Then Jesus said to the man with the withered hand, "Get up and stand in front of everyone." So the man got up and stood there. Jesus asked the religious leaders "Which is lawful on the Sabbath, to do good or to do evil? To save life or to kill?" But they did not say anything. Jesus looked around at them with anger because he was deeply troubled by their stubborn hearts. Then Jesus said to the man, "Stretch out your hand!" When the man stretched out his hand, it was totally healed.

After Jesus healed the man's hand in the synagogue, the religious leaders became furious. So they quickly left the synagogue and began to plot together with the Herodians on how they could go against Jesus and how they could kill him. The Herodians were a Jewish political party that supported the sons of King Herod the Great, who were closely aligned with the Roman rulers.

When Jesus learned that the religious leaders were planning to kill him, he and his disciples left Capernaum and walked out to the northwest coast of Lake Galilee. A large crowd of people from Galilee followed Jesus, and he healed all who were sick. Jesus told the people he healed not to tell anyone. But when the people heard about all the miracles that Jesus was doing, a huge crowd of people came to him from Judea, Jerusalem, Idumea, the region of Perea east of the Jordan River, and from around Tyre and Sidon.

Because of the growing crowd Jesus told his disciples to get a small boat ready for him, so that the people would not crush him. Because Jesus had healed so many people, those with diseases were pushing forward to touch him. Whenever demons saw Jesus, those who were demon-possessed fell down before him and cried out, "You are the Son of God!" But Jesus commanded the demons not to tell others who he was. All this happened to fulfill the words written in *Isaiah 42:1-4*, "Here is my chosen servant, the one I love and in whom I delight. I will put my Spirit on him, and he will proclaim justice to the nations. He will not argue or cry out. No one will hear his voice in the streets, for a bruised reed he will not break, and a smoldering wick he will not snuff out. He will lead justice to victory, and the nations will put their hope in his name."

CHAPTER 7

Jesus left Capernaum and walked up a hill west of Lake Galilee to pray. He spent the whole night praying to God. In the morning Jesus called his disciples and gathered around him those he wanted. He selected and appointed 12 of these disciples to be with him, and to be his apostles. The term 'apostle' means "one who is sent." He chose his apostles so that he could send them out to preach and have God's authority to cast out demons from people. These are the names of the Twelve Apostles that Jesus selected: the brothers Peter and Andrew; the brothers James and John; Philip; Bartholomew (Nathanael); Matthew; Thomas; James son of Alphaeus; Simon called the Zealot; Jude (Thaddaeus); and Judas Iscariot, who would betray Jesus.

Jesus walked down the hill with his apostles and stood on a plateau area of land. A large crowd of his disciples was there and a great number of people who had come from all over Judea, from Jerusalem, and the Mediterranean coastal region of non-Jewish Tyre and Sidon. The crowd came to hear Jesus teach and to be healed of their diseases. Those who were tormented by demons were set free, and the people tried to touch Jesus, for God's power was coming from his body and healing everybody.

When Jesus saw the large crowds following him, he went back up on the hill, sat down, and taught his disciples the blessings of the kingdom of God that are known as the "Beatitudes." He taught, "Blessed are the poor in spirit, for theirs is the kingdom of God. Blessed are those who weep now, for they will laugh. Blessed are those who mourn, for they will be given comfort. Blessed are those who hunger and thirst for the right ways of God, for they will be filled. Blessed are the humble, for they will inherit the earth. Blessed are the merciful, for they will be shown mercy. Blessed are the pure in heart, for they will see God. Blessed are those who work for peace, for they will be called the children of God. Blessed are those who are persecuted for obeying the right ways of God, for theirs is the kingdom of God. Blessed are you when people insult you, persecute you, and say false words about you because of me. Rejoice and be happy, for your reward in heaven will be great, for in the same way they persecuted the Old Testament prophets who came before you. Blessed are you when people hate you, exclude you, and insult you, and call you evil, for you are a follower of the Son of Man. Rejoice in that day and jump for joy, for great is your reward in heaven, for that is how their ancestors treated the Old Testament prophets."

Then Jesus continued to teach them what is today called the Sermon on the Mount.

"How terrible for you who are rich now, for you have already received your comfort. How terrible for you who are well fed now, for you will be hungry. How terrible for you who are laughing now, for you will mourn and weep. How terrible for those who say good things about you, for that is how their ancestors treated the false prophets.

"You are the salt of the earth! But if salt loses its taste, it cannot be made to taste like salt again. It is no longer good for anything except to be thrown on the ground and walked on. You are the light of the world! A city built on a hill cannot be hidden. People do not light a lamp and put it under a bowl. Instead they put a lamp on a stand, so that it gives light to everyone in the house. In the same way, let your light shine before others, so that they will see your good works and praise your Father in heaven.

"Do not think that I came to eliminate the law of Moses or the prophets. I did not come to destroy them, but to fulfill them! For I tell you the truth: Until heaven and earth disappear, not the smallest mark of a letter from the law of Moses will be taken away until everything in it is fulfilled. Therefore, whoever eliminates one of the least of God's commandments and teaches others to do the same will be called the least in the kingdom of God. But whoever obeys and teaches God's commandments will be called the greatest in the kingdom of God. For I tell you the truth: Unless your righteousness is greater than that of the religious leaders, you will certainly not enter the kingdom of God.

"You have heard that it was said to the people long ago in *Exodus 20:13*, 'Do not murder.' But I say to you that anyone who is angry with another believer will be subject to judgment. Again, anyone who insults another believer will be brought before the Jewish governing council. And anyone who says, 'You are a fool,' to another believer will be in danger of the fire of hell.

"If you are offering your gift at God's altar and there remember that your fellow believer has something against you, leave your gift at the altar. First go and heal the relationship with your fellow believer; then go back and offer your gift to God. Immediately settle matters with your adversary who is taking you to court. Do it while you are walking together to the courthouse, or he will hand you over to the judge, and the judge will hand you over to a guard, and you will be thrown into prison. I tell you the truth: You will not get out of prison until you have paid the very last penny you owe that person.

"You have heard that it is written in *Exodus 20:14*, 'Do not commit adultery.' But I say to you that anyone who looks at a woman with sexual lust has already committed adultery with her in his heart.

"If your right eye causes you to sin, pull it out and throw it away. For it is far better for you to lose one eye than for your whole body to be thrown into hell. And if your right hand causes you to sin, cut it off and throw it away. For it is far better for you to lose one hand than for your whole body to be thrown into hell.

"It has been written in *Deuteronomy 24:1*, 'Whoever divorces his wife must give her a certificate of divorce.' But I say to you that whoever divorces his wife, except for marital unfaithfulness, makes her commit adultery, and whoever marries a divorced woman commits adultery.

"You have heard that it was said to the people long ago in *Leviticus 19:12*, 'Do not break your oath, but fulfill to the Lord any vows you have made.' But I say to you: Do not make any oaths—either by heaven, for it is God's throne; or by the earth, for the earth is God's footstool; or by Jerusalem, for it is the city of the Great King. And do not make an oath by your head, for you cannot make even one hair white or black. I tell you to say either 'Yes' or 'No.' To say anything more than this comes from Satan, the evil one.

"You have heard that it was said in *Exodus 21:24*, 'An eye for an eye and a tooth for a tooth.' But I say to you: Do not use violence to resist an evil person. If anyone slaps you with a backhand on your right cheek in an attempt to humiliate you, turn your left cheek to them. And if anyone sues you in court and takes your inner shirt, give them your outer coat also. If anyone forces you to go one mile, insist on going with them for two miles. If anyone asks you to give them something, give it to them; do not turn away a person who wants to borrow from you.

"You have heard that it was written in *Leviticus 19:18*, 'Love your neighbor,' and others have said, 'hate your enemy.' But I say to you: Love your enemies and pray for those who persecute you. If you do this, you will be children of your Father in heaven. For God causes his sun to rise on the good and the evil, and sends rain on the righteous and the unrighteous. If you love only those who love you, why should you get a reward for that? For even tax collectors love those who love them. And if you greet only your friends, you are no better than anyone else. For even unbelievers greet their friends. Therefore, you must be holy like your heavenly Father is holy.

"Be careful not to practice your righteousness in front of other people, with the desire to be seen by them. If you do, you will not receive a reward from your Father in heaven. Therefore, when you give to people in need, do not draw attention to yourselves by blowing trumpets like the religious hypocrites do in the synagogues and on the streets. They simply want to be praised by people who see them. I tell you the truth: They have received their full reward. But when you give to people in need, do not let your left hand know what your right hand is doing, so that your giving to others will be done in private.

Then your Father—who sees everything that is done in private—will reward you.

"This is how you should pray: 'Our Father in heaven, holy is your name, your kingdom come, your will be done, on earth as it is in heaven. Give us today our daily bread. And forgive us our debts, as we also have forgiven our debtors. And lead us not into temptation, but deliver us from Satan, the evil one.'

"For if you forgive other people when they sin against you, your Father in heaven will also forgive you. But if you do not forgive the sins of others, your Father will not forgive your sins.

"When you fast, do not fast like the religious hypocrites, who put on a sad face to show other people that they are fasting. I tell you the truth: They have received their full reward. But when you fast, comb your hair and wash your face, so that other people will not know that you are fasting, but only your Father, who is unseen; and your Father, who sees everything that is done in private, will reward you.

"Do not store up treasures for yourselves on earth, where moths and rust destroy, and where thieves break in and steal. Instead, store up for yourselves treasures in heaven. Sell what you own and give to the poor. Pursue money bags for yourselves that will not wear out, a treasure in heaven that will never fail. For where your treasure is, there your heart will be also.

"Your eyes are the lamp of your body. When your eyes are good and sincere, then your whole body will be full of shining light. If your whole body is full of shining light—having no darkness—then it will be just as when a lamp shines its light on you. But when your eyes are evil, your body will radiate darkness. Therefore, watch carefully that the light within you does not become darkness, for your darkness will be great!

"You cannot serve two masters: You will either love one and hate the other, or you will be devoted to one and despise the other. You cannot serve God and money.

"I tell you the truth: Do not worry about your life, what you will eat or drink, or about the clothes you will wear. For life is much more than food, and your body is much more important than what clothes you will wear. Watch the birds flying in the sky. Watch how the birds live. They do not work. They do not plant or harvest. They have no storerooms or barns for their food, but God, your Father in heaven, feeds them! And you are much more valuable than birds! You cannot add a single hour to your life by worrying. Since you can't do this, why do you worry about everything else? Why do you worry about what clothes you will wear? Watch the wild flowers grow in the field. Look, they do not labor or work. I tell you the truth: Not even Solomon in all his kingly splendor was dressed like the beauty of the flowers. So if that is how God clothes the grass of the field—which is here today and tomorrow is thrown into the fire—how much more will God clothe you, you of little faith! Do not worry about your life. Do not set your heart on what you will eat or drink. Stop saying, 'What will we eat?' or 'What will we drink?' or 'What will we wear?' Do not worry about all these things of life! For the people of this world live for all these things, and your Father in heaven knows what you need in life. Instead, seek first the kingdom of God and his righteousness and all these things you need in life will be given to you. Do not be afraid, little flock, for your Father in heaven is pleased to give you the kingdom of God. Therefore, do not worry about tomorrow, for tomorrow will have its own worries. Today has enough trouble of its own.

"Do not judge others, so that you will not be judged. Do not condemn others, and you will not be condemned. For in the same way you judge others, you will be judged. The measure you use to judge others will be the same measure used against you. Forgive others, and you will be forgiven. Give to others, and it will be given to you. You will receive much. It will be poured over into your lap, for the amount you give is the amount that you will receive. Can the blind lead the blind? Won't they both fall into a hole? The student is not above his teacher. But everyone who is fully trained will be like their teacher. Why do you notice the small piece of sawdust in a fellow believer's eye, but ignore the large piece of wood in your own eye? How can you say to a fellow believer, 'Let me take the small piece of sawdust out of your eye,' when you have a large piece of wood in your own eye? You religious hypocrites! First remove the large piece of wood out of your own eye, and then you can see clearly to remove the small piece of sawdust from the eye of your fellow believer.

"A good tree produces good fruit, and a bad tree produces bad fruit. Each tree is recognized by the kind of fruit it produces. We do not pick figs from thorn bushes, or grapes from thistles. A good man brings good treasure out of the good stored up in his heart, and an evil man brings evil things out of the evil stored up in his heart. For a man speaks out of the abundance that has been stored up in his heart.

"Do not give dogs what is holy, or throw pearls before pigs. If you do, they will trample them, and then attack you and tear you to pieces.

"Suppose you go to your friend at midnight and tell him, 'My dear friend, please lend me three loaves of bread, for another friend on a long journey has come to visit my home, and I have no food to give him.' But suppose the friend you asked for bread tells you, 'Don't bother me! My door is already locked, and my family is all sleeping. I can't get up out of bed and give you any bread.' I tell you the truth: Even though your friend will not at first get out of bed to give you bread, yet if you are persistent and keep asking, he will finally get up and give you as much as you need. Keep asking and it will be given to you; keep seeking and you will find; keep knocking and the door will be opened to you. For everyone who asks receives; everyone who seeks finds; and to the one who knocks, the door will be opened to you. Tell me, which of you fathers, if your son asks for a fish or bread, will give him a stone or a snake? Or if he asks you for an egg, will give him a scorpion? Not one of you! Therefore, if you earthly fathers give good gifts to your children, how much more will your Father in heaven give good gifts and the Holy Spirit to those who ask him!

"So in all things, do to others what you would have them do to you, for this way of living fulfills the teaching of the entire Old Testament.

"Enter through the narrow gate! For the gate is wide and the road is easy that leads to destruction, and many people choose to go this way. The gate is narrow and the road is hard that leads to eternal life, and only a few people choose to go this way. Make every effort to enter through the narrow gate, for I tell you the truth, many people will try to enter and will not be able to.

"Watch out for false prophets. They come to you wearing sheep's clothing, but on the inside they are ferocious wolves. You can recognize false prophets by their fruits—how they live their lives. People do not pick grapes from thorn bushes, or figs from thistles. Good trees produce good fruit, but bad trees produce bad fruit. Every tree that does not produce good fruit is cut down and thrown into the fire. For not everyone who says to me on the final day, 'Lord, Lord,' will enter the kingdom of God, but only those who do the will of my Father who is in heaven. Many will say to me on the final day, 'Lord, Lord, we prophesied in your name, drove out demons in your name, and performed many miracles in your name.' Then I will tell them directly, 'I never knew you. Away from me! You have lived evil lives!'

"Why do you call me, 'Lord, Lord,' and do not do what I teach? Therefore, whoever comes to me, hears my teaching, and puts it into practice is like a wise man building a house. He dug down deep and built the house on a rock foundation. And when the rains came, the rivers rose, the winds blew, and the rushing waters hit against that house, the house did not shake and fall, for its foundation was built on the solid rock and was built well. But whoever hears my teaching and does not put it into practice is like a foolish man who built his house on sand without a rock foundation. And when the rains came, the rivers rose, the winds blew, and the rushing water hit that house, it fell with a great crash and it was completely destroyed."

After Jesus had finished his teaching, the crowds of people were amazed at what he said, for he taught as one who had God's authority, and not like their religious teachers. When Jesus came down from the hillside, large crowds of people followed him.

CHAPTER 8

After Jesus' teaching he walked back into the town of Capernaum. In Capernaum a Roman military officer heard about Jesus and sent some Jewish elders to ask him to come and heal his servant who was about to die. When they came to Jesus, they pleaded with him saying, "This Roman deserves to have you heal his servant because he loves our nation, and he is the one who built our synagogue." Then the military leader came and begged Jesus for his help saying, "Lord, my servant lies at home paralyzed, and he is in great suffering. Jesus said to him, "Should I come and heal him?" The military leader said, "Lord, I am not worthy for you to come into my house. Instead, just give a command, and my servant will be healed. For I work under the authority of military leaders, and my soldiers work under my command. And I tell a soldier under me to 'Go,' and he goes. I tell a soldier to 'Come,' and he comes. I tell my servant, 'Do this,' and he does it." When Jesus heard this, he was amazed and said to those following him, "I tell you the truth: I have not found anyone in Israel with such great faith. I tell you that many people will come from the east and the west to take their places at the final banquet with Abraham, Isaac, and Jacob in the kingdom of God. But many people in Israel will be thrown out into the darkness, where people will be weeping and grinding their teeth." Then Jesus said to the military leader, "Go! Let your servant be healed as you believed he would." And his servant was healed that very moment.

After healing the servant of the military officer, Jesus left Capernaum and walked to a small town called Nain that was located six miles southeast of Nazareth. His disciples and a large crowd of people followed him. As Jesus approached the town gate, he saw a dead man being carried out of the town. The man was the only son of his mother, who was a widow. And a large crowd was walking with her. When the Lord saw the woman, his heart was filled with compassion for her and he said, "Don't cry." Then Jesus went up and touched the wooden board on which they were carrying her son. Those carrying him stopped. And Jesus said, "Young man, I tell you to get up!" The dead man sat up and began to talk, and Jesus gave him back to his mother. All the people who saw this were filled with awe and praised God and declared, "A great prophet has walked among us today; God has come to help his people." The news about Jesus raising the dead man at Nain spread everywhere in the land of the Jews and the surrounding country.

After hearing Jesus' teaching and seeing his miracles, the disciples of John the Baptist went and told John in prison about all that Jesus was teaching and doing. John had been imprisoned for about one year at the Fortress Machaerus in the region of Perea, located on the eastern side of the Dead Sea. After John the Baptist heard what Jesus was doing, he called two of his disciples and sent them to ask Jesus, "Are you the one who is to come, or should we expect and look for someone else?" When they came to Jesus they said, "John sent us to ask you, 'Are you the one who is to come, or should we expect someone else?' At that very time Jesus was healing many people who had diseases, sicknesses, and were blind. He was also casting demons out of people. Jesus told John's disciples, "Go back and tell John what you see and hear: The blind see, the lame walk, the lepers are cleansed, the deaf hear, the dead are raised to life, and the good news of God is proclaimed to the poor. Blessed is everyone who does not stumble or fall away because of me."

After the two disciples of John the Baptist had left, Jesus said this to the crowd of people about John: "What did you go out to see in the Wilderness of Judea? A weak and fragile desert reed blowing in the wind? What did you go out to see? A man dressed in expensive

Chapter 8

clothes? No, those who wear expensive clothes and indulge in luxury live in the palaces of kings. Then what did you go to see? A prophet? Yes, I tell you the truth: He is much more than a prophet. For John is the one written about in *Malachi 3:1*, 'I will send my messenger ahead of you, who will prepare your way before you.' I tell you the truth: Among those born of women there is no one who is greater than John; yet whoever is least in the kingdom of God is greater than John. From the days of John until now, the kingdom of God has advanced in power and people of strong faith enter it. For the entire Old Testament foretold of all these things until the coming of John. And if you are willing to accept it, John is the Elijah who was to come. Whoever has ears to hear, let them hear!"

When all the people and the tax collectors heard Jesus' teaching, they confessed that God's way was right, for they had been baptized by John. But the Jewish religious leaders rejected God's plan for them, for they had not been baptized by John.

Then Jesus said, "John the Baptist did not come eating bread or drinking wine, and the religious leaders say, 'He has a demon.' The Son of Man came eating bread and drinking wine and they say, 'Look at him! He is a glutton and a drunkard, and a friend of tax collectors and sinners!'"

At that time a Jewish religious leader named Simon invited Jesus to have dinner with him. Simon's house also served as a synagogue for the community. Jesus entered into the house and reclined at the table. And a woman in that town who lived a life of sin came to the house with an alabaster jar filled with expensive fragrant oil because she heard that Jesus was eating at the house. As she stood at his feet weeping, her tears dripped onto his feet. Then she wiped his feet with her hair, kissed them, and poured perfume on them. When Simon saw this, he said to himself, "If Jesus was a true prophet, he would know what kind of woman is touching him—for she is a sinner." Then Jesus said to him, "Simon, I have a story to tell you." Simon said, "Tell me, teacher." Jesus said, "Two men were in debt to a moneylender; one man owed him 500 coins and the other 50 coins. Neither of these men had the money to repay the loan, so the moneylender forgave their debts.

Now tell me, which man will have a greater love for the moneylender?" Simon said, "The man who was forgiven the largest debt." Jesus said to him, "You are correct." Then Jesus turned toward the woman and said to Simon, "Look at this woman. I came into your house and you did not give me water to wash my feet, but she washed my feet with her tears and wiped them with her hair. You did not give me a kiss, but she has not stopped kissing my feet. You did not put oil on my head, but she has poured fragrant oil on my feet. Therefore, I tell you the truth: For her many sins have been forgiven, she has shown me great love. But whoever has been forgiven little shows little love." Jesus said to the woman, "Your sins are forgiven." The other guests said to one another, "Who is this Jesus who forgives sins?" Jesus said to the woman, "Go in peace, for your faith has saved you." Then Jesus declared, "Come to me, all you who are tired of carrying the heavy burdens of life, and I will give you rest. Live the way I live and learn from me, for I am gentle and humble in heart, and you will experience rest within your inner life. For my way of life is easy and my burden is light."

After this Jesus walked through the villages and towns of Galilee proclaiming the good news of the kingdom of God. The apostles were with him, and also some women who had been healed of demons and diseases: Mary Magdalene, who had seven demons cast out of her; Joanna the wife of Cuza, the house manager of Herod Antipas; Susanna; and a large number of other women. These women were helping to support them out of their own possessions.

Then the people brought to Jesus a demon-possessed man who could not see or talk. Jesus healed the man by casting the demon out. All the people were amazed. They said to one another, "Could this be the Son of David, the Messiah?" Some Jewish religious leaders came down from Jerusalem. When they heard that Jesus healed a demon-possessed man they said, "He is possessed by Satan! He casts out demons by Satan, the ruler of demons." Other people tested Jesus by asking him to show them a miraculous sign from heaven.

Jesus knew what the religious leaders were thinking, so he called them over and said to them: Every kingdom divided against itself cannot stand, it will fall into ruin. Every city divided against itself cannot stand. Every family divided against itself cannot stand. How can Satan cast out demons? If Satan fights himself and is divided, he cannot stand and that would be his end.

Jesus said to the religious leaders, "I tell you this because you accuse me of casting demons out of people by the power of Satan. But I cast out demons by God's power, and so the kingdom of God has already come upon you. Whoever is not with me is against me, and whoever does not gather with me scatters."

Because the religious leaders were saying that Jesus was possessed by Satan, he said to them, "I tell you the truth: People will be forgiven of all their sins and every blasphemous and slanderous word they say. And whoever speaks a word against the Son of Man will be forgiven. But whoever blasphemes the Holy Spirit will never be forgiven. For they will be guilty of an eternal sin." The eternal sin that will not be forgiven is attributing to Satan what is accomplished by the Holy Spirit. This sin is committed by unbelievers who deliberately reject the ministry of the Holy Spirit in calling them to salvation.

Then Jesus said to the religious leaders, "Make a tree good and its fruit will be good, or make a tree bad and its fruit will be bad, for a tree is known by its fruit. You are a group of snakes! How can you who are evil say anything good? For what a person says comes out of what fills his heart. A good person speaks good things out of the good stored up in his heart, and an evil person speaks evil things out of the evil stored up in his heart. I tell you the truth: On the day of God's judgment, everyone will give an account for every false word they have said. For by your words you will either be set free or condemned."

Then some of the religious leaders said to Jesus, "Teacher, we want to see you do a miraculous sign." As the crowd of people got bigger, Jesus said, "You are a wicked generation in Israel because it seeks a miraculous sign, but the only sign I will give is the sign of the prophet Jonah. Jonah was a sign to the people of Nineveh, and the Son of Man will be a sign to this generation of Israel. For as Jonah was three days and three nights in the stomach of a large fish, so the Son of Man will be three days and three nights in the heart of the earth." Jesus was speaking about his burial. The non-Jews of Nineveh will stand up at

God's judgment and condemn this generation of Israel, for the people of Nineveh repented at the preaching of Jonah; and now someone greater than Jonah is here! The Queen of Sheba will stand up at God's judgment and condemn this generation in Israel, for she came from the ends of the earth to listen to the wise teaching of Solomon, and now someone greater than Solomon is here!

Then Jesus condemned the religious leaders saying, "This is how it will be with this evil generation of religious leaders. When a demon comes out of a person, it goes through dry and waterless places seeking rest, but does not find any. Then it says, 'I will go back inside the house where I used to live.' When the demon returns, it finds the house empty, swept clean, and put in order. Then the demon goes and brings back seven other demons more evil than itself, and they go live inside the house."

Jesus went into Peter's house in Capernaum, and once again a large crowd gathered so that he and his disciples were not even able to eat a meal. When Jesus' family in Nazareth heard what was happening in Capernaum, they went to stop Jesus because they said, "He is out of his mind." When his mother and brothers arrived, they stood outside the house for they were not able to get near him because of the crowd of people inside the house. So they asked to talk to Jesus, and sent someone inside to tell him that they were there. A crowd was sitting around Jesus, and they said to him, "Your mother and brothers are outside and want to talk with you." Jesus said, "Who are my mother and my brothers?" Then Jesus pointed to those sitting in a circle around him and said, "These are my mother and my brothers! For whoever hears God's word and puts it into practice—doing the will of my Father in heaven—is my mother, brother, and sister."

CHAPTER 9

Jesus left Peter's house in Capernaum and sat on the northwest coast of Lake Galilee, and large crowds of people were gathering around him. The crowds became so large that he sat down in a fishing boat out on the lake, while all the people stood along the shore at the water's edge. Then Jesus taught them many things in stories called parables.

Turning to the crowd, Jesus told the story of a farmer. He said, "A farmer went out and threw seed on his field. As he was throwing the seed, some of the seed fell on the walking path. The seed was trampled on, and the birds came and ate the seed. Some seed fell onto rocky ground that had little soil. Because the soil was shallow, the seed grew very quickly, but the sun burned the plants. The plants withered because they had no roots in the soil to get water and keep them alive. Other seed fell among thorns, but the thorns grew up and choked the plants, so they did not produce grain. But other seed fell on good, deep soil. The seed grew and produced an abundant harvest that was 30, 60, and 100 times more than what was planted." Then Jesus declared, "Whoever has ears to hear, let them hear!" In private Jesus told his disciples the meaning of his story. He said, "The seed that the farmer threw into his field was the word of God. Some people are like the seed the farmer threw onto the walking path. They are people who when they hear the message of the kingdom of God do not accept it.

As soon as they hear the word of God, Satan comes and quickly steals the word of God that was planted in their hearts, so that they will not believe and be saved. Some people are like the seed the farmer threw onto the rocky ground. They hear God's word and immediately receive it with joy, but since they do not have deep roots, they believe for only a short time. When times of testing, trouble, and persecution come because of the word of God, they quickly fall away. Some people are like the seed the farmer threw into the thorns. They hear God's word, but the worries of this life, the deception of wealth, pleasures, and the desire for earthly things come in and choke the word of God. So they are unfruitful and do not grow and mature. Some people are like the seed the farmer threw on the good deep soil. These people have honest and good hearts. They hear God's word, and accept it, understand it, and hold fast to it. And by persevering, they produce an abundant crop—some 30, some 60, some 100 times more than was planted.

Then Jesus told the story of light and understanding. He said, "No one lights a lamp and hides it under a clay bowl or puts it under a bed. Instead, they put the lamp on a stand, so that those who come into the house can see the light. For there is nothing hidden that will not be revealed, and nothing kept secret that will not be known or brought out into the open." Then Jesus said, "Whoever has, will be given more; whoever has very little, even what they have will be taken away. Whoever has ears to hear, let them hear!"

Then Jesus spoke about the kingdom of God by telling the story of the weeds. He said, "The kingdom of God is like a landowner who threw good seeds of wheat on his field. But while everyone was sleeping, his enemy came and threw seeds of weed among the wheat and ran away. When the good seed grew and produced wheat, the weeds also appeared. These weeds were called darnel, a weedy rye grass with poisonous black seeds which resembles wheat in its early growth. The landowner's servants came to him and said, 'Sir, didn't you throw good seed on your field? Where then did these weeds come from?' The landowner said to them, 'An enemy did this.' The servants asked him, 'Do you want us to pull up the weeds?' 'No, for when you pull up the weeds, you will also pull out the wheat. Let both grow together until the harvest. At that time I will tell the harvesters: 'First pull up the weeds and tie them in bundles to be burned; then gather the wheat and store it in my barn.'" In private Jesus told his disciples the meaning of his story. He said, "The one who threw the good seed in the field is the Son of Man. The field is this world, and the good seed refers to the people of the kingdom of God. The weeds are the people of Satan, and the enemy who sows them is Satan. The harvest is the end of this world, and the harvesters are angels. As the weeds are pulled up and burned in the fire, so it will be at the end of this world. The Son of Man will send out his angels, and they will remove from his kingdom everyone that causes sin and all who do evil. They will all be thrown into the blazing furnace of fire, where people will be weeping and grinding their teeth. Then the righteous will shine like the sun in the kingdom of their Father."

Then Jesus spoke about the kingdom of God by telling the story of the mustard seed and yeast. He said, "The kingdom of God is like a small mustard seed that a man planted in his field. Although the mustard seed is one of the smallest seeds, it grows larger than all the plants and becomes a large bush in the field, so that birds come and make nests in its large branches. The kingdom of God is like yeast that a woman mixed in her flour until the yeast spreads through all the dough.

Then Jesus told these stories about the kingdom of God.

"The kingdom of God is like treasure hidden in a field. When a man discovered the treasure, he buried it again, and then in his joy went and sold all he owned and bought that field.

"The kingdom of God is like a merchant searching for valuable pearls. When he found a pearl of great value, he went away and sold everything he owned and bought the pearl. Therefore, every teacher of the law of Moses who has become a disciple in the kingdom of God is like the owner of a house who brings out of his storeroom both old and new treasures.

"The kingdom of God is like a fishing dragnet that was thrown into the lake and caught all kinds of fish. When it was full, the fishermen pulled the dragnet up on the shore. Then they sat down and put the good fish in baskets, but threw the bad fish away. This is how it will be at the end of this world. God's angels will come and separate the wicked from the righteous and throw them into the blazing furnace of fire, where there will be weeping and grinding of teeth." Jesus asked his disciples, "Do you understand?" And they said, "Yes."

Jesus spoke the word of God to the crowd of people using many other stories. He did not teach anything to them without using a story. So this fulfilled what is written in *Psalm 78:2*, "I will speak in stories, I will speak about things hidden since the creation of the universe."

When Jesus was alone, the disciples asked Jesus, "Why do you teach the people in stories? Jesus said to them, "The knowledge of the mysteries of the kingdom of God have been given to you, but to the people on the outside I teach everything by telling stories. Whoever has a receptive heart, an abundance will be given to them. But whoever does not have a receptive heart, what they have will be taken from them. This is why I teach the people in stories: Though seeing, they do not see; though hearing, they do not hear or understand. This fulfills what is written in *Isaiah 6:9-10*, 'so that they may be always looking, but never perceiving, and always hearing, but never understanding; otherwise they might turn to God and be forgiven!' For the people's hearts have become dull. They are hard of hearing and have closed their eyes. Otherwise they might hear with their ears, see with their eyes, and understand with their heart and turn to me, so that I can heal them. But blessed are your eyes because they see, and blessed are your ears because they hear. For I tell you the truth: Many prophets and righteous people longed to see what you see, but did not see it, and to hear what you hear, but did not hear it."

CHAPTER 10

One evening Jesus saw a crowd of people gathering around him, so he told his disciples to prepare a fishing boat so that they could go to the east side of Lake Galilee. Leaving the crowd, Jesus and his disciples got into the boat and set across the northern end of the lake.

As Jesus and his disciples were crossing Lake Galilee, suddenly a violent windstorm came upon the lake and large waves splashed over the boat. The boat was full of water and was in danger of sinking. Jesus was sleeping in the back of the boat on a pillow, and his disciples woke him up yelling, "Lord, Lord! Teacher! Save us! Don't you care that we are going to die!" Then Jesus got up and rebuked the wind and shouted to the waves to stop. He yelled, "Quiet! Be still!" Then the wind immediately stopped blowing, and the lake became completely calm. Jesus said to his disciples, "Why are you so afraid? Where is your faith?" The disciples were amazed and filled with great fear. They asked one another, "What kind of man is this? Who is Jesus? For even the winds and the waves obey his commands!"

After being blown off course by the strong wind, Jesus and his disciples landed on the east coast of Lake Galilee in the non-Jewish region of the Gerasenes. As soon as Jesus stepped out of the boat onto the shore, a demon-possessed man ran to meet Jesus. This man was from the local town, but for a long time he had been naked and homeless and lived among the burial tombs. No one could tie him up anymore, not even with a chain. For he had chains put around his hands and feet, but he tore the chains apart and broke the irons around his ankles. No one was strong enough to control him. Day and night he wandered among the tombs and in the hills; he would scream out and cut himself with sharp rocks. The man was so violent that people could not walk by that area of the tombs. When the man came to Jesus he screamed and fell on his knees in front of him. Jesus began to command the demon to come out of the man saying, "Come out, you evil spirit!" The demon shouted through the man at the top of his voice, "What do you want with us Jesus, Son of the Most High God? Have you come here to torture us before God's appointed time? I beg you, in God's name don't punish us!" Then Jesus asked the demon, "What is your name?" The demon said, "My name is Legion, for we are many demons." And then the demon begged Jesus again and again not to send them out of that region and into the world of the dead. Now there was a large herd of pigs eating on the hillside nearby. Then the demons begged Jesus, "If you cast us out, send us into the herd of pigs." Jesus gave them permission and said to them, "Go!" So the demons left and went into the pigs, and the herd of pigs—about 2,000—ran down the steep bank and drowned in Lake Galilee. The herders watching the pigs saw what had happened and ran into the town and countryside telling the people everything that had taken place. Then the whole town ran out to meet Jesus and see what had happened. When they came to Jesus, they saw the demon-possessed man sitting at Jesus' feet. He was dressed and in his right mind, and the people became very afraid. The pig herders told the people everything that had happened to the pigs and how the demon-possessed man was healed. Then the people begged Jesus to leave their region of the country because they were filled with fear. As Jesus was getting into the boat to leave, the man who had been set free begged to go with Jesus. But Jesus would not let him and said, "Go home and tell everyone the great things the Lord has done for you, and how he has had mercy on you."

When Jesus and his disciples returned to the northwest coast of Lake Galilee in a fishing boat, a large crowd of people were waiting and welcomed him on the shore at Capernaum.

Chapter 10

At that time a Capernaum synagogue leader named Jairus ran and fell on his knees at Jesus' feet. He pleaded with Jesus to go to his house saying, "My only daughter—a young girl about 12 years old—is about to die. Please come to my house and touch her, and she will be healed and live." Jesus and his disciples got up and went with Jarius.

As Jesus was walking toward the house a large crowd followed and pressed all around him. The crowd was almost crushing Jesus. Just then there was a woman in the crowd who had suffered from continual bleeding for 12 years, but no one could heal her. She had suffered tremendously under the care of many doctors and had spent all of her money, but instead of getting better she became much worse. When she heard about Jesus, she said to herself, "If I just touch his clothes, I will be healed."

The woman came up behind Jesus in the crowd and touched his clothes. Immediately she was healed, her bleeding stopped, and she felt in her body that she had been healed from her suffering. At once Jesus realized that power had gone out from his body. Jesus turned around in the crowd and asked everyone, "Who touched me? Who touched my clothes?" When the people denied touching Jesus, Peter and the disciples said to him, "Master, you can see the crowd of people pressing against you, so why do you ask us who touched me?" But Jesus kept looking around the crowd to see who had touched him. Jesus said, "I know someone touched me, for God's power went out from my body." When the woman realized that she could no longer hide, she came trembling to Jesus. She was shaking in fear and fell at Jesus' feet. With the crowd of people standing around her, she told Jesus the whole truth. She told him that she was the one who touched him and how she was instantly healed. Jesus turned and said to her, "My daughter, take heart, your faith has healed you. Go in peace, you are now free from your suffering."

While Jesus was still talking with the woman, some men came from the house of the synagogue leader and said to Jairus, "Your daughter is dead, do not bother the teacher anymore." Overhearing what they told Jairus, Jesus said to him, "Don't be afraid; just believe, and your daughter will be healed." Jesus did not allow anyone to follow him except Peter, James, and John. When Jesus arrived at Jairus' house, he only allowed his three disciples and the girl's parents inside. When they entered the house, a crowd of people were crying and wailing very loudly over the daughter and playing funeral flutes. Jesus said to them, "Go away! Why are you crying and wailing? The girl is not dead; she is only sleeping." The crowd of people laughed at Jesus because they knew she was dead. After Jesus had sent the crowd of people outside the house, he took the girl's parents, the three disciples, and went into the daughter's room. Jesus took the girl's hand and said to her, "Little girl, I tell you, get up!" And Jesus raised her from the dead. Immediately the girl's spirit came back into her, and she stood up and began to walk around the house. When the parents and people saw her, they were exceedingly amazed. Then Jesus told them to give her something to eat. But Jesus gave them strict orders not to tell anyone that he had healed the girl.

As Jesus left the house of Jairus, two blind men followed him. They cried out, "Have mercy on us, Son of David!" When Jesus had entered the house of Peter, the blind men came to him. Jesus asked them, "Do you believe that I am able to make you see?" They said, "Yes, Lord." Then Jesus touched their eyes and said, "You will see because of your faith." Immediately their eyes were healed, and they could see. Then Jesus commanded the healed blind men, "Do not tell anyone that I have healed your eyes." But they went out and spread the news about Jesus all over that region of Galilee.

While Jesus and his disciples were leaving the house of Peter in Capernaum, a demon-possessed man who could not talk was brought to Jesus. Jesus cast the demon out and then the man could speak. The crowd of people following Jesus was amazed and said, "Nothing like this has ever been seen in Israel." But the religious leaders said, "Jesus drives demons out of people by the power of Satan, the ruler of demons."

Then Jesus and his disciples left Capernaum and once again walked to his hometown of Nazareth. On the Sabbath day, Jesus taught in the synagogue and many who heard his teaching were amazed. The people of Nazareth asked each other, "Where did Jesus get these things? Where did Jesus get this wisdom? What are these miracles he is doing? Isn't Jesus the carpenter? Isn't this Mary's son and the brother of James, Joseph, Judas, and Simon? Aren't his sisters here with us?" Then the people of Nazareth took offense and went against Jesus. Jesus said to them, "A prophet is honored except in his hometown, among his relatives, and in his own family." Because of their unbelief, Jesus did only a few miracles in Nazareth. He was astonished at the people's lack of faith.

Jesus left Nazareth and walked through the villages and towns of Galilee teaching the people in their synagogues, proclaiming the good news of the kingdom of God, and healing every disease and sickness. When Jesus saw the crowds of people following him, he had deep compassion for them because they were harassed and helpless like sheep without a shepherd. Then Jesus said to his disciples, "The harvest is great, but the workers are few. Therefore, ask the Lord of the harvest to send out workers into his harvest field."

CHAPTER 11

Jesus called his Twelve Apostles together and through the Holy Spirit he gave them God's authority to cast demons out of people and to heal every disease and sickness.

Before Jesus sent out his apostles on their mission journey, he gave them these instructions: "Do not go among the non-Jews or enter any town of the Samaritans. Instead go only to the lost sheep of the house of Israel. As you go, proclaim this message to them, 'The kingdom of God has arrived.' Heal the sick, raise the dead, cleanse the lepers, and cast out demons. Freely you have received, so freely give to others. And whatever Jewish village or town you enter, search there for a worthy person and stay at his home until you leave. As you enter the house, give a greeting. Give a blessing of peace to the homes that deserve it, but do not bless the homes that do not deserve it. If anyone refuses to welcome you or listen to your teaching, leave that home or town and shake the dirt off your feet as a witness against him. For I tell you the truth: It will be much better for Sodom and Gomorrah on the day of God's judgment than for that Jewish town. Because the worker deserves his livelihood, do not take anything extra with you on your mission journey.

Then Jesus said to his apostles, "I send you out like sheep among wolves, so be as wise as snakes and as harmless as doves. Be on your guard, for you will be handed over to Jewish courts and be flogged in synagogues. And for my sake you will be dragged before governors and kings as witnesses to them and to the non-Jews. When you are arrested, do not worry about what to say or how to say it. At that time, you will be given what to say, for it will not be you speaking, but the Spirit of your Father speaking through you. Brother will betray brother to death, a father will give his child to be put to death, and children will go against their parents and have them put to death. People will hate you because you are my disciples, but whoever stands strong to the end will be saved. When you are persecuted in one place, flee to another. A student is not above his teacher, and a servant is not above his master. It is enough for students to be like their teachers, and servants to be like their masters. If they call me Satan, how much more will they persecute my followers? So do not be afraid of those who persecute you, for there is nothing concealed that will not be made public, or hidden that will not be revealed. What I tell you in the dark of night, shout it in the light of day; whatever is whispered in your ear in private, proclaim it from the housetops. Do not be afraid of those who can kill your body, but cannot kill your soul! Instead, you should fear God who can destroy both your body and soul in hell. Two birds are sold for a penny, but no bird dies without your Father's care. So don't be afraid, for you are much more valuable than birds! Whoever tells others about me, I will tell my Father in heaven about them. But whoever denies me before others, I will deny them before my Father in heaven. Do not think that I came to bring peace to the earth! I did not come to bring peace, but a sword of separation. For I came into the world to turn a son against his father, a daughter against her mother, a daughter-in-law against her mother-in-law, and a person's enemies will be the members of his own family. Anyone who loves his father, mother, son, or daughter more than me is not worthy of me. Whoever does not take up his cross and follow me is not worthy of me. Whoever finds his life will lose it, and whoever loses his life for my sake will find it. Whoever welcomes you welcomes me, and whoever welcomes me welcomes my Father who sent me. Whoever welcomes a prophet will receive a prophet's reward, and whoever welcomes a righteous person will receive a righteous person's reward. For I tell you the truth: If anyone gives a single cup of cold water to one of my disciples, that person will not lose his reward."

Then Jesus sent out his apostles two by two throughout the villages and towns of Galilee. They proclaimed the good news of the kingdom of God, and called people to repent and turn to God. They cast out many demons from people, and anointed many sick people with olive oil and healed them. After Jesus had sent out his apostles, he began to proclaim and teach throughout the towns of Galilee.

Herod Antipas was one of the sons of Herod the Great, and the Roman governor of the regions of Galilee and Perea. One day he gave a banquet for his high officials, military leaders, and the leading men of Galilee at the Fortress of Machaerus in the region of Perea, east of the Dead Sea. When the daughter of Herodias named Salome came into the birthday celebration and danced, she pleased Antipas and his dinner guests. Antipas was so pleased, he said to the girl, "Ask me for anything you want, and I'll give it to you." Antipas promised her with an oath, "Whatever you ask of me I will give you up to half of my kingdom." The daughter went out and told her mother, Herodias, what Antipas had promised her. She asked her mother, "What should I ask for?" Herodias said, "Ask for the head of John the Baptist on a plate!" Immediately the girl hurried in to Antipas and said, "I want you to give me the head of John the Baptist on a plate." When Antipas heard the daughter's request, he was very troubled. But because of his oath in front of his guests, he ordered that the head of John be cut off. The executioner went into the prison and cut off John's head. The head was brought in on a plate, presented to the girl, and she showed it to her mother. On hearing about John's beheading, his disciples came and took his body and laid it in a tomb. Then they went and told Jesus that John was dead.

At that time Herod Antipas heard the news about all that Jesus was doing in Galilee, for Jesus' name had become very well known. Antipas became very troubled because some people were saying that John the Baptist had been raised from the dead, and that is why these miracles of power are at work in Jesus. Others said that Jesus was Elijah." And still others said, "He is a prophet who has come back to life." Antipas heard this and said to his servants, "I cut off the head of John, and he has risen from the dead. That is why miraculous powers are working in him. Who is this person I hear so much about?" From then on, Antipas looked for an opportunity to meet Jesus.

Then the apostles returned to Jesus from their mission journey and gathered around him in Capernaum and told him all they had done and taught.

CHAPTER 12

It was springtime and the time of the Jewish Passover Feast was near. When so many people were coming and going that they did not have time to eat, Jesus said to his disciples, "Come with me and let's go to an isolated place on the other side of Lake Galilee where we can be alone and get some rest."

Jesus and his disciples withdrew by boat privately across the northern end of Lake Galilee to the isolated region of Bethsaida on the northeast side of Lake Galilee. But some people became aware that Jesus and his disciples had left Capernaum. So they ran from all the towns and followed Jesus by foot, and they arrived at Bethsaida before Jesus. When their boat landed at the Bethsaida Plain, Jesus saw a large crowd of people waiting for them.

He welcomed them and had compassion on them, for they were like sheep without a shepherd. Jesus taught the people many things about the kingdom of God and healed the sick.

When it was getting dark the disciples said to Jesus, "It is evening and this is a very isolated place, send the people away so that they can go to the surrounding villages and countryside to buy food and find lodging." Jesus said to them, "They do not need to go away. You give them something to eat." The disciples said, "Are we to go and spend that much money on bread and give it to them to eat? It will cost more than a half year's wages." When Jesus looked up and saw a large crowd of people rushing toward him, he said to Philip, "Where will we buy bread for all these people to eat?" Philip said to Jesus, "It would take a lot of money to buy enough bread for everyone to just take a single bite." Jesus said to them, "Go and see how many loaves of bread you have." Then Andrew spoke up, "Here is a boy who has five small barley loaves and two small fish, but we will need much more to feed so many people." Jesus told his disciples to have the people sit down in groups on the green grass. They sat down in groups of 50 and 100. There were about 5,000 men. Jesus took the five loaves of bread and two small fish, looked up to heaven, gave thanks to God, and then broke the loaves of bread. He gave the pieces to his disciples, who then distributed them to the people. The people ate and were full. Jesus told his disciples, "Gather up the pieces of food that are left over; let nothing be wasted." So the disciples collected 12 basketfuls of broken pieces of bread and fish that had not been eaten. After the people saw Jesus' miracle, they began saying to one another, "This must be the Prophet that Moses said would come into the world." Jesus knew the people were planning to come and make him the king of Israel by force, so he withdrew again up a hillside so he could be alone.

Jesus told his disciples to take the boat and go back to Capernaum, while he dismissed the crowd. Jesus' disciples went down to Lake Galilee that night. It was now dark and they got into a boat and started across the north end of the lake toward Capernaum. After he had dismissed the people, Jesus withdrew onto a hillside by himself to pray.

Later that night the disciples' boat was in the middle of the north end of Lake Galilee. Suddenly a storm arose making huge waves on the lake. The waves smashed against the boat. From the shore Jesus could see the disciples straining to row the boat against the waves. Shortly before dawn Jesus walked on the lake toward the disciples' boat. Jesus was about to walk by the boat, when the disciples saw him walking on the water and they were terrified. They cried out in fear, "It is a spirit, a ghost!" Jesus immediately called out to them, "It is me! Take courage! Don't be afraid!" Then Peter said to Jesus, "Lord, if it's you, tell me to come to you on the water." Jesus said, "Come!" Then Peter got out of the boat and walked on the water toward Jesus. But when he saw the wind and waves, he became afraid and began to sink. He cried out, "Lord, save me!" Immediately Jesus reached out his hand and grabbed him. Jesus said, "You have such little faith, why did you doubt?" And then Jesus and Peter climbed into the boat, and the wind stopped. The disciples were completely amazed. Then the disciples were filled with joy when Jesus got into the boat. The disciples worshiped Jesus saying, "It is true, you are the Son of God!"

When they had crossed back over to the western coast of Lake Galilee, their boat was blown off course and landed in the region of Gennesaret. The fertile Plain of Gennesaret is crescent-shaped and is located on the northwestern coast of Lake Galilee between Tiberias and Capernaum. As soon as Jesus and the disciples got out of the boat the people recognized Jesus, so they ran and sent word throughout the whole surrounding region of Galilee. The people carried the sick on stretchers to wherever they heard Jesus was. And wherever Jesus went—into villages, towns, or the countryside—they put the sick in the public marketplaces. The people begged Jesus to let the sick touch the edge of his clothes, and everyone who touched him was healed.

The next day a large crowd of people who had stayed on the east side of the lake realized that neither Jesus nor his disciples were there. They got into their boats and went to Capernaum in search of Jesus.

When the people found Jesus in the synagogue of Capernaum, they said to him, "Teacher, when did you get here?" Jesus said to them, "I tell you the truth: You are following me not because you saw my miracles, but because your stomachs were filled with bread. Stop working for food that rots, but live for food that endures to eternal life which the Son of Man will give to you."

Then the people asked Jesus, "What are the works that God requires of us?" Jesus said, "This is the work of God: To believe in the one God has sent into this world." They said to Jesus, "Show us a miracle, then we will believe in you! Our ancestors ate bread from heaven in the desert, as *Psalm 78:24* says, 'God gave them bread from heaven to eat.'" Jesus said to them, "I tell you the truth: It was not Moses who gave you the bread from heaven, but it is my Father who gives you the true bread from heaven. For God's bread is the one who comes down from heaven and gives life to this world." They said to Jesus, "Sir, give us this bread forever!"

Then Jesus declared, "I am the bread of life! Whoever comes to me will never be hungry, and whoever believes in me will never be thirsty. But as I said, you have seen me and still you do not believe in me. Whoever the Father gives me will come to me, and whoever comes to me, I will never turn away. For I came from heaven not to do my will, but to do the will of the one who sent me into the world. And this is the will of the one who sent me: That I would not lose anyone he has given me, but raise them up at the last day. For this is my Father's will: That whoever comes to the Son and believes in him will receive eternal life, and I will raise him from the dead on the last day."

After Jesus said these things, the Jewish religious leaders were upset because he said, "I am the bread that came down from heaven." They said, "How can he say that he came down from heaven? Isn't this Jesus, the son of Joseph? We know his father and mother." Jesus said to them, "Stop complaining! No one can come to me unless the Father who sent me brings him to me, and I will raise him from the dead on the last day. For it is written in *Isaiah 54:13*, 'They will all be taught by God.' Whoever hears and learns from the Father comes to me. No human has ever seen the Father, but only the one who is from God; only he has seen the Father. I tell you the truth: Whoever believes in me has eternal life. I am the bread of life! Your ancestors ate the bread in the wilderness, yet they died. But this is the bread that comes down from heaven, which anyone can eat and not die. I am the living bread that came down from heaven! Whoever eats this bread will live forever. This bread is my body, which I will give for the life of this world."

Then the Jews began to argue with each other saying, "How can Jesus give us his body to eat?" Jesus said to them, "I tell you the truth: Unless you eat the body of the Son of Man and drink his blood, you have no life in you. Whoever eats my body and drinks my blood has eternal life, and I will raise him from the dead on the last day. For my body is true food, and my blood is true drink. Whoever eats my body and drinks my blood lives in me, and I live in them. Just as the living Father sent me into this world, and I live because of the Father, so whoever eats my body will also live. This is the bread that came down from heaven. Your ancestors ate bread and died, but whoever eats this bread will live forever."

When Jesus was speaking about eating his body and drinking his blood, he was speaking symbolically about his death on the cross for the sins of the world. This is a foreshadow of what is today known as the Lord's Supper or Communion.

When many of his disciples heard Jesus' teaching, they said to one another, "This is a very difficult teaching to believe. Who can accept it?" Jesus knew that his disciples were complaining about his teaching and said to them, "Does my teaching offend you? Then what if you see the Son of Man ascend to heaven where he came from! It is the Holy Spirit who gives life; the flesh means nothing. The words of my teaching are full of the Holy Spirit and life. But some of you still refuse to believe in me." For Jesus knew from the beginning which of them would not believe and who would leave him. And Jesus said, "This is why I told you that no one can come to me unless the Father enables them."

Because of Jesus' teaching, many of his disciples stopped following him. Jesus looked at his apostles and said, "Are you going to leave me too?" Peter said, "Lord, who are we going to follow? You are the only one who has the words of eternal life. We believe in you! We know that you are the Holy One of God!" Jesus said, "Although I have chosen you as my apostles, one of you is a demon." Jesus was talking about Judas Iscariot, who would later betray him.

Then some Jewish religious leaders who had come from Jerusalem gathered around Jesus. The religious leaders saw some of the disciples of Jesus eating food with unwashed hands. So they considered them to be religiously unclean, for the Jews would not eat unless their hands were ritually washed. They also observed many other religious traditions, such as ritually washing cups, pitchers, and copper kettles.

So the religious leaders asked Jesus, "Why do your disciples disobey the tradition of the Jewish elders?" Jesus said to them, "The prophet Isaiah was right when he prophesied about you religious hypocrites in *Isaiah 29:13*, 'These people honor me with their lips, but their hearts are far from me. They worship me in vain; their teachings are simply human rules.' You have rejected God's commandments and are obeying human traditions and rules. You are experts at ignoring God's commands! For God said through Moses in *Exodus 20:12*, 'Honor your fathers and mothers.' But you teach the people that money dedicated to help their father and mother should be given to God's temple instead. So you nullify the word of God by your religious tradition, and you do many things like this."

Once again, Jesus gathered the crowd of people together and said to them, "Listen to me and understand what I am telling you: It is not what you eat that makes you unclean, but it is what you say that makes you unclean. There is nothing outside a person that can make him unclean. Rather, a person is made unclean by what comes out from inside him." Then the disciples came and asked Jesus, "Did you know that the religious leaders were offended by what you said?" Jesus said to them, "Every plant that my Father in heaven has not planted will be pulled up by the roots. Leave them alone; they are blind leaders. And if the blind lead the blind, they will both fall into a hole."

After Jesus left the crowd of people and went into the house, Peter and his disciples asked Jesus to explain his teaching to them. Jesus said to them, "Don't you understand that it is not what a person eats that makes him unclean? It is what comes out of a person's heart that makes him unclean. For it is out of a person's heart that comes evil thoughts, sexual perversion, theft, false testimony, murder, adultery, greed, hate, deceit, envy, slander, pride, and foolishness. All these evil things come from a person's heart and make him unclean, but eating with unwashed hands does not make anyone unclean."

By this teaching, Jesus made all foods clean to eat. Then Jesus left Capernaum and walked through Galilee, for he knew the Jewish religious leaders were looking for a way to kill him.

CHAPTER 13

It was time to celebrate Israel's journey from Egypt to the Promised Land at the Jewish Feast of Tabernacles in Jerusalem. The brothers of Jesus said to him, "Leave Galilee and go to Judea, so that your disciples can see the miraculous works you are doing. For no one who wants to become a public figure hides what he does. Since you are doing these miracles, show yourself to the world!" For even Jesus' brothers refused to believe in him. Jesus said to his brothers, "It is not God's time for me, but any time is right for you. This world does not hate you, but it hates me because I testify that the ways of this world are evil. You go to the Feast. I'm not going, for my time has not yet fully come." After Jesus said this, he stayed in Galilee. However, after Jesus' brothers had left for the Feast of Tabernacles, he also walked to Jerusalem in secret.

Now the Jewish religious leaders were looking for Jesus in Jerusalem. They asked the people, "Where is Jesus?" The crowds of people were whispering many things about Jesus. Some said, "He is a good man." Others said, "No, he deceives the people." But no one would talk about Jesus in public, for they were afraid of the religious leaders.

When the week-long Feast of Tabernacles was about half over, Jesus entered the temple courts and began to teach. The Jews who heard him were amazed and asked, "How does this man have such learning, for he has never been formally taught?" Jesus said, "My teaching is not my own, but it comes from the one who sent me into this world. Whoever chooses to do the will of God discovers whether my teaching is from God or whether I speak on my own authority. Whoever speaks on his own authority seeks his own glory, but whoever seeks the glory of the one who sent him is a man of truth for there is no falsehood in him. Moses gave you the law, but none of you obey it. So why are you trying to kill me?" The crowd of people said, "You are demon-possessed! Who is trying to kill you?" Jesus said to them, "You were amazed at one miracle that I did. Yet, because the patriarchs gave you circumcision, you circumcise a boy on the Sabbath day. Now if you circumcise a boy on the Sabbath so that the law will not be broken, why are you angry with me for healing a man's body on the Sabbath? Stop judging by outward appearances, but judge according to what is right."

At this time some of the people in Jerusalem began to ask, "Isn't this the man who the religious leaders are trying to kill? Look! He is teaching publicly, and they are not trying to stop him. Do the authorities now believe that he is the Messiah? But we know he comes from Galilee, and no one knows where the Messiah will come from." Then while Jesus was still teaching in the temple courts, he shouted out, "Yes, you know me, and you know I am from Galilee! I am not here on my own authority, but he who sent me is true. You do not know him, but I know him because I came from him. He sent me into this world. I am with you for only a short time more, and then I am going back to the one who sent me. You will look for me, but you will not find me. Where I am going, you cannot come." The Jews said to one another, "Where is Jesus planning to go that we cannot find him? Does he plan to go where our people live scattered among the non-Jews? Is he going to teach the non-Jews? What is he talking about?'"

On the last and greatest day of the Feast of Tabernacles, Jesus stood up in the temple courts and shouted with a loud voice, "Whoever is thirsty come to me and drink! Whoever believes in me, as it is written in *Isaiah 58:11*, 'Out of their hearts will flow rivers of living water.'" By this Jesus was talking about the Holy Spirit that people who believed in him would later receive at Pentecost. Up to that time the Holy Spirit had not been given, for Jesus had not yet been glorified.

When some of the people heard Jesus, they said, "This man is truly the Prophet that Moses told us about." Others said, "He is the Messiah!" Still others said, "How can the Messiah come from Galilee? Doesn't the Bible tell us that the Messiah will be a descendant of David and come from Bethlehem, the town where David lived?" Therefore, the people were divided about Jesus. The religious leaders wanted to arrest Jesus, but they did not touch him because God's time had not yet come.

Many in the crowd of people believed in Jesus. They said, "When the Messiah comes, will he do more miracles than this man?" The religious leaders heard the people whispering these things about Jesus, so they sent temple guards to arrest him. But when the temple guards returned to them without Jesus, the religious leaders asked them, "Why didn't you bring Jesus to us?" The guards said, "We have not heard anyone speak the way he does." The religious leaders snapped back saying, "You mean you have been fooled too? Have any of the religious rulers believed in him? No! But this mob of people that knows nothing about the law of Moses is under a curse!" Nicodemus, who had previously talked with Jesus and who was a member of the Jewish religious council said, "Our law does not condemn a man until we first hear from him and learn what he is doing." The religious leaders yelled back and said, "Nicodemus, are you from Galilee, too? Search through the Bible! For no prophet comes from Galilee." Then the religious leaders left for their homes.

Early the next morning, Jesus again entered the temple courts, sat down, and began teaching a crowd of people that had gathered around him. The religious leaders brought in a woman who had been caught in the act of adultery. They made her stand in front of the people and said to Jesus, "Teacher, this woman was caught in the act of adultery. As you know, the law of Moses commands us to kill her with rocks. Do you agree with Moses?" They were using this question to trap Jesus, so that they could have evidence to bring charges against him. But Jesus bent down and began to write on the ground with his finger. When the religious leaders continued questioning him, Jesus stood up and said to them, "Whoever among you is without sin should throw the first rock at her." Then Jesus bent down again and continued to write on the ground. Those who heard Jesus' words began to leave one by one—the older ones left first, until Jesus was left alone with the woman standing there. Jesus stood up and asked her, "Woman, where are your accusers? Did any of them condemn you?" She said, "Sir, no one." Jesus replied, "I don't condemn you either. Go now and leave your life of sin."

At that time a crowd of people gathered around Jesus in the area of the temple where the offerings were given. He declared to them, "I am the light of this world! Whoever follows me will never live in darkness, but will have the light that gives life." When some of the religious leaders heard Jesus they confronted him saying, "You are giving witness about yourself. Your testimony is false." Jesus said, "Even if I testify about myself, my testimony is true, for I know where I came from and where I am going. But you do not know where I came from or where I am going. You judge me by human standards, but I do not judge anyone. Yet, if I do judge anyone, my judgments are true, because I am not alone. I judge with the Father, who sent me into this world. As Moses wrote in *Deuteronomy 17:6*, 'The testimony of two witnesses is true.' I am one who testifies about myself, and my other witness is the Father." Then the religious leaders asked Jesus, "Where is your father?" Jesus said, "You don't know me or my Father. If you knew me, you would also know my Father." Yet no one tried to arrest him, for God's time had not yet come.

Jesus began to teach once again saying, "I am going away, and you will search for me, but you will die in your sin. Where I am going, you cannot come." The Jews asked one another, "Where is he going? Is he going to kill himself? Jesus said, "You are from this world below, but I am from heaven above. You are of this world, but I am not of this world. I tell you the truth: You will die in your sins if you refuse to believe that I am the Messiah. Yes, you will die in your sins." They said, "Who are you?" Jesus said, "From the beginning, I have told you many times. I have much more to say in judgment of you, but the one who sent me into this world is true, and what I have heard from him I have told this world." They did not understand that Jesus was speaking to them about his Father. So Jesus said, "When you have lifted up the Son of Man, then you will know that I am he and that I do nothing on my own authority. For I speak only what I have learned from the Father. The one who sent me into this world is with me; he has never left me alone, for I always do what pleases him."

Even while Jesus was speaking, many people believed in him. Jesus said to those who had believed in him, "If you continue to follow my teaching, then you are truly my disciples. Then you will know the truth, and the truth will set you free." But they said, "We are Abraham's descendants, and we have never been slaves of anyone. How can you say that we can be set free?" Jesus said, "I tell you the truth: Whoever sins is a slave to sin. A slave has no permanent status in the family, but a son always belongs to the family. So if the Son sets you free, you will be truly free."

Then Jesus said to the religious leaders, "I know that you are Abraham's descendants, but you are looking for a way to kill me because my teaching finds no place in your hearts. I tell you what I have seen in the Father's presence, but you are doing what you have heard from your father." But they said to Jesus, "Our father is Abraham." Jesus said, "If you were Abraham's children then you would live the life that Abraham did. But instead, you are looking for a way to kill me, even though I tell you the truth that I heard from God. Abraham did not do these things. You are doing the works of your real father." They said, "We aren't illegitimate children, for God alone is our father." Jesus said, "If God were your Father, you would love me, because I came into this world from God. He sent me into this world, I did not come on my own authority. You are not able to understand what I am saying because you are not able to hear my teaching. I tell you the truth: You belong to your true father, the devil, and your desire is to do your father's will. He was a murderer from the beginning, never holding to the truth, for there is no truth in him. He is a liar and the father of lies. Yet, even though I tell you the truth, you still refuse to believe me! Which one of you can prove that I am guilty of sin? If I am telling you the truth, why don't you believe me? Whoever belongs to God hears what God says. The reason you do not hear God is because you do not belong to God."

The religious leaders were angry and said to Jesus, "Aren't we right to say that you are a Samaritan and demon-possessed?" Jesus said, "I'm not possessed by a demon, but I honor my Father and you dishonor me. I do not seek my own glory, but there is one who seeks it, and he is the true judge. I tell you the truth: Whoever obeys my teaching will never die." They declared, "Now we know that you are demon-possessed! Abraham died and so did the prophets, but you say that whoever obeys your teaching will never die. Who do you think you are? Are you greater than our father Abraham and the prophets who died?" Jesus said, "If I glorify myself, it is worth nothing. But my Father—whom you claim is your God—is the one who glorifies me. I know God, but you do not. I would be a liar like you if I said I did not know him. For I do know him and obey his word. Your father Abraham rejoiced at the thought of seeing my day. And indeed he did see it and was glad." The religious leaders said, "You are not yet 50 years of age, and you have seen Abraham?" Jesus said, "I tell you the truth: Before Abraham was born, I AM. For as Moses wrote in *Exodus 3:14*, 'I AM WHO I AM.'" When they heard this, they picked up rocks to kill Jesus, but he hid himself and left the temple courts.

While Jesus was walking away from the temple, he saw a man who was blind from birth. His disciples asked Jesus, "Teacher, why was this man born blind? Was it because of his sins or the sins of his parents?" Jesus said, "Neither this man nor his parents sinned, but he was born blind so that the acts of God would be seen in what happens to him. While it is still day, we must do the work of him who sent me into this world. The darkness of night is coming, when no one can work. As long as I am in this world, I am the light of the world!" After saying this, Jesus spit on the ground, made mud with his saliva, and smeared it on the blind man's eyes. Jesus said to him, "Go, wash the mud from your eyes in the Pool of Siloam." So the man went and washed the mud off his eyes, and he went to his home seeing. His neighbors and those who knew him as a blind man said, "Look! Isn't this the blind beggar?" Some said he was. Others said, "No, he only looks like him." But the healed blind man kept insisting, "I am the man!" They asked him,

Chapter 13

"How can you now see?" He said to them, "The man called Jesus made some mud and put it on my eyes. He told me to go wash my eyes in the Pool of Siloam. So I went and after I washed my eyes I could see." They asked, "Where is this Jesus?" The man said, "I don't know."

Then they took the man who was once blind to the religious leaders. Now it was on the Sabbath day that Jesus had healed his eyes. Therefore, they asked the man how he had received his sight. The man said, "Jesus put mud on my eyes, and after I washed my eyes I could see." Some of the religious leaders said, "This Jesus is not from God, for he violated the Sabbath." But others said, "How can a sinner do these miracles?" Then they turned again to the man and asked, "Since it was your eyes that were healed, what do you think about this man Jesus?" The man said, "He is a prophet!"

The religious leaders still would not believe that the man was born blind and that his eyes were healed, so they sent for his parents. They asked his parents, "Is this your son? Was he born blind? How can he now see?" His parents said, "Yes, this is our son, and he was born blind. But we don't know how he can now see, nor who it was that healed him. Ask him; he is an adult. He can speak for himself." His parents said this because they were afraid of the religious leaders, who had already said that anyone who believed that Jesus was the Messiah would be put out of the synagogue.

Now a second time, the religious leaders called for the man born blind and they told him, "Give all the glory to God by telling the truth, for we know that this Jesus is a sinner." The man said, "I don't know whether he is a sinner or not, but one thing I do know: I was once blind, and now I see!" Then the religious leaders asked him again, "What did this man Jesus do to you? How did he heal your eyes?" The man said, "I have told you already, but you refuse to listen. Why do you want me to tell you over and over again? Do you want to become his disciples too?" Then the religious leaders heaped insults on him saying, "You are this man's disciple! But we are disciples of Moses! We know that God spoke to Moses, but as for this man, we don't even know where he comes from." The man said, "I am amazed! He healed my eyes, and you say you don't know where he comes from? We all know that God does not listen to sinners. He only listens to those who worship him and do his will. Nobody has ever heard of someone who heals the eyes of a man born blind. If this Jesus did not come from God, he could not do anything." The religious leaders said, "You were completely steeped in sin at birth! How dare you lecture us?" And they threw the man out of the synagogue.

Jesus heard that the religious leaders had thrown the man out of the synagogue. When Jesus found him, he said, "Do you believe in the Son of Man?" The man said, "Sir, who is he? Tell me so that I can believe in him." Jesus said, "You are now looking at him; he is the one speaking with you." Then the man said, "Lord, I believe in you," and he worshiped Jesus. Jesus said to him, "I came into this world to bring judgment so that the blind will see, and those who see will become blind."

Some religious leaders who were with him heard Jesus say this and asked him, "What? Are you saying that we are blind?" Jesus said, "If you were blind, you would not be guilty of sin. But since you claim you can see, you remain guilty in your sins."

Jesus said, "You religious hypocrites, I tell you the truth: Whoever does not enter the sheep pen by the gate, but climbs in by any other way, that one is a thief and a robber. The one who enters by the gate is the shepherd of the sheep. The gatekeeper opens the gate for him, and the sheep listen to his voice. He calls his sheep by name and leads them out. When the shepherd brings out all his sheep, he walks ahead of them, and his sheep follow him because they know his voice. But his sheep will never follow a stranger; in fact, they will run away from him because they do not recognize a stranger's voice. I tell you the truth: I am the gate of the sheep! All who have come before me are thieves and robbers, but the sheep would not listen to them. I am the gate! Whoever enters through me will be saved. The thief comes only to steal and kill and destroy, but I have come into this world that they will have life abundantly. I am the good shepherd! The good shepherd lays down his life for his sheep. A hired worker is not the shepherd and does not own the sheep. So when he sees a wolf coming, he runs away and leaves the sheep. Then the wolf attacks and kills the sheep and scatters them. The hired worker runs away because he is simply an employee and does not care about the life of the sheep. I am

Chapter 13

the good shepherd! I know my sheep, and my sheep know me—just as the Father knows me and I know the Father. I lay down my life for my sheep! I have other sheep that are not from this sheep pen. I must bring them also. They too will listen to my voice, so that there will be one flock under one shepherd. The reason my Father loves me is because I lay down my life, and I will take it up again. No one takes my life from me, but I lay it down by my own choice. I have authority to lay my life down, and I have the authority to take it up again. This command I received from my Father."

Once again, the Jews were divided over who Jesus was and what he was saying. Many of them said, "He is demon-possessed! He is insane! Why even listen to him?" But others said, "These are not the sayings of someone who is possessed by a demon. A demon cannot heal a man who was born blind."

CHAPTER 14

When Jesus returned to Galilee from the Feast of Tabernacles in Jerusalem, he withdrew to regions outside of Galilee. Jesus and his disciples left Capernaum and walked northwest of Galilee to the non-Jewish region of Tyre and Sidon. When Jesus arrived, he entered a house and did not want anyone to know that he was there. But he could not keep it a secret. As soon as a woman from that region heard that Jesus was there, she came to Jesus and fell at his feet crying out, "Lord, Son of David, have mercy on me! My little daughter is demon-possessed and suffers terribly." She begged Jesus to cast the demon out of her daughter. Jesus did not answer her. So his disciples came to him and told him, "Send her away, for she keeps crying out after us." Jesus said, "Yes, I was sent to the lost sheep of the house of Israel." But then the woman came and fell on her knees before Jesus and said, "Lord, help me!" Jesus said to her, "It is not right to take the bread the children are eating and throw it to the dogs." The woman said, "This is true, Lord, but even the dogs eat the children's crumbs that fall from their master's table." Then Jesus said, "This is a good answer; you have great faith! I will do what you asked me. Go, the demon has left your daughter." And her daughter was healed immediately. The woman went home and found her daughter lying on the bed, and the demon was gone.

Then Jesus left the region of Tyre and walked north through Sidon, down to Lake Galilee, and then into the region of the Decapolis. The Decapolis was located southeast of Lake Galilee where there were ten Greek cities. At that time some people brought Jesus a man who was deaf and could hardly talk. They begged him to place his hand on him. After Jesus took the man away from the crowd of people, he put his fingers into the man's ears. Then he spit and touched the man's tongue. Jesus looked up to God in heaven, took a deep sigh, and said to the man, "Be opened!" Immediately the man could hear, his tongue was released, and he began to talk. Jesus commanded the crowd not to tell anyone about the healing, but the more Jesus told them this, the more they kept talking about it publicly. People were overcome with amazement and said, "Everything Jesus does is good; he even makes deaf people hear and mute people speak." News about Jesus spread throughout the region of the Decapolis.

Then Jesus walked along the east coast of Lake Galilee. He went up on a hillside and sat down. Large crowds of people brought the lame, the blind, the crippled, those who could not speak, and many others. They laid them at the feet of Jesus, and he healed them. The people were amazed when they saw the mute speak, the crippled made whole, the lame walking, and the blind seeing. And they all praised the God of Israel.

During those days another large crowd of people gathered around Jesus. Since the people had nothing to eat, Jesus called his disciples to him and said to them, "I have compassion for these people. They have been with me for three days and have had nothing to eat. I do not want to send them away hungry. They will faint walking back to their homes, for some of them have walked a long distance to be with me." The disciples said to Jesus, "Where in this isolated place could we get enough bread to feed so many people?" Jesus asked them, "How many loaves of bread do you have?" They said, "We have seven loaves of bread and a few small fish." Jesus told the people to sit down on the ground. Then he took the seven loaves and the fish. After he had given thanks to God, he broke the bread and fish into pieces and gave them to his disciples, and they distributed them to the people. All the people ate until they

Chapter 14

were full. Afterward the disciples picked up seven baskets full of broken pieces of bread and fish that were not eaten. There were 4,000 men who ate, not including the women and children.

After Jesus had sent the people away to their homes, he and his disciples got into a fishing boat, crossed Lake Galilee, and landed at Magdala on the west coast of the lake. Magdala was the home town of Mary Magdalene that was located about six miles south of Capernaum on the Plain of Gennesaret. Magdala had a population of about 40,000 and was the center of Galilee's fish-processing industry. It was one of the most important fishing centers in Galilee.

In Magdala some religious leaders came and began to question Jesus in order to trap him. Confronting Jesus, they demanded that he show them a miraculous sign from heaven. Jesus said to them, "When it is evening you say, 'It will be good weather, for the sky is red.' And in the morning you say, 'It will be stormy weather today, for the sky is red and overcast.' You know how to interpret the sky's appearance, but you cannot interpret the signs of the times." Jesus took a deep breath and said, "Why does this wicked generation of Israel demand a miraculous sign? I tell you the truth: I will not show this generation of Israel a sign except the sign of the prophet Jonah." Just as the prophet Jonah was three days and three nights in the belly of a huge fish, so Jesus would be three days and three nights in a burial tomb before his resurrection. Then Jesus left them and walked back into Capernaum.

After Jesus and his disciples left the religious leaders, they once again took a fishing boat from Capernaum and crossed over to Bethsaida on the northeast coast of Lake Galilee. While Jesus and his disciples were rowing across the northern end of the lake, the disciples noticed that they had forgotten to bring bread. At that time Jesus warned his disciples, "Be careful! Be on your guard against the yeast of the religious leaders. The disciples talked about Jesus' warning with one another and said, "Jesus knows that we did not bring any bread with us." Jesus was aware of what his disciples were talking about and said to them, "You have so little faith! Why are you talking about not bringing any bread? Do you not see or understand? Are your hearts so hard? Don't you remember when we fed 5,000 men with five loaves of bread? How many baskets of bread did you collect?" The disciples said, "We had baskets full of bread. We collected 12 baskets full." Then Jesus said, "Don't you remember when I broke seven loaves of bread and fed 4,000 men. How many baskets full of bread did you collect?" The disciples said, "We collected seven baskets full." Jesus said, "How can you not understand that I am not talking about bread." Then the disciples finally understood that Jesus was telling them to be on guard against false teaching of the religious leaders.

When the fishing boat landed at the town of Bethsaida some people brought a blind man and begged Jesus to touch him. Jesus took the hand of the man and led him outside of the town. After Jesus had spit on the man's eyes and put his hands on them, he asked the man, "Do you see anything?" The man looked around and said, "I see people, but they look like trees walking around." Once again, Jesus put his hands on the man's eyes. Then his eyes were healed, and he could see everything clearly. Jesus sent the man home saying, "Do not go back into town."

Then Jesus and his disciples left Bethsaida and walked north to the villages of Caesarea Philippi, where Jesus prayed alone with his disciples. This region was primarily non-Jewish and was located about 25 miles north of Lake Galilee near Mount Hermon. When Jesus and his disciples came to Ceasarea Philippi, he asked them, "Who do the people say the Son of Man is? Who do the people say that I am?" The disciples said to him, "Some say John the Baptist, others say Elijah, and still others say Jeremiah, or one of the other Old Testament prophets who had come back to life." Then Jesus asked his disciples, "Who do you say I am?" Peter said to Jesus, "You are the Messiah, the Son of the living God!" Jesus said to him, "Blessed are you Peter because this was not revealed to you by flesh and blood, but by my Father in heaven. I tell you the truth: You are Peter and on this rock I will build my church, and the gates of death will not be strong enough to stop it. I will give you all the knowledge of the kingdom of God." Then Jesus told his disciples not to tell anyone that he was the Messiah.

From that time on, Jesus began to teach and explain to his disciples that he—the Son of Man—must travel to Jerusalem and suffer many things at the hands of the religious leaders. He told them that he must be put to death, and that he would rise from the dead on the third day. Jesus spoke boldly and clearly about these things.

After Peter heard Jesus tell his disciples about his crucifixion and resurrection, he was offended and pulled Jesus away from the others and rebuked him. He said to Jesus, "Never, Lord! This will never happen to you!" Jesus turned and looked at the other disciples, then he rebuked Peter saying, "Get behind me, Satan! You are a stumbling block to me. You are not thinking about God's purposes, but only human concerns!"

Then Jesus gathered his disciples and the crowd of people and said to them, "Whoever wants to be my disciple must surrender himself and pick up his cross daily and follow me. For whoever wants to save his life will lose it, but whoever gives up his life for my sake and for the gospel will find it. Tell me, what good is it for someone to gain the whole world, yet lose his life? What can anyone give in exchange for his soul? For the Son of Man will come again in his Father's glory with his angels, and then he will reward each person according to how he has lived on earth. If anyone is ashamed of me and my words in this sinful generation of Israel, the Son of Man will be ashamed of him when he comes in his Father's glory with the holy angels. I tell you the truth: There are some standing here who will not die before they see the Son of Man coming in his kingdom, for they will see the kingdom of God come with power."

About a week later, Jesus led Peter, James, and John up on a mountainside to pray. When they arrived, Jesus and the disciples were alone. Jesus was praying and his appearance was transformed in front of the disciples' eyes. The face of Jesus changed and shone as bright as the sun. His clothes became as white as light. Suddenly Moses and Elijah appeared before them in glorious light and began talking with Jesus. They spoke to him about his coming ascension back to heaven, which he was about to bring to fulfillment in Jerusalem. Peter, James, and John slept, but when they woke up, they saw the glory of Jesus, and Moses and Elijah standing with him. As Moses and Elijah were leaving, Peter said to Jesus, "Teacher, it is good for us to be here together. I can put up three tents—one for you, one for Moses, and one for Elijah." The disciples were terrified, and Peter was confused and did not know what to say. While Peter was still talking, suddenly a bright cloud—the presence of God— appeared and covered them. They shook in fear when the cloud surrounded them, and a voice from the cloud said, "This is my Son, who I love and have chosen, with him I am very pleased. Be sure to listen to him!" When the disciples heard the voice from heaven, they fell facedown to the ground because they were so afraid.

The next day, while Jesus, Peter, James, and John were walking down the mountainside, Jesus said to his disciples, "Do not tell anyone what you have seen, until the Son of Man has been raised from the dead." The disciples asked each other, "What does 'rising from the dead' mean?" Puzzled, the disciples asked Jesus, "Why do the teachers of the law of Moses say that Elijah must come first?" Jesus said, "It is true, Elijah will come first and restore all things. I tell you the truth: Elijah has already come, and the religious leaders did not recognize him, but they mistreated him. Then the disciples understood that Jesus was talking to them about John the Baptist. Jesus said, "In the same way, the Son of Man is going to suffer at their hands."

When Jesus and his disciples came down from the mountainside, they met the other disciples and a large crowd of people. The crowd was around the disciples, and the religious leaders were arguing with them. As soon as the crowd saw Jesus, they were overcome with wonder and ran to greet him. Jesus asked his disciples, "What are you arguing about?"

But before they could answer, a man suddenly jumped out from the crowd and fell on his knees before Jesus and cried out, "Lord, have mercy on my son! I beg you to help my son, for he is my only child. Teacher, my son is demon-possessed and he can't speak. The demon attacks him and throws him to the ground. He foams at the mouth, grinds his teeth, and his body becomes stiff. The demon seizes him and he screams; it causes him to have convulsions. He has seizures and experiences tremendous suffering. The demon seldom leaves him and is destroying his life. I asked your disciples to cast the demon out of my son, but they could not heal him."

Then Jesus said to the father, "Bring your son to me." So as the boy was being brought to Jesus, the demon immediately threw the boy to the ground in a severe convulsion. The boy rolled around on the ground, foaming at the mouth. Jesus asked the boy's father, "How long has your son been acting like this?" The father said, "Since he was a child. The demon tries to kill him by throwing him into fire or water. But if you can do anything, please have mercy on us and help us." Jesus said, "Why do you ask me if I can help you? Everything is possible for a person who believes." Immediately the boy's father yelled out, "I do believe! Help me overcome my unbelief!" When Jesus saw that a crowd of people was running toward them, he rebuked the demon saying, "You evil spirit, I command you to come out of him and never enter him again!" The demon cried out and shook the boy violently. He was healed immediately. When the demon left, the boy looked like a corpse, so that many people said, "He's dead." But Jesus took the hand of the boy and lifted him to his feet. When he gave the boy back to his father, all the people were amazed at the majesty of God.

After Jesus had entered a house nearby, his disciples were troubled and came to him in private and asked him, "Why couldn't we cast out that demon from the boy?" Jesus said, "Because you have so little faith. I tell you the truth: If you have faith as small as a mustard seed, you can say to this mountain, 'Move from this place to another place.' And it will move. Nothing will be impossible for you. For this kind of demon can only be cast out by prayer and fasting."

While everyone was still in awe at all that Jesus had done, Jesus and his disciples left the region of Caesarea Philippi and walked through Galilee. Jesus did not want anyone to know where they were, for he was teaching his disciples. Jesus gathered his disciples and said, "Listen carefully to me! I tell you the truth: The Son of Man will soon be delivered over to the custody of men. They will kill him, but on the third day he will be raised to life." The disciples were very afraid to ask him what he meant.

When Jesus and his disciples arrived back in Capernaum, collectors of the annual temple tax worth about two days' wages came to

Peter and asked him, "Doesn't your teacher pay the temple tax?" Peter said, "Yes, he does." When Peter went into his house, Jesus asked him, "What do you think, Peter? From whom do the kings of the earth collect duty and taxes—from their own children or from others?" Peter said, "From others." So Jesus said, "Then their children do not pay taxes. But so that we will not offend anyone, go to the lake and throw out your fishing line. Open the mouth of the first fish you catch, and you will find a coin in its mouth. Take it and give it to them for my tax and yours."

Once again, the disciples began arguing among themselves about which one of them would be the greatest in the kingdom of God. After they went into Peter's house, Jesus asked them, "What were you arguing about?" Embarrassed, his disciples did not say anything. Then Jesus sat down, called them together, and had a young child stand beside him. He then took him in his arms and said to his disciples: "I tell you the truth: Unless you change and become like a young child, you will not enter the kingdom of God. Therefore, whoever humbles himself like this child will be the greatest in the kingdom of God. Whoever wants to be first must be the last, and the servant of all. For it is the one who is least among you who is the greatest. Whoever receives and welcomes a young child in my name receives me; and whoever receives me, receives the one who sent me into the world. If anyone causes one of these little children—who believe in me—to sin, it would be much better for him to have a large millstone hung around his neck and be thrown into the deep sea to drown. Make sure that you do not mistreat one of these little children. For I tell you the truth: Their angels always see the face of my Father in heaven.

Then Jesus told them this story of lost sheep, "Tell me what you think: If a man owns 100 sheep, and one of them wanders away and gets lost, will he not leave the 99 sheep on the hill grazing and go to search for the one that is lost? I tell you the truth: When he finds the lost sheep, he is happier for that one sheep than for the 99 that were not lost. In the same way, your Father in heaven does not want one of these little children to be lost."

Jesus looked into the eyes of his disciples and said, "How terrible

Chapter 14

for the world because of the temptations that cause people to sin! If your hand causes you to sin, you should cut it off. It is much better for you to enter eternal life with one hand than to be thrown into the eternal fire of hell with two hands. For in hell the fire never goes out. And if your foot causes you to sin, you should cut it off. It is much better for you to enter eternal life with one foot than to be thrown into the eternal fire of hell with two feet. And if your eye causes you to sin, pluck it out and throw it away. For it is much better for you to enter eternal life with one eye than be thrown into the fire of hell with two eyes. Be warned, in hell the worms that eat them do not die, and the fire does not go out."

Then the apostle John abruptly said to Jesus, "Teacher, we saw a man casting demons out of people in your name. We told him to stop, because he was not one of us." Jesus said, "Do not stop him, for whoever is not against us is for us." For no one who does a miracle in my name can then speak evil about me."

Jesus continued to teach saying, "If your brothers or sisters sin against you, go in private and tell them their sin against you. If they listen to you, you have restored your relationship with them. But if they refuse to listen to you, take one or two other believers along with you, for as it is written in *Deuteronomy 19:15*, 'Let every matter be settled by the testimony of two or three witnesses.' If they still refuse to listen, tell it to the church; and if they refuse to listen to the church, treat them as you would a religious pagan or a tax collector. I tell you the truth: When two believers on earth agree about anything they ask for, it will be done for them by my Father in heaven. For where two or three believers gather in my name, there I am with them!"

Looking puzzled, Peter asked Jesus, "Lord, how many times must I forgive a fellow believer who sins against me? Do I have to forgive him up to seven times?" Jesus said to him, "I tell you the truth: No, you must never stop forgiving a fellow believer."

Then Jesus told them the story of the unforgiving servant: "The kingdom of God is like a king who told his servants to pay back all the money they owed him. As he began to settle his accounts, a servant who owed the king about 20 years' wages was brought to him. Because the servant was not able to pay his debt, the king ordered that he and his family and all that he owned be sold to repay his debt. After hearing this, the servant fell on his knees before him begging, 'Please be patient with me, and I will pay you back everything I owe you.' The king showed mercy toward the servant and forgave him his entire debt and let him go. But when the forgiven servant left, he found a fellow servant who owed him about a day's wages. He grabbed him and began to choke him demanding, 'Pay me back all that you owe me!' The fellow servant fell to his knees and begged him, 'Please be patient with me, and I will pay you back everything I owe you.' But the servant refused to forgive his fellow servant his debt. Instead, he had the man thrown into prison until he could pay his entire debt. When the other servants saw what had happened, they were very angry and went and told their king everything. Then the king called the forgiven servant in and said, 'You are a wicked servant! I forgave you of all your debt because you begged me. You should have had mercy on your fellow servant just as I had mercy on you.' In his anger the king handed him over to the jailers to be punished, until he paid back all he owed."

PART THREE

CHAPTER 15

After Jesus finished his final teaching in Capernaum, he left Galilee and began walking toward Jerusalem because the time for his ascension back to heaven was getting close.

When Jesus began to walk toward Jerusalem he sent messengers ahead of him. They went into a Samaritan village to prepare for the arrival of Jesus. But the Samaritans would not welcome him, because he was traveling to Jerusalem. When the apostles James and John saw this, they asked Jesus, "Lord, do you want us to call fire of judgment down from heaven to destroy them?" Jesus was upset. He turned and rebuked them.

Then Jesus and his disciples walked east into the region of the Jews in Perea on the other side of the Jordan River. And a large crowd of people followed Jesus, and he taught them and healed those who were sick.

As Jesus and his disciples were walking along the road in Perea, a religious leader came to him and said, "Teacher, I will follow you wherever you go." Jesus said to him, "Foxes have holes to live in, and birds have nests, but the Son of Man has no place to lay his head." Jesus said to another disciple, "Follow me!" But the disciple said to Jesus, "Lord, first let me go and bury my father when he dies." Jesus said to him, "No, follow me and go proclaim the kingdom of God." And another man said to Jesus, "Lord, I will follow you, but first let me go back and say goodbye to my family." Jesus said to him, "No one who puts his hand to the plow and then looks back is ready to serve in the kingdom of God."

Then Jesus chose 72 from the crowd of disciples and sent them two by two ahead of him to every town he would pass through in the region of Perea on his way to Jerusalem. Before they left, Jesus said to them, "There is an abundant harvest, but there are only a few workers to gather it in. Therefore, ask the Lord of the harvest to send out workers into his harvest field. Go now! I send you out like lambs among wolves. Do not take a money bag or extra sandals; and do not stop to greet anyone along the road. When you enter a home say, 'God's peace be on this home.' If a person of peace lives there, your blessing of peace will rest on him; if not, it will return to you. Stay only in that home and do not move around from house to house; eat and drink whatever is given you. When you enter a town and are welcomed, heal the sick who are there and tell them, 'The kingdom of God has arrived.' But when you enter a town and are not welcomed, stand in its streets and declare, 'We wipe the dirt of your town from our feet as a warning to you. You can be sure of this: It will be much better on the day of God's judgment for Sodom than for that town.'"

Then Jesus turned to his disciples and denounced the Jewish towns around Lake Galilee that they had just left. It was in these towns where Jesus did most of his miracles, but they refused to repent and turn to God. Jesus declared: "How terrible it will be for the Jewish towns of Chorazin and Bethsaida! For if the miracles that I did in you were done in the non-Jewish cities of Tyre and Sidon, they would have repented long ago. But I tell you the truth: It will be better for Tyre and Sidon on the day of God's judgment than for you. And you, Capernaum, will you be lifted to the heavens? Absolutely not! You will go down to the realm of the dead! For if the miracles that were done in you had been done in Sodom, it would still exist today. I tell you the truth: It will be better for Sodom on the day of God's judgment than for you." Then Jesus said, "Whoever listens to you listens to me. Whoever rejects you rejects me. And whoever rejects me rejects him who sent me into the world."

After their mission journey, the 72 disciples returned full of joy and said to Jesus, "Lord, even the demons obey what we say in your name." Jesus said to them, "I saw Satan fall like a lightning bolt from heaven. I gave you God's authority to walk over snakes and scorpions and to overcome all the power of Satan our enemy; nothing can hurt you! However, do not rejoice that demons obey your commands, but rejoice that your names are written in heaven."

At that time Jesus was full of joy through the Holy Spirit and prayed: "I praise you, Father—Lord of heaven and earth—because you have hidden these things from the wise and educated, and have revealed them to little children. Yes, Father, for this was your gracious will and good pleasure. Then Jesus turned to his disciples and said, "All things have been given to me by the Father. No one knows who the Son is except the Father, and no one knows who the Father is except the Son and those to whom the Son chooses to reveal him. Blessed are your eyes because you see what you see. For I tell you the truth: Many prophets and kings wanted to see and hear what you have. But they did not see or hear what you have seen and heard."

Then suddenly a religious leader spoke up to test Jesus. He asked him, "Teacher, what must I do to inherit eternal life in the kingdom of God?" Jesus said to him, "What is written in the law of Moses? How do you understand what it says?" The man said, "It is written in *Deuteronomy 6:5*, 'Love the Lord your God with all your heart and with all your soul and with all your strength and with all your mind,' and in *Leviticus 19:18*, 'Love your neighbor as yourself.'" Jesus said, "Very good, your answer is correct; do this and you will live."

But then the religious leader became shaken and wanted to prove that he was a righteous person. He asked Jesus, "Who is my neighbor?" So Jesus told him this story of the Good Samaritan: "A man was walking down the road that leads from Jerusalem to Jericho, and he was attacked by robbers. They took his clothes, beat him, and left him lying there nearly dead. A Jewish temple priest walked down the same road, but when he saw the dying man, he passed by him on the other side of the road. Another temple priest walked down the same road and saw the dying man, but he passed by him on the other side of the road. But when a Samaritan walked down that road and saw the dying man, he had compassion on him. He poured oil and wine on his wounds and bandaged them. Then, putting him on his donkey, he took the man to a hotel and took care of him. The next day the Samaritan paid the hotel manager two coins, and told him, 'Take care of him, and when I return from my journey I will pay you for any extra costs you may have.'"

Then Jesus asked the religious leader, "Which of these three men do you think was a neighbor to the man who was attacked by robbers?" He said, "The one who had compassion for him and showed him mercy." Jesus said to him, "You are right, now go and do the same for others."

CHAPTER 16

It was December and it was the time to celebrate Hannukah—the Festival of Lights in Jerusalem. When Jesus and his disciples entered the town of Bethany on the eastern slope of the Mount of Olives, a woman named Martha extended hospitality to Jesus and opened her home to him. Martha had a sister named Mary, and a brother named Lazarus.

When they were in the house, Mary sat at the Lord's feet listening to his teaching, but Martha was distracted by all the preparations of hospitality that had to be done. So Martha asked Jesus, "Lord, Mary has left me to serve all alone; don't you care? Tell her to help me!" Jesus said to her, "Martha, Martha, why are you so anxious and worried about so many things? For there is only one thing that is truly important, and Mary has chosen what is truly good."

At that time a crowd of people had gathered and were trampling one another, and suddenly someone jumped out from the crowd and said to Jesus, "Teacher, tell my brother to divide the inheritance with me." Jesus said to him, "Who appointed me to be a judge between you two brothers? Watch out! Be on your guard against all kinds of greed, for true life does not consist of the abundance of one's possessions." Then Jesus told the people the story of a rich man's greed. He said, "The land of a rich man produced an abundant harvest. So he thought to himself, 'What should I do? I have no more space to store all my crops.' Then he said to himself, 'I know what I will do. I will tear down my small barns and build big ones, and then I can store all my extra crops. And I'll say to myself: 'I now have an abundant amount of food stored up for many years, so I will take life easy. I will eat, drink and be happy.' But God said to the man, 'You rich fool! For this very night your life will be taken from you. Then who will get all the food that you have stored up for yourself?' This is how it will be with whoever stores up things for themselves on earth, but is not rich toward God."

Turning to his disciples, Jesus told them a story about faithfulness. "Be dressed ready to serve and make sure you keep your lamps burning, like servants waiting for their master to return home from a wedding banquet, so that when he knocks on the door you will immediately open it for him. Blessed are those servants whose master finds them ready, even if he comes in the middle of the night or early in the morning." Then Jesus said, "You also must be ready, because the Son of Man will come at a time when you do not expect him."

Then some people were frantic and rushed to tell Jesus about the Galilean Jews whose blood Pontius Pilate had mixed with their sacrifices. Jesus said to them, "Do you think these Galileans were worse sinners than the other Galileans because they suffered in this way? No, they were not! I tell you the truth: Unless you repent and turn to God, you too will perish. Then Jesus said, "What about those 18 people who died when the tower of Siloam fell on them—do you think they were more guilty than all the others living in Jerusalem? No! I tell you the truth: Unless you repent and turn to God, you too will perish."

One day Jesus was teaching in a synagogue on the Sabbath day, and a woman was there who had been crippled by a demon for 18 years. She was bent over and could not stand up straight. When Jesus saw her, he called her to the front of the synagogue and said to her, "Woman, you are set free from your deformity." Then Jesus put his hands on her, and immediately she stood up straight and praised God. The synagogue leader was furious with Jesus because he healed someone on the Sabbath. He told the people, "Come to be healed on the six days we can work, but do not come to be healed on the Sabbath."

Then Jesus said to the synagogue leader, "You are a religious hypocrite! Don't you on the Sabbath untie your ox or donkey from the feeding trough and lead it out to drink water; then shouldn't this woman, a daughter of Abraham, who Satan has kept crippled for 18 years, be set free on the Sabbath?" When Jesus said these things, all his religious opponents were ashamed, but the people were full of joy because of all the wonderful things he was doing.

Then Jesus walked in Solomon's Colonnade along the eastern side of the temple complex, and the Jews were frustrated with Jesus and said to him, "How long will you keep us wondering? If you are the Messiah, tell us in plain language." Jesus said to them, "I have already told you, but you refuse to believe. The miracles that I do in my Father's name tell you who I am, but you don't believe because you are not my sheep. I know my sheep. My sheep listen to my voice and follow me. And I give them eternal life, and they will never perish; because no one has the power to seize them out of my hand. My Father, who has given them to me, is greater than all things; no one has the power to seize my sheep out of my Father's grasp. The Father and I are one!"

Because Jesus said that he was one with the Father, his Jewish opponents were furious and picked up rocks to throw at him. But Jesus said to them, "I have shown you many good works of power from the Father. For which one of these good works do you want to stone me to death?" The Jews said, "We do not want to stone you because you do good works, but because you blaspheme—you are a mere man, but claim to be God." Jesus to them, "Why do you accuse me of blasphemy because I said to you, 'I am the Son of God'? For the Father is in me, and I am in the Father."

Once again, the religious leaders tried to arrest Jesus, but he escaped.

CHAPTER 17

Because the Jewish religious leaders were planning to arrest Jesus, he left Jerusalem with his disciples and walked east across the Jordan River to Bethany, the place where John had been baptizing people in the early days. Then Jesus taught through the towns and villages of Perea, and many people believed in him. They said, "Although John never did a miracle, everything he said about Jesus was true."

All of a sudden, a man spoke up and asked Jesus, "Lord, are only a few people going to be saved and enter the kingdom of God?" Jesus said to him, "Make every effort to enter through the narrow door. For I tell you the truth, many people will try to enter and will not be able to. Once the owner of the house gets up and closes the door, you will stand outside knocking and begging, 'Sir, open the door for us.' But the owner will declare, 'I don't know you or where you come from!' Then you will tell him, 'We ate and drank with you, and you taught in our streets.' But the owner will declare, 'I don't know you or where you come from! Go away from me, all you workers of evil!' There will be weeping and grinding of teeth there when you see Abraham, Isaac, Jacob, and all the Old Testament prophets in the kingdom of God, but you have been thrown out. People will come from east and west and north and south, and will take their places at the banquet feast in the kingdom of God." Then Jesus said, "For there are some people who are last who will be first, and there are some people who are first who will be last."

At that time some religious leaders rushed forward and said to Jesus, "Hurry, leave Perea because Herod Antipas wants to kill you." Jesus said to the them, "Go tell that fox, 'Today and tomorrow I will continue to cast out demons, heal the sick, and on the third day I will reach my goal. Believe me, I will keep walking today and tomorrow and the next day—for surely no prophet can die outside of Jerusalem! Jesus was speaking about his crucifixion and resurrection from the dead.

During that time Jesus went to eat in the house of a prominent religious leader on the Sabbath day, which also served as a synagogue. He was being carefully watched to see what he would do. There was a man there in front of Jesus who was suffering from a swollen body. Jesus asked the religious leaders, "Is it lawful to heal on the Sabbath?" But they did not say anything to him. So Jesus took hold of the man, healed him, and sent him away. Then Jesus said to the religious leaders, "If one of you had a child or an ox that fell into a well on the Sabbath, you would immediately pull them out." Again, they did not say anything to Jesus.

As they were about to eat, Jesus saw how the guests chose the places of honor at the table. The places of honor were to sit on the right and left side of the host. So he told them this story: "When someone invites you to a wedding feast, do not take the place of honor, for a more important person than you may have been invited. And then the wedding host who had invited both of you will tell you, 'Give this person your seat of honor.' Then you will be put to shame, and you will have to sit in a less honorable seat. Instead, when you are invited, take the least important place, so that when your host comes, he will tell you, 'Friend, move to a more honored place at the table.' Then you will be honored in the presence of all the other guests. For whoever exalts himself will be humbled, and whoever humbles himself will be exalted."

Then Jesus turned and said to the religious leader, "When you give a luncheon or dinner, do not invite your friends, family, relatives, or your rich neighbors; if you do, they might invite you back to repay you. Instead, when you give a banquet, invite the poor, crippled, lame, and blind. If you do, you will be blessed. Although they cannot repay you, you will be repaid at the resurrection of the righteous." When someone at the table heard this, he said to Jesus, "Blessed is the one who will eat at the feast in the kingdom of God."

Then Jesus told the story of a great banquet. He said, "A man was preparing a great banquet and invited many guests. At the time of the banquet he sent his servant to tell everyone who had been invited, 'Come, for everything is now ready!' But all of those invited made excuses. The first person said, 'I have just bought some land, and I must go and see it. Please excuse me.' Another person said, 'I have bought five teams of oxen, and I'm on my way to try them out. Please excuse me.' Still another person said, 'I just got married, so I can't come.' The servant returned and told his master about all the excuses that those who were invited had made. Then the owner of the house became angry and ordered his servant, 'Go out quickly into the streets and alleys of the town and bring in the poor, the crippled, the blind, and the lame.' The servant said, 'Sir, what you asked us to do, we have already done, but there is still space in the banquet room.' Then the master told his servant, 'Go out to the roads and country paths and persuade people to come in, so that my house will be full. For I tell you the truth: Not one of those people who were invited will ever eat at my banquet.'"

Large crowds of people were walking with Jesus through Perea, and he turned to them and said, "Whoever comes to me and loves his father and mother, wife and children, brothers and sisters—yes, and even his own life—more than me cannot be my disciple. Whoever does not carry his cross and follow me is not worthy of me. He cannot be my disciple. Whoever finds his life will lose it, and whoever loses his life for my sake will find it. For those of you who do not give up everything cannot be my disciples."

Then Jesus said to those who were following him, "Listen to me. Whoever can be trusted with little can also be trusted with much, and whoever is dishonest with very little will also be dishonest with much. So if you have not been faithful in handling worldly wealth, who will trust you with true riches? And if you have not been faithful with someone else's property, who will give you property of your own?"

Jesus turned to the crowd of people around him and said, "No servant can serve two masters. Either you will hate the one and love the other, or you will be devoted to the one and despise the other. You cannot serve both God and money." When the religious leaders heard this, they made fun of Jesus because they were lovers of money. Jesus said to them, "You are those who justify yourselves in the eyes of other people, but God knows your hearts. The money people value in this world is detestable in God's sight. Jesus was disturbed with the religious leaders and said, "The law of Moses and the Old Testament prophets were proclaimed until the coming of John the Baptist. Since the coming of John the Baptist, the good news of the kingdom of God is being preached, and whoever has strong faith is entering it. For it is easier for heaven and earth to disappear than for the smallest stroke of a pen to be left out of the law of Moses.

Then Jesus told the religious leaders the story of the rich man and Lazarus. "There was a rich man who was dressed in purple and fine linen and lived in luxury every day. A poor beggar named Lazarus—whose body was covered with sores—was laid at the rich man's gate, hoping to eat what fell from the rich man's table. Even the dogs came and licked Lazarus' sores. The time came when Lazarus died and the angels carried him to Abraham's side. Then the rich man also died and was buried. As the rich man was being tormented in the realm of the dead, he looked up and saw Abraham far away and Lazarus at his side. The man called out, 'Father Abraham, have mercy on me and send Lazarus to dip his finger in water and cool off my tongue, for I am suffering in this fire.' But Abraham said to the rich man, 'You received all your luxurious things during your life on earth, while Lazarus only received bad things, but now he is comforted here and you are suffering. And besides, a great canyon has been placed between us, so that no one is able to cross to either side.' The rich man said, 'Then I beg you, Father Abraham, send Lazarus to my family, for I have five brothers. Have Lazarus warn them, so that they will not come to this place of torment.' Abraham said, 'They can believe Moses and the Old Testament prophets; let them listen to them.' But the rich man said, 'No, Father Abraham, for if someone from the dead goes to them, they will repent and turn to God.' Abraham said to him, 'If they will not listen to Moses and the Old Testament prophets during their life on earth, they will not be convinced even if someone rises from the dead.'"

At that time many tax collectors and sinners were all crowding around to hear Jesus. But the religious leaders complained, "Jesus welcomes sinners and eats with them." So Jesus told them these stories:

"Suppose someone has 100 sheep and loses one of them. Wouldn't he leave the 99 sheep in the field and search for the one lost sheep until he finds it? And when he finds the lost sheep, he puts it on his shoulders rejoicing and goes home. Then he calls together his friends and neighbors and says, 'Rejoice with me; I have found my lost sheep!' Jesus said, "I tell you the truth: In the same way, there is more rejoicing in heaven over one sinner who repents and turns to God than over 99 righteous people who do not need to repent.

"Suppose a woman has 10 silver coins and loses one of them. Wouldn't she light a lamp, sweep the house, and look everywhere until she finds it? And when she finds the lost coin, she calls together her friends and neighbors and says, 'Rejoice with me; I have found my lost coin!' Jesus said, "I tell you the truth: In the same way, there is rejoicing in the presence of God's angels over one sinner who repents and turns to God.

"There was a man who had two sons. The younger son said to his father, 'Father, give me my share of the estate.' So the father divided his property between his two sons. Not long after that, the younger son took all that he owned, and went on a journey to a faraway, non-Jewish country where he wasted his wealth in sinful living. After he spent all his money there was a severe famine in that country, and he began to be in desperate need. So he went and was hired to feed the pigs in the field. He became so hungry that he even wanted to eat the pigs' food, but no one gave him anything. When the son realized that his life had hit bottom, he said to himself, 'My father's servants have plenty of food to eat, but here I am starving to death! I will go back to my father and tell him, "Father, I have sinned against God and against you. I am no longer worthy to be called your son, so just make me one of your servants. So the son left that country and walked back to his father. His father saw his son in the distance walking toward him, and was filled with compassion for him; he ran to meet his son, threw his arms around him, and kissed him. The son said to his father, 'I have sinned against God and against you. I am no longer worthy to be called your son.' But the father told his servants, 'Go! Bring the best robe and put it on my son. Put a ring on his finger and sandals on his feet. Bring the well-fed calf and kill it. Let's have a feast and celebrate the return of my son. For my son was dead, but he is alive again; he was lost, but now he is found.' So they began to celebrate. Meanwhile, the father's older son was working in the field. When he came near to the house, he heard music and dancing. So he called one of the servants and asked him why everyone was celebrating. The servant said, 'Your younger brother has come home, and your father has killed the well-fed calf because he is back home safe and sound.' The older brother became very angry and refused to go into the house and join the celebration. So his father went outside and pleaded with him. But the older son told his father, 'Look! For many years I've worked like a slave for you, and I have done everything you have told me to do. But you never gave me even a young goat so that I could celebrate with my friends. But when this son of yours who wasted your property with prostitutes comes home, you kill a well-fed calf for him!' The father said to him, 'My son, you are always with me, and everything I own is yours. But we had to celebrate and rejoice, because your brother was dead and is alive again; he was lost, but now he is found.'"

At that time, Mary and Martha—Lazarus' sisters—sent this message to Jesus saying, "Lord, our brother Lazarus, the one you love is very sick." Jesus was sad because he loved Mary, Martha, and Lazarus. He turned to his disciples and said, "Lazarus' sickness will not lead to his death. No, his sickness is for God's glory, so that the Son of God will be praised through it." Jesus stayed east of the Jordan River in the region of Perea for two more days. Then he said to his disciples, "Let us go back to Jerusalem." His disciples said, "But Teacher, a short while ago the religious leaders in Jerusalem were trying to kill you. Why are you going back there?" Jesus said, "There are 12 hours of light in a day. Whoever walks during the day will not stumble, because they see by this world's light. But it's when a person walks in the darkness of night that they stumble, for they have no light to see. Our friend Lazarus has

Chapter 17

fallen asleep, but I am going there to wake him up." His disciples were puzzled and said, "Lord, if he is asleep, he will wake up on his own." Jesus was telling them of Lazarus' death, but his disciples thought he was saying that Lazarus was just sleeping. Then Jesus told them directly, "Lazarus is dead. Get ready we are going to Jerusalem." Then Thomas said to the other disciples, "Let's go and die with him."

When Jesus arrived at Bethany on the Mount of Olives, Lazarus had already been in a rock tomb for four days, and many Jews had come to comfort Mary and Martha because of their brother's death. When Martha heard that Jesus was coming to Bethany, she ran to meet him, but Mary stayed home. Martha said to Jesus, "Lord, if you had been here, my brother Lazarus would not have died. But I know that God will do whatever you ask him." Jesus said to her, "Your brother will be raised from the dead." Martha said, "I know he will rise from the dead in the resurrection at the last day." Jesus said to her, "I am the resurrection and the life! Whoever believes in me will live, even though he dies. Whoever lives by believing in me will never die. Do you believe what I tell you is true?" Martha said, "Yes, Lord! I believe that you are the Messiah, the Son of God, who has come into this world."

After saying this, Martha hurried back to Bethany and called her sister Mary aside and said, "The Teacher is here and he is asking to see you." When Mary heard this, she left quickly and ran to meet him. When the Jews, who were with Mary in the house, saw how quickly she got up and left, they followed her. When Mary came to Jesus, she fell at his feet and said, "Lord, if you had been here, my brother Lazarus would not have died."

When Jesus saw Mary and the others weeping, he was deeply moved in his spirit and was greatly troubled. Then Jesus asked them, "Where did you put Lazarus' body?" They said, "Lord, come and we will show you." Jesus wept. Then the Jews said to one another, "See how much he loved Lazarus." But some of the Jews said, "He healed the man who was born blind, why couldn't he have stopped Lazarus from dying?"

Jesus arrived at Lazarus' tomb, and he was deeply moved in his spirit. Now it was a cave tomb, and a large stone had been rolled across its entrance. Jesus yelled, "Roll away the stone." Martha was confused and said, "But Lord, he has been dead four days and by this time his body will stink." Then Jesus said to her, "Didn't I tell you that if you believe you will see the glory of God?" So finally they rolled the stone away from the tomb's entrance. Then Jesus looked up to heaven and prayed, "Father, I thank you that you hear me. I know that you always hear me." After Jesus had prayed, he shouted, "Lazarus, come out of the tomb!" Lazarus walked out of the tomb, his hands and feet wrapped with linen strips, and his face wrapped with a cloth. Jesus told the people, "Take off his grave clothes and set Lazarus free!"

At that time, many of the Jews who had come to visit Mary believed in Jesus after they saw him raise Lazarus from the dead. But some other Jews went and told the religious leaders what Jesus had done. So they called a meeting of the Jewish religious council. They asked, "What are we going to do? For this man Jesus is doing many miracles. If we do not stop him, everyone will believe in him, and then the Romans will come and destroy our temple and our nation." Then the high priest Caiaphas said, "You know nothing at all! Jesus must die to protect the Jewish nation."

So from that day on the religious leaders made plans to kill Jesus.

CHAPTER 18

Because the Jewish religious leaders were making plans to kill him, Jesus would not walk around openly among the people in Jerusalem. So Jesus and his disciples left and traveled to the village of Ephraim, about 15 miles north of Jerusalem.

From Ephraim, Jesus began walking back toward Jerusalem along the border between Galilee and Samaria. As Jesus was going into a village, 10 men with a severe skin disease met him. They stood at a distance and yelled out, "Jesus, have mercy on us!" When Jesus saw them, he said, "Go, show yourselves to the temple priests in Jerusalem." As the 10 men were going to the temple priests, they were healed. One man saw that he was healed, and so he went back to Jesus, praising God in a loud voice. He was a Samaritan and threw himself at Jesus' feet and thanked him. Jesus asked him, "I healed 10 of you. Where are the other nine? No one has come back to praise God except this foreign Samaritan." Then Jesus said to the Samaritan man, "Stand up and go; your faith has healed you."

At this time some religious leaders asked Jesus when the kingdom of God would come. Jesus said to them, "The kingdom of God is not something that you can see with your eyes, nor will people say, 'Here it is,' or 'There it is,' because the kingdom of God is within you—it is in your midst."

When Jesus was alone with his disciples he told them, "The time is coming when you will want to see the Son of Man, but you will not see him. People will tell you, 'There he is!' or 'Here he is!' But do not run after them or follow them. For the coming of the Son of Man will be like flashes of lightning that will light up the sky from one end to the other. But first the Son of Man must suffer many things and be rejected by the religious leaders of Israel. Just as it was in the time of Noah, so also will it be in the time of the Son of Man. At the time of Noah people were eating, drinking, and marrying up to the day Noah entered the ark. Then the flood came and destroyed them all. It was the same in the time of Lot. People were eating and drinking, buying and selling, and planting and building. But the day Lot left Sodom, fire and sulfur thundered down from heaven and destroyed them all. And this is how it will be on the day the Son of Man comes.

Then Jesus told his disciples that they should always pray and never give up. He told them this story, "In a certain town there was a judge who did not fear God or care about people. But there was a widow in that town who kept going to the judge pleading, 'Give me justice against my enemy.' For a long time the judge refused to listen, but finally he said to himself, 'I do not fear God or care about people, but because this widow keeps bothering me, I will give her justice, so that she won't one day come back and attack me!'" And the Lord said to his disciples, "Listen to what this unjust judge said. Will not God give justice to his chosen ones, who cry out to him day and night? Will he continue to ignore them? I tell you the truth: God will give justice to them, and quickly. However, when the Son of Man comes, will he find faith on the earth?"

Because some people trusted in their own righteousness and looked down with religious pride on everyone else, Jesus told this story: "Two men went up into the temple to pray—one was a religious leader and the other was a tax collector. The religious leader stood by himself and prayed, 'God, I thank you that I am not like sinners—robbers, evildoers, adulterers—or even like this tax collector. I fast twice a week and give a tenth of all I get.' But the tax collector stood at a distance. He would not even lift his eyes to God, but beat his chest and prayed, 'God, have mercy on me, a sinner.'" Then Jesus said to his disciples, "I tell you the truth: This tax collector is the only one who went home in a right relationship with God. Believe me, whoever exalts himself will be humbled, and whoever humbles himself will be exalted."

Some religious leaders who opposed Jesus came to test him. They asked him, "Is it lawful for a man to divorce his wife for any reason?" Jesus said to them, "What did Moses teach you?" They said, "Moses allowed a man to write a certificate of divorce and send his wife away." Jesus said, "Moses wrote you this command because your hearts were hard. But it was not this way from the beginning of creation. From the beginning of creation, God 'created them male and female,' as it is written in *Genesis 1:27*. And it is written in *Genesis 2:24*, 'For this reason, a man will leave his father and mother and be united to his wife, and the two will become one body. I tell you the truth: They are no longer two in marriage, but one body. Therefore, what God joined together as one, let no one separate." I tell you the truth: A man who divorces his wife—except for marital unfaithfulness—and marries another woman commits adultery."

When they were alone with Jesus in a house, the disciples asked him about his teaching on divorce. Jesus said to them, "Whoever divorces his wife and marries again commits adultery against her. And if she divorces her husband and marries again, she commits adultery." The disciples said to Jesus, "If what you taught is true between a husband and wife, then it is better not to marry." Jesus said, "Not everyone can accept my teaching, but only to those who have been given understanding. For there are some men who are spiritually gifted not to marry, there are some men who have been made eunuchs by being castrated, and there are some men who choose not to marry for the sake of the kingdom of God. Whoever can accept my teaching should receive it."

Then some people brought little children to Jesus for they wanted him to put his hands on them and pray for them. But when the disciples saw this, they rebuked them and told the people to stop bringing children to Jesus. When Jesus saw this he became very angry. Then he called the children around him and told his disciples, "Let these little children come to me. Do not stop them, for the kingdom of God belongs to them. I tell you the truth: Whoever does not receive the kingdom of God like a little child will never enter it." Then Jesus took the little children in his arms, put his hands on them, and blessed them. Then he left that place.

As Jesus was walking along the road toward Jerusalem, a young ruler ran and fell on his knees before Jesus. He asked Jesus, "Good teacher, what must I do to enter eternal life?" Jesus said, "Why do you call me good? Why do you ask me about what is good? God is the only one who is good. If you want to enter eternal life, then keep God's commandments. You know God's commandments." The man asked Jesus, "Which commandments?" Jesus said, "Do not murder, do not commit adultery, do not steal, do not give false testimony, honor your father and mother, and love your neighbor as yourself." The young man said, "Teacher, I have kept all of these commandments since I was a boy. What else must I do?" Jesus looked at him and loved him. When Jesus heard his answer, he said to him, "There is one thing that you lack. If you want to be perfect, go and sell everything you own, give it to the poor, and then you will have treasure in heaven. After you do this, come and follow me." When the young ruler heard this, he went away sad, because he was very rich.

Seeing the sadness on the face of the young ruler, Jesus looked around at his disciples and said to them, "I tell you the truth: It is hard for a rich person to enter the kingdom of God. It is easier for a camel to go through the hole of a sewing needle than for a rich person to enter the kingdom of God." When the disciples heard Jesus, they were astonished. And then they asked Jesus, "Who then can be saved? Jesus stared at his disciples and said, "For humans this is impossible, but with God all things are possible."

Then Peter was flustered and said to Jesus, "What about us? We have left everything to follow you! What is our reward?" Jesus said to his disciples, "Whoever has left houses, father, mother, brothers, sisters, wife, children or lands for my sake and the kingdom of God, will receive 100 times more in this present age and eternal life in the age to come. But many people who are first will be last, and many who are last will be first. I tell you the truth: At the creation of a new heaven and earth, when the Son of Man sits on his glorious throne, you who have

Chapter 18

followed me will also sit on 12 thrones judging the 12 tribes of Israel."

Then Jesus spoke to them about the kingdom of God. He said, "The kingdom of God is like a landowner who went out before 6 a.m. to hire men to work in his vineyard. He agreed to pay them a day's wage and sent them into his vineyard. Then the landowner went out again about 9 a.m. and saw men standing in the public market doing nothing. He told them, 'You also can go and work in my vineyard, and I will pay you a day's wage.' So they went out to work. Then the landowner went out around noon and again at 3 p.m. and hired more workers. Again, the landowner went out about 5 p.m. and found more men standing around doing nothing. So he asked them, 'Why have you been standing here all day doing nothing?' They answered, 'Because no one has hired us to work for them.' The landowner replied, 'You also can go and work in my vineyard.'" At 6 p.m. the landowner told his foreman, 'Call all the workers in from the vineyard and pay them their day's wage—beginning with the last ones hired to the first ones hired.' The workers who were hired last came and each received a day's wage. So when those came who were hired first, they expected to receive more money than the others, but they also received only a day's wage. When they received their pay, they began to complain to the landowner. They said, 'The men you hired last worked for only one hour. And you gave them the same wage as us, even though we did most of the work. We labored through the heat of the day!' But the landowner said to one of them, 'Friend, I am not being unfair to you. Didn't you agree to work for a day's wage? Take your money and leave. I want to give the same wage to the one who was hired last. Don't I have the right to do what I want with my own money? Or are you envious because I am generous?'" Then Jesus said, "So the last will be first, and the first will be last."

As Jesus was leading his disciples along the road toward Jerusalem, the disciples were amazed; but the crowd following behind them were afraid. Then once again Jesus took his apostles away from the crowd and said to them, "We are going up to Jerusalem, and everything that is written about the Son of Man in the Bible will be fulfilled. For the Son of Man will be delivered over to the Jewish religious leaders. They will condemn him to death and will turn him over to the

Romans to be mocked, spit upon, flogged, and crucified. But God will raise him to life on the third day!" The disciples did not understand anything he was saying.

Thinking the kingdom of God was going to appear soon in Jerusalem, the apostles James and John came to Jesus. They said, "Teacher, we want you to do something for us, whatever we ask." Jesus said to them, "What do you want me to do for you?" They answered, "Let us sit in the place of honor in your kingdom. Let one of us sit at your right side in your glory, and the other one sit at your left side in your glory." Jesus said, "You don't know what you are asking me." Then Salome, the mother of James and John, kneeled before Jesus and asked him for a favor. Jesus asked, "What is it that you want?" She said, "Let one of my sons sit at your right and the other sit at your left in your kingdom." Jesus said, "You don't know what you are asking me." Then Jesus said to James and John, "Can you drink the cup of suffering that I am going to drink and be baptized with the baptism I am baptized with?" They answered, "Yes, we can." Jesus said to them, "You will drink from my cup of suffering, and be baptized with the baptism I am baptized with. But I can't grant who will sit at my right or my left. For these places of honor belong to those for whom they have been prepared by my Father."

When the other apostles heard about the request of James and John, they became very angry with them. So Jesus called the apostles together and said to them, "You know that the rulers of the non-Jews lord it over their people. And their high officials exercise authority over them. But this is not true with you. Instead, whoever wants to become great among you must be your servant. Whoever wants to be first among you must become a servant of all. For even the Son of Man did not come to be served, but to serve, and to give his life as a ransom payment for many people."

With a large crowd of people, Jesus and the disciples walked through Jericho toward Jerusalem. Jericho was located near the Jordan River in the Wilderness of Judea. In Jericho, a man named Bartimaeus and another blind man were sitting by the road begging. When Bartimaeus heard the crowd, he asked what was happening. They told him, "Jesus of Nazareth is walking by." When Bartimaeus heard this, he began shouting, "Jesus, Son of David, have mercy on me!" The crowd walking in front of Jesus rebuked him and told him to be quiet, but he shouted even louder, "Son of David, have mercy on me!" Then Jesus stopped walking and told his disciples to bring the blind man to him. So the disciples called to the man, "Take heart! Stand on your feet! Jesus is calling for you." Throwing his garment aside, he jumped to his feet and went to Jesus. When Bartimaeus came to Jesus, he asked him, "What do you want me to do for you?" Bartimaeus said, "Teacher, I want you to heal my eyes so that I can see." Jesus had compassion on him and touched his eyes. He said, "Receive your sight; go, your faith has healed you. Immediately Bartimeaus could see, praised God, and followed Jesus as he walked along the road toward Jerusalem. When all the people saw this, they also praised God.

There was a man living in Jericho named Zacchaeus. Zacchaeus was the chief tax collector and was very rich. Zacchaeus wanted to see Jesus, but because he was short he could not see over the crowd of people. So he ran ahead of the crowd and climbed a sycamore tree to see Jesus as he walked by. When Jesus walked by, he looked up into the tree and said to Zacchaeus, "Come down immediately from the tree, for I will stay at your house tonight." So Zacchaeus came down and welcomed Jesus with joy. All the people saw this and began to complain, "He is going to be a house guest of a sinner." But Zacchaeus stood up and said to Jesus, "Lord! I will give half of what I own to the poor, and I will pay back the people that I have cheated. I will give them four times the amount of money I took from them." Jesus said to him, "Zacchaeus, today salvation has come to your house. You are also a son of Abraham. For the Son of Man came to seek and to save the lost!"

It was Friday morning and Jesus was walking ahead of the people up the steep winding road from Jericho to Jerusalem, which was about 18 miles long and ascended through the dry desert of Judea. They were coming closer to Jerusalem and the people were listening carefully to Jesus.

Because the time of the Feast of Passover was near, many people went up from the countryside to Jerusalem for their ceremonial purification before the Passover began. The people were looking for Jesus, and when they were in the temple courts they asked each other, "What do you think? Isn't Jesus coming to celebrate the Passover?" The religious leaders gave orders that whoever found out where Jesus was must report it so that they could arrest him.

PART FOUR

CHAPTER 19

It was six days before the start of the Passover, and Jesus, his disciples, and a large crowd of followers walked up the eastern slope of the Mount of Olives. The Mount of Olives was a mountain ridge that was separated from Jerusalem by the Kidron Valley. On the Mount of Olives were the towns of Bethphage and Bethany. The village of Bethphage was located less than a mile east of Jerusalem, and Bethany was located about 2 miles east of Jerusalem.

When Jesus and his disciples arrived at Bethany at the beginning of the Sabbath on Friday evening, a dinner was given for Jesus at the house of Simon the Leper. Martha served, and Lazarus reclined with Jesus at the table. While Jesus was eating, Mary came to him with an alabaster jar containing a pound of very expensive fragrant oil. She broke the jar and poured it on his head. The whole house was filled with the smell of the fragrance. When the disciples saw this, they became very angry and said to her, "Why are you wasting this expensive oil? This oil could have been sold for lots of money—for more than a year's wages—and the money given to the poor. They rebuked her. But Jesus said to his disciples, "Leave her alone! Why are you rebuking her? Why are you causing her so much trouble? For she has done a beautiful thing to me. The poor you will always have with you. You can help the poor any time you want. But you will not always have me with you. She poured this fragrant oil on my body to prepare it for my burial. I tell you the truth: Wherever the gospel is proclaimed around the world, what she did to me will be told in her memory."

On Sunday morning Jesus said to Peter and John, "Go to Bethphage. When you enter the village you will find a donkey tied there. Her colt that has not been ridden will be tied beside her. Untie them and bring them to me. If anyone asks you, 'Why are you taking this colt?' tell them, 'The Lord needs it. We will send it back here soon.' And they will let you take them." Peter and John did what Jesus had told them to do. They went to the village and found the colt tied at a doorway in the street. As they untied the colt, its owners asked them, "Why are you taking this colt?" The disciples said, "The Lord needs it." And so the people let them go. Peter and John brought the donkey and her colt to Jesus in Bethany. They placed their clothes on the colt and put Jesus on it. This happened to fulfill what is written in *Zechariah 9:9*, "Say to the Daughter of Zion: See, your king comes to you, gentle and riding on a colt, the colt of a donkey."

As Jesus rode the colt from Bethany along the Mount of Olives toward Jerusalem, large crowds of people went out to meet him and waved palm branches. Many of the people saw Jesus raise Lazarus from the dead, and they never stopped telling others about him. Other people spread their outer clothes and branches from the fields on the road. The people who walked ahead of Jesus and those who followed him were shouting *Psalm 118:26*, "Hosanna in the highest heaven! Blessed is the king of Israel! Hosanna to the Son of David! Blessed is the coming kingdom of our father David! Blessed is he who comes in the name of the Lord!" When Jesus came near the place where the road descends the Mount of Olives to Jerusalem, the whole crowd of disciples began to rejoice and praise God in loud voices for all the miracles they had seen. They shouted, "Blessed is the king who comes in the name of the Lord! Peace in heaven and glory in the highest!" Then some of the religious leaders in the large crowd of people said to Jesus, "Teacher, command your disciples to stop shouting these things!" Jesus said to them, "I tell you the truth: If my disciples keep quiet, the rocks on the ground will cry out!"

When Jesus approached Jerusalem and saw the city, he wept over it and said, "If you had only known on this day what would bring you peace—but now it is hidden from your eyes. The days will come upon you when your Roman enemies will set up an embankment against you, and encircle you on every side. You will not be able to escape. They will tear Jerusalem down to the ground, with you and your children within its walls. They will not leave one stone upon another, because you did not recognize the time of God's visitation." Once again, Jesus predicted that the Romans would destroy Jerusalem and the temple, which was fulfilled in AD 70.

When Jesus crossed the Kidron Valley and was entering Jerusalem, the whole city was stirred up and full of excitement. The crowd of people asked one another, "Who is this?" The people yelled, "This is Jesus, the prophet from Nazareth in Galilee!" But the religious leaders said to one another, "Look! We are accomplishing nothing. The whole world is following Jesus!" At first Jesus' disciples did not understand what was going on. Only after Jesus was glorified did they remember what had been written about him and all the things that had been done to him.

Jesus rode the colt into Jerusalem, and then he went into the temple courts. He looked around at everything. But because it was already late on Sunday, he left Jerusalem with his apostles and walked back along the Mount of Olives to spend the night in Bethany.

CHAPTER 20

Early Monday morning, Jesus left Bethany and was walking along the Mount of Olives toward Jerusalem. As he was walking, he became hungry. Jesus saw a fig tree in the distance by the road. He went over to it, but it had no figs. Then the disciples heard Jesus say to the fig tree, "You will never produce figs again!" Immediately the tree dried up and died. The cursing of the unfruitful fig tree was a symbolic judgment upon Israel. When the disciples saw this, they were amazed and asked each other, "How did the fig tree die so quickly?" Jesus said to them, "I tell you the truth: If you have faith and do not doubt, you will not only be able to do what I did to this fig tree, but you can also tell this mountain, 'Go, throw yourself into the sea,' and it will happen. If you believe, you will receive whatever you ask for in prayer."

When Jesus and his disciples entered Jerusalem, they went into an area of the temple. Then Jesus began driving out those who were buying and selling sacrifices there. He turned over the wooden tables of the money changers, and the chairs of those selling doves for sacrifices. He would not allow anyone to carry merchandise and other objects through the temple court. Jesus was teaching and said to them, "It is written in I*saiah 56:7*, 'My house will be called a house of prayer for all nations. But as it is written in *Jeremiah 7:11*, 'You are making it a den of robbers.'"

The religious leaders became furious when they heard what Jesus was saying and saw the wonderful things that he was doing. The children were shouting in the temple courts, "Hosanna to the Son of David." The religious leaders asked Jesus, "Don't you hear what these children are shouting?" Jesus said to them, "Yes, haven't you ever read *Psalm 8*:2? It says, 'From the lips of children, you Lord, have called forth your praise.'" So the religious leaders began looking for a a way to kill Jesus, but they were afraid of all the people who were listening intently to every word he spoke.

At that time there were some non-Jews among the people who went up to worship at the Passover Festival. They went to Philip and said to him, "Sir, we want to meet Jesus." Philip went and told Andrew, and they went and told Jesus. Jesus said to them, "The time has come for the Son of Man to be glorified. I tell you the truth: Unless a grain of wheat falls to the ground and dies, it remains a single seed. But if it dies, it produces many seeds. Whoever loves his life will lose it, but whoever hates his life in this world will keep it for eternal life. Whoever serves me must follow me; and where I am, my servant also will be. My Father will honor the one who serves me."

Jesus was greatly troubled and prayed, "Father, deliver me from this time of suffering. Yet I know it was for this very reason that I came to this hour. Father, glorify your name!" Then a voice came from heaven and said, "I have glorified it, and I will glorify it again."

A crowd of people that was there heard the voice and said it sounded like thunder. Others said, "An angel spoke to him!" Jesus said, "This voice was for your good, not mine. Now is the time for judgment to come on this world. And now, Satan—the ruler of this world—will be cast out. And when I am lifted up from the earth, I will draw all people to myself!" Jesus said this to tell the people about his crucifixion— the kind of death he was going to die.

The crowd of people were confused and said, "We have heard that the Messiah will stay in this world forever. So how can you say, 'The Son of Man must be lifted up? Who is this 'Son of Man?'" Then Jesus said to them, "The light is with you for a little while longer. Walk while you have the light, before darkness overcomes you. Whoever walks in the dark does not know where he is going. Believe in the light while you have light, so that you will become children of light." When Jesus finished teaching, he left and hid himself from them.

Even after Jesus had performed many miracles in their presence, the religious leaders still refused to believe in him. This fulfilled the words of *Isaiah 53:1*, "Lord, who has believed our message and to whom has the arm of the Lord been revealed?" For this is why they did not believe, because as it is written in *Isaiah 6:10*, "He has blinded their eyes and hardened their hearts, so they cannot see with their eyes, nor understand with their hearts, nor turn to God and be healed." The prophet Isaiah said this because he saw Jesus' glory and spoke about him. Although many people—even among the religious leaders—believed in Jesus, they did not tell anyone about their faith because they were afraid that they would be put out of the synagogue. They loved to receive human praise more than praise from God.

Then Jesus shouted out in the temple, "Whoever believes in me also believes in the one who sent me into this world. Whoever sees me, sees the one who sent me. I came into this world as the light, so that whoever believes in me will not remain in darkness. If anyone hears my teaching, but does not practice it, I do not judge that person. For I did not come to judge this world, but to save this world. There is a judge for the person who rejects me and does not believe in my teaching; because the very words I have spoken will condemn them at the last day. For I do not speak on my own, but the Father who sent me commanded me to say all that I have spoken. I know that his commandment leads to eternal life. So whatever I say is exactly what the Father told me to say."

It was getting late on Monday evening, so Jesus and his disciples left the temple and walked back across the Kidron Valley and along the Mount of Olives to the village of Bethany where they spent the night.

CHAPTER 21

On Tuesday morning as Jesus was walking along the Mount of Olives from Bethany toward Jerusalem, his disciples saw the dead fig tree; it was dried up from its roots. Peter remembered and said to Jesus, "Teacher, look! The fig tree you cursed has withered up and is dead!" Jesus said, "Have faith in God! For I tell you the truth: Whoever says to this mountain, 'Go throw yourself into the sea,' and does not doubt in his heart, but believes that what he says will happen, it will be done for him. Therefore, I tell you the truth: Whatever you ask for in prayer, believe that you have received it, and it will be yours. And whenever you pray, if you hold anything against anyone, forgive him, so that your Father in heaven will forgive your sins."

Then Jesus and his disciples arrived in Jerusalem and entered the temple courts. Jesus was walking around the temple, teaching, and proclaiming the good news of the kingdom of God. At that time the Jewish religious leaders walked up to Jesus and asked him, "By what authority are you doing these things? Who gave you this authority?" Jesus said to them, "I will ask you a question. If you answer me, I will tell you by what authority I do these things." Jesus asked them, "Tell me, was the baptism of John from God or was it from man?" The religious leaders talked with each other and said, "If we say, 'From God,' he will ask, 'Then why did you not believe John?' But if we say, 'It was from man,' then we fear what all the people might do. They will throw rocks at us because they believe that John was a prophet of God." So they answered Jesus, "We do not know where John's baptism came from." Then Jesus said to them, "Neither will I tell you by what authority I do these things".

Then Jesus asked the religious leaders, "What do you think about this story? "There was a man who had two sons. He went to the first and said, 'Son, go and work today in the vineyard.' The son answered, 'No, I will not go,' but later he changed his mind and went into the vineyard to work. Then the father went to his second son and said the same thing, "Go work today in the vineyard.' He answered, 'Yes, I will, father,' but he did not go into the vineyard to work. Tell me, which of the two sons did the will of his father?" The religious leaders answered, "The first son." Then Jesus said to them, "I tell you the truth: The tax collectors and the prostitutes are entering the kingdom of God before you! For John the Baptist came to show you the way of righteousness, and you refused to believe him, but the tax collectors and the prostitutes did believe him. And even after you saw this, you still would not repent and believe."

Turning to the religious leaders, Jesus told them the story of the vineyard owner saying, "There was a landowner who planted a vineyard. He built a wall around it, dug a hole for a winepress, and built a watchtower. Then he rented his vineyard to some farmers and went away on a long journey to another place. When it was time for the harvest, the landowner sent a servant to the farmers to collect his share of the vineyard's fruit. But the farmers grabbed the servant, beat him, and sent him away without any fruit. Then the landowner sent another servant to them, but they hit him on the head, beat him, and sent him away with nothing. The owner sent a third servant, and they hurt him and threw him out of the vineyard. Finally, the landowner sent his only son who he loved, for he was the only one left to send. The landowner thought, 'They will respect my son.' But when the farmers saw the son coming, they said to one another, 'This is the landowner's son, the inheritor of the vineyard; come, let's kill him and take his inheritance.' So they killed the son, and threw his body out of the vineyard."

Then Jesus asked the religious leaders, "when the vineyard's owner comes, what will he do to those evil farmers?" They said, "He will destroy those evil men, and he will rent his vineyard to other farmers, who will give him his share of the crops at harvest time." Jesus said, "Yes, the vineyard owner will go and kill the farmers and then give the vineyard to others. When the religious leaders heard this, they said, "God forbid! May this never be!" Jesus looked directly at them and asked them, "Haven't you ever read *Psalm 118:22-23*? 'The stone the builders rejected has become the cornerstone; the Lord has done this, and it is marvelous in our eyes.' I tell you the truth: The kingdom of God will be taken away from you and given to people who will produce its fruit."

When the religious leaders heard Jesus' stories, they knew that Jesus was talking about them. So the religious leaders looked for a way to arrest Jesus. But they were afraid of the crowd of people because they believed that Jesus was a prophet. The religious leaders left Jesus and went away.

Then Jesus spoke to the people about the kingdom of God. "The kingdom of God is like a king who prepared a wedding banquet for his son. He sent his servants to those who had been invited to the banquet to tell them to come, but those who were invited refused to come. Then the king sent out more servants and told them, 'Tell those who have been invited that I have prepared my dinner: My oxen and cattle have been butchered and everything is ready to eat. Come to the wedding banquet!' But the invited guests ignored them and left—one went to his field, and another went to his business. The others grabbed the king's servants, mistreated them, and killed them. The king was furious. He sent out his soldiers and destroyed those murderers, and burned their city. Then the king told his servants, 'The wedding banquet of my son is ready, but those that I invited do not deserve to come. Therefore, go to the street corners and invite everyone to the banquet.' So the servants went out into the streets and gathered all the people they could find—the good and the bad—and the wedding hall was filled with guests. But when the king came in to see the guests, he noticed a man there who was not dressed in wedding clothes. The king asked him, 'Friend, how did you get in here without wedding clothes?' The man was speechless. Then the king told the servants, 'Tie this man hand and foot, and throw him outside into the outer darkness, where people will be weeping and grinding their teeth.'" Then Jesus said, "For many people are called but only a few are chosen."

At that time the Jewish religious leaders were keeping a very close watch on Jesus. They sent some of their followers to Jesus along with some Herodian spies to trap him in what he was teaching. They pretended to be friendly to Jesus. They hoped to catch him in what he said, so that they could hand him over to the power and authority of the Roman governor Pontius Pilate. The religious leaders said to Jesus, "Teacher, we know that you are a man of integrity and show no favoritism because you do not worry about who they are. You speak the truth and teach the true way of God. Tell us what you think: Is it right to pay the imperial tax to the Roman Emperor Tiberius or not?" Jesus knew they were deceptive and filled with evil intent. He said to them, "You are religious hypocrites! Why are you trying to trap me in what I teach?" Then Jesus said, "Bring me a coin—a Roman denarius—used for paying the imperial tax and let me look at it." They brought Jesus a coin. Then Jesus asked them, "Whose image and inscription is stamped on the coin?" The religious leaders said, "It is Caesar's." Jesus said to them, "So give to Caesar what is Caesar's, and give to God what is God's." When they heard this, the religious spies were amazed by his answer, and failed to trap Jesus in his public teaching. So they no longer asked Jesus any more questions and walked away.

That same day some religious leaders called Sadducees—who denied the resurrection from the dead—came to Jesus in the temple and asked him this question to test him, "Teacher, Moses told us that if a man dies without having children, his brother must marry the widow and have children for him. Now there were seven brothers. The first one married and died without children, so he left his wife to his brother. The same thing happened to all seven brothers. Finally, the woman died. Tell us, which one of the seven brothers will the woman be married to at the resurrection from the dead, for she had married all the brothers." Jesus said to them, "The people of this world get married, but the worthy at the resurrection of the dead will not get married. They will not die, for they will be like the angels. They are God's children, since they are children of the resurrection. You are wrong because you do not know the Bible or the power of God. Why do you not believe in the resurrection of the dead, for even Moses believed in the resurrection of the dead. Haven't you read the words of Moses in *Exodus 3:6* when God appeared and spoke to him at the burning bush? God said to Moses, 'I am the God of Abraham, the God of Isaac, and the God of Jacob.' And Moses responded by calling him 'the God of Abraham, the God of Isaac, and the God of Jacob.' So God is not the God of the dead, but of the living. You are very wrong!" When the crowds of people heard Jesus speak, they were amazed at his teaching.

Then some religious leaders called Pharisees—who did believe in the resurrection of the dead—said to Jesus, "Teacher, very good!" The Pharisees met together when they heard that Jesus had silenced the Sadducees. So one of them came and heard the Sadducees debating Jesus in the temple court. The religious leader heard the wisdom of Jesus, so he tried to test Jesus by asking him, "Teacher, what must I do to inherit eternal life? Of all of God's commandments, which one is the most important? Which is the greatest commandment in the law of Moses?" Jesus said to him, "What is written in the law of Moses? How do you understand what it says?" The religious leader said, "It is written in *Deuteronomy 6:5*, 'Love the Lord your God with all your heart and with all your soul and with all your strength and with all your mind,' and in *Leviticus 19:18*, 'Love your neighbor as yourself.'" Jesus said, "Very good, your answer is correct; do this and you will live. The first and greatest commandment is *Deuteronomy 6:4-5*, 'Hear, O Israel, the Lord is our God, the Lord is one. Love the Lord your God with all your heart and with all your soul and with all your mind and with all your strength.' And the second greatest commandment is *Leviticus 19:18*, 'Love your neighbor as yourself.' There is no commandment greater than these two. For the whole truth of the Old Testament is contained in these two commandments." The religious leader said, "Teacher, well said. You are right in saying that God is one and there is no other but him. To love him with all your heart, with all your understanding, and with all your strength, and to love your neighbor as yourself is much more important than all the burnt offerings and sacrifices in the temple." From that time on, none of the religious leaders dared to ask Jesus any more questions.

When Jesus was teaching in the temple courts, the religious leaders gathered around him. Jesus asked them, "What do you think about the Messiah? Whose son is he?" They said, "The son of David." Then Jesus responded, "Why do you teach that the Messiah is the son of David? Why is it then that David, speaking by the Holy Spirit, declared in *Psalm 110:1*, 'The Lord said to my Lord, "Sit at my right hand until I put your enemies under your feet.' Therefore, David calls him 'Lord.' So how then can the Messiah be his son?" The religious leaders had no answer for Jesus, and from that day on, they dared not ask Jesus any more questions. And a large crowd of people were listening with excitement.

Jesus turned and said to his disciples and the crowd of people, "Beware of the Jewish religious leaders. Be careful to obey what they teach, but do not live as they live. For they do not practice what they preach, for everything they do is to be seen by other people. They like to walk around in flowing robes and make their garment tassels long for everyone to see. They love to be greeted with respect in the public market. They love to sit in places of authority in the synagogues that are called the seats of Moses. They like to sit at places of honor at banquets. They defraud widows' houses and for a show make long prayers before people. But you can be assured that they will receive a most severe judgment from God. They tie heavy burdens onto the shoulders of the people, but they are not willing to lift a finger to remove them. They love to be called teachers, but you should not be called teachers because you have only one true Teacher, and you are all fellow believers. The greatest among you will be your servant. For whoever exalts themselves in pride will be humbled, and whoever humbles themselves will be exalted by God. And don't call anyone on earth 'father.' You have only one Father in heaven.

Then Jesus continued to condemn the religious leaders. He said, "How terrible for you! You slam the door of the kingdom of God in people's faces. And you yourselves do not even enter it, nor will you let those enter who are trying to enter. You travel over land and sea to win a single convert, but when they convert, you make them twice the child of hell as you are. How terrible for you. You are blind leaders! You say, 'Whoever makes a promise by the temple, it means nothing; but whoever promises by the gold of the temple is bound to keep his oath.' You are blind fools! Which is greater—the gold, or the temple that makes the gold holy? You also say, 'Whoever makes a promise by the altar, it means nothing; but whoever promises by the gift that is on the altar is bound to keep his oath.' Which is greater—the gift, or the altar that makes the gift holy? Therefore, whoever makes a promise by the altar swears an oath by it and by all the offerings on it. And whoever makes a promise by the temple swears an oath by it and by God who dwells in it. And whoever makes a promise by heaven swears an oath by God's throne and by the one who sits on it. You give to God a tenth of your spices, but you neglect the more important matters of the law—justice, mercy, and faithfulness. You should have practiced these, without neglecting the former things. You are blind leaders! You remove insects from your drinks, but you swallow a camel. You clean the outside of the cup and dish you use, but your hearts are full of greed and self-indulgence. You are spiritually blind! First clean the inside of the cup and dish, and then the outside will also be clean. You are like tombs that are painted white and are beautiful on the outside, but on the inside they are full of rotting bones of the dead people, and everything unclean. In the same way, on the outside you appear righteous, but on the inside you are full of hypocrisy and wickedness. How terrible for you! You build tombs for the prophets and decorate the graves of the righteous. And you say, 'If we lived in the days of our ancestors, we would not have helped kill the prophets.' In saying this, you testify against yourselves that you are the children of those who murdered the prophets. Go ahead, then, and finish what your ancestors started! You are snakes! You are the children of snakes! Why do you think you will escape being condemned to hell? Therefore, I am sending you prophets, wise men, and teachers. Some of them you will kill and crucify; others you will flog in your synagogues, and chase them from town to town. And so upon you will come all the righteous blood that has been shed on earth, from the righteous blood of Abel to the righteous blood of Zechariah who you murdered. I tell you the truth: This will all come on this generation of Israel."

Then Jesus declared in the temple, "Jerusalem, Jerusalem, you who kill God's prophets and stone to death those sent to you! How often I have longed to gather your children together, as a mother bird gathers her chicks under her wings. But you were not willing!. Look! Your house has been forsaken by God and left desolate. I tell you the truth: You will not see me again until you shout *Psalm 118:26*, 'Blessed is he who comes in the name of the Lord!'"

Frustrated with the religious leaders, Jesus sat down opposite the place where the offerings were given in the temple. He watched the crowd putting their money into the temple treasury. He looked up and saw many rich people putting their gifts into the treasury; they were throwing in large amounts of money. Then Jesus saw a poor widow come and put in two very small copper coins, worth only a few cents. Jesus called his disciples and said to them, "I tell you the truth: This poor widow has put more money into the temple treasury than all the rich people. For the rich gave out of their abundant wealth, but she gave out of her poverty. She gave all she had to live on."

CHAPTER 22

It was Tuesday afternoon and Jesus and his disciples left the temple courts and began walking to the Mount of Olives toward Bethany. As they were walking away, the disciples were talking about how the temple complex was decorated with beautiful stones and with gifts dedicated to God. Then the disciples came to Jesus and one of them said to him, "Teacher, look at the temple buildings! Look at the massive stones and the magnificent buildings of the temple!

Jesus was distressed with his disciples and said to them, "Do you admire all these things about the temple? Do you see all these great buildings? I tell you the truth: A time is coming when these temple buildings will be destroyed. Every stone will be thrown down, not one stone will be left on another. When you see Jerusalem surrounded by Roman armies, you will know that its destruction is near. Jerusalem will be trampled by the Romans until the times of the non-Jews are fulfilled. For this is the time of punishment in fulfillment of all that has been written in the Old Testament. There will be great trouble in the land and wrath against this people. They will die by the sword and will be taken as prisoners to all the nations. So when you see standing in the holy place 'the abomination that causes destruction,' as it is written in *Daniel 9:27*, those living in Judea flee to the mountains for refuge. Let those in Jerusalem leave, and let those in the country not enter Jerusalem. Those who are on their rooftops should not go down to take anything out of their houses, and those working in their fields should not go back to their homes to get their extra clothes. Pray that your flight will not take place in winter or on the Sabbath. For then there will be great distress, unequaled since God's creation of the world, until now—and never to be equaled again. Those days will be horrifying for pregnant women and nursing mothers. If the Lord had not cut short these terrible days, no one would survive, but for the sake of the chosen those days will be kept short." Once again, Jesus predicted the Romans' destruction of Jerusalem and the temple that took place in AD 70.

After walking across the Kidron Valley, Jesus sat on the Mount of Olives opposite the temple. His disciples—Peter, Andrew, James, and John—asked Jesus in private, "Teacher, tell us, when will all these things happen? What will be the sign that these things are about to take place? What will be the sign of your coming and the end of this age?"

Jesus looked at his disciples and said, "Watch out that no one deceives you. Stay alert so that you will not be deceived and led astray, for many people will come in my name claiming that they are the Messiah and that the time is near. Do not follow them! Many false prophets will appear and lead many people to believe in things that are false. At that time if anyone declares to you, 'Look, here is the Messiah!' or 'Look, there is the Messiah!' do not believe them. For false messiahs and false prophets will appear and do miraculous signs and wonders to deceive, if possible, even the chosen. So be on your guard, because I am telling you these things before they happen.

"When you hear of wars and rumors of uprisings, do not be afraid. Nations will rise up and fight against nations, and kingdoms will rise up and fight against kingdoms. There will be great earthquakes, famines, and plagues in various places. And there will be terrifying events and great signs from heaven. But these things are only the beginning of the pains of childbirth. For they must happen first, but the end of the world is still to come."

"At that time, before all these things happen, you will be persecuted, arrested, punished, and killed because you are my disciples.

People from all over the world will hate you because you believe in me. You must be on your guard and be alert, for you will be handed over to the Jewish local councils, and flogged in the synagogues. You will be put in prison. Because you are my disciples, you will be brought before kings and governors as witnesses to them. But determine in your minds not to worry beforehand about how you will defend yourselves, because I will give you words and wisdom that none of your enemies will be able to oppose or argue against. Whenever you are arrested and brought to trial, do not worry about what you will say. Just say whatever words of wisdom that are given to you at that time, for it is the Holy Spirit within you speaking and not you.

"You will be betrayed by parents, brothers, sisters, relatives and friends, and they will put some of you to death. Brother will betray brother to death, and a father will have his child put to death. Children will rebel against their parents and have them put to death. At that time many believers will turn away from the faith. They will hate and betray each other. Because of the increase of wickedness, the love of many people will grow cold. Everyone will hate you because you are my disciples, but those who stand strong to the end will be saved. Stand strong, and you will gain your lives. Be assured, not a hair of your head will perish.

"But in the days following the time of great tribulation, what is written in *Isaiah 13:10* will come true, 'The sun will be darkened, and the moon will not give forth its light; the stars will fall from the sky, and the powers in heaven will be shaken.' There will be signs in the sun, moon, and stars. On the earth, nations will experience great turmoil and anguish at the roaring and tossing of the sea. People will faint from overwhelming fear at what is coming on this world, for the elements of the heavens will be shaken.

"But the good news of the kingdom of God will be proclaimed throughout the whole world as a witness to all nations, and then the end will come.

"The coming of the Son of Man will be like lightning that flashes in the sky from the east to the west. At that time the sign of the Son of Man will appear in the sky. And then all the peoples of the earth will mourn when they see the Son of Man coming in the clouds with great power and brilliant glory. When these things begin to take place, stand up and lift up your heads, because your salvation is coming soon. For he will send out his angels with a loud trumpet call, and they will gather his chosen ones from the four winds—from the ends of the earth to the ends of the heavens.

"No one knows the day or hour of the coming of the Son of Man, not even the angels in heaven, nor the Son, but only the Father. Be on your guard! Be alert! Pay close attention! For you do not know when that time will come. Be careful, or your hearts will be weighted down with partying, drunkenness, and the worries of life, and the day of the Lord will come upon you suddenly like a trap. For the day of the Lord will come on everyone living on the whole earth. Be always alert, and pray that you will have the strength to escape all that is about to happen, and that you will be able to stand before the Son of Man.

"As it was in the days of Noah, so it will be the same at the coming of the Son of Man. For in those days before the great flood, people were living normal lives—eating and drinking, marrying and giving in marriage—up to the day Noah entered the ark; and they did not know what would happen until the great flood came and washed them away. That is how it will be at the coming of the Son of Man.

"It's like a man who goes away on a trip: He leaves his servants in charge of his house and gives each one a job, and tells the one at the door to keep watch. Therefore, keep watch because you do not know when the owner of the house will return—it could be in the evening, or at midnight, or at dawn when the rooster crows. If he comes suddenly, do not let him find you sleeping. What I say to you, I declare to everyone: Keep watch! But understand this: If the owner of the house had known at what time of night a thief was coming, he would have kept watch and would not have let the thief break into his house. So you also must be ready, because the Son of Man will come at an hour when you do not expect him.

"When the Son of Man comes in his glory along with all the angels, he will sit on his glorious throne. All the nations will be gathered before him, and he will separate the people from one another as a shepherd separates the sheep from the goats. He will put the sheep on his right side and the goats on his left. Then the King will say to those on his right, 'Come, you who are blessed by my Father; receive your inheritance, the kingdom prepared for you since the creation of the universe. For I was hungry and you gave me something to eat; I was thirsty and you gave me something to drink, I was a stranger and you invited me in, I needed clothes and you clothed me, I was sick and you took care of me, and I was in prison and you came to visit me.' Then the righteous will ask him, 'Lord, when did we see you hungry and feed you, or thirsty and give you something to drink? When did we see you as a stranger and invite you in, or needing clothes and clothe you? When did we see you sick or in prison and go visit you?' The King will reply, 'I tell you the truth: Whatever you did for one of the least of my followers, you did for me.' Then the King will say to those on his left, 'Depart from me, you who are cursed, into the eternal fire prepared for the devil and his demons. For I was hungry and you gave me nothing to eat, I was thirsty and you gave me nothing to drink, I was a stranger and you did not invite me in, I needed clothes and you did not clothe me; I was sick and in prison and you did not take care of me.' They also will ask, 'Lord, when did we see you hungry or thirsty or a stranger or needing clothes or sick or in prison, and did not help you?' The Lord will say 'I tell you the truth: Whatever you did not do for the least of my followers, you did not do for me.' Then the wicked will go away to eternal punishment, and the righteous to eternal life."

Then Jesus told his disciples the story of the faithful servant. He said, "Who is the faithful and wise servant? Who is the servant that the master put in charge of his servants to give them their food at the proper time? Blessed is the servant whose master finds him faithful and doing what he was told to do. I tell you the truth: The master will put that wise and faithful servant in charge of all his possessions, over everything he owns. But if that servant is wicked and says to himself, 'My master is staying away a long time.' He then beats his fellow servants, and lives the life of a drunkard. The master of that wicked servant will come on a day and at a time when he does not expect him. And then the master will send him to the place with the religious hypocrites and unbelievers, where people will be weeping and grinding their teeth." Then Jesus said, "From everyone who has been given much, much will be demanded; and from the one who has been entrusted with much, much more will be required."

Then Jesus told them these stories about the kingdom of God.

"At that time the kingdom of God will be like ten young girls who took their lamps and went out to meet the bridegroom. Now five of the young girls were foolish, and five were wise. The foolish girls took their lamps, but did not take any oil with them. However, the wise girls took oil in jars along with their lamps. The bridegroom was delayed a long time in coming, so they all became tired and fell asleep. At midnight the cry rang out, 'Here comes the bridegroom! Come out to meet him!' Then all the young girls woke up and lit their lamps. The foolish girls said to the wise girls, 'Give us some of your oil because our lamps are going out.' The wise girls said, 'No! There is not enough oil for both of us. Go and buy your own oil.' But while they were away buying oil, the bridegroom arrived. The wise girls went in with him to the wedding banquet. And the door was shut. Later the foolish young girls came and said, 'Sir! Sir! Open the door for us!' But he replied, 'I tell you the truth: I don't know you.' Therefore, keep watch, for you do not know the day or the hour of the coming of the Son of Man.

"The kingdom of God will be like a man going on a journey, who called his servants and entrusted his riches to them. To one servant he gave five bags of money, to another two bags of money, and to another one bag of money, each according to his ability. Then the man went on his journey. The servant who received five bags of money immediately went and invested the money and earned another five bags of money. So also, the servant with the two bags of money earned another two bags. But the servant who was given one bag of money went and dug a hole in the ground and buried it. After a long time the master of the servants returned and settled the accounts with them. The servant who had been given five bags of money brought the other five bags that he earned. He said, 'Master, you gave me five bags of money, and I now have 10 bags of money to give to you.' His master said, 'Well done, good and faithful servant! You have been faithful with a few things; so I will put you in charge of many things. Come and share your master's happiness.' The servant who was given two bags of money also came and said, 'Master, you gave me two bags of money, and now I have four bags of money to give to you.' His master said, 'Well done, good and faithful servant! You have been faithful with a few things; so I will put you in charge of many things. Come and share in your master's happiness!' Then the servant who was given one bag of money came and said, 'Master, because I knew that you are a hard man, I was afraid and went out and buried the bag of money in the ground. So, here is the bag of money that you gave me.' In anger, his master said, 'You wicked and lazy servant! You should have put my bag of money in the bank, so that when I returned I would have received it back with interest. So he took the one bag of money from him and gave it to the servant who had ten bags of money. For whoever has will be given more, and he will have an abundance. Whoever has very little, even what he has will be taken away from him. And the worthless servant will be thrown outside into the darkness—where people will be weeping and grinding their teeth."

After Jesus finished teaching all these things, he said to his disciples, "The Passover is coming soon. It is only two days away. At that time, the Son of Man will be handed over to the Romans to be crucified." Then Jesus and his disciples spent the night in Bethany.

It was Wednesday and many Jews who had come to visit Mary believed in Jesus after they saw him raise Lazarus from the dead, but other Jews went and told the Jewish religious leaders what Jesus had done. Hearing what Jesus was teaching, the religious leaders met together in the palace of Caiaphas the high priest. They asked each other, "What are we going to do? For this man Jesus is doing many miracles. If we do not stop him, everyone will believe in him, and then the Romans will come and destroy our temple and our nation." Then Caiaphas shouted, "You know nothing at all! You don't realize that it is better that Jesus should die than our whole nation be destroyed." From that day forward the Jewish religious council made plans to deceive Jesus, arrest him in private, and kill him. But because they were afraid of the people, they said to one another, "We can't arrest Jesus during the Passover because the people will riot.

Then Satan entered the heart of Judas Iscariot. He went to the religious leaders and the officers of the temple guard, and talked to them about how he could betray Jesus. Judas asked them, "How much money will you give me to turn Jesus over to you?" The religious leaders were thrilled to hear that Judas would betray Jesus, and agreed to give him money. So they paid Judas 30 silver coins, worth about $5,000. From then on Judas looked for an opportune time to betray Jesus and have him arrested when people were not present.

CHAPTER 23

It was Thursday when the Passover lamb was sacrificed in the temple. So Jesus said to Peter and John, "Go and make preparations for us, so that we can eat the Passover meal together." Peter and John asked Jesus, "Where do you want us to prepare Passover?" Jesus said, "Go into Jerusalem. As you enter the city, a man carrying a jar of water will meet you. Tell the man, 'The Teacher says: My appointed time is near. I will celebrate the Passover meal at your guest room with my disciples.' Follow him to his house, and he will show you a large furnished guest room upstairs. Make preparations for us there." So Peter and John went into Jerusalem from the Mount of Olives, and they found everything as Jesus had told them. So they prepared the Passover meal in the upper room.

When it was Thursday evening, Jesus and his apostles arrived at the upper room in Jerusalem. They reclined on a couch around the table to eat the Passover meal together. Jesus said to them, "I have been eager to eat this Passover with you before I suffer. I tell you the truth: I will not eat it again until the Passover is fulfilled in the kingdom of God."

While they were eating together, the devil had already put into the heart of Judas Iscariot to betray Jesus. But Jesus knew that the Father had put everything under his power, and that he had come from God and was going back to God. I am telling you now before it happens, so that when it does happen you will believe that I am who I am. I tell you the truth: Whoever receives anyone I send receives me; and whoever receives me receives the one who sent me into this world."

After Jesus had said this, his heart was troubled in spirit and he told his apostles, "I tell you the truth: One of you eating with me is going to betray me." Jesus said, "I am not speaking about all of you, because I know those I have chosen. But this is to fulfill *Psalm 41:9*, 'He who ate my bread has gone against me.' His apostles stared at one another, because they were confused about what he was saying. All the apostles were very troubled, and one by one they said to Jesus, "Lord, is it me?" The apostle John was reclining next to Jesus at the table. Peter motioned to him and said, "Ask Jesus which one of us he is talking about." John leaned against Jesus and asked him, "Lord, which one of us is going to betray you?" Jesus said to him, "The one sitting next to me will betray me. The Son of Man will suffer just as it is written about him in God's word, but how terrible for the one who betrays the Son of Man! It would be much better for him if he had not been born."

Then Jesus dipped the piece of bread into the dish and gave it to Judas Iscariot. As soon as Judas took the piece of bread, Satan entered his heart. Then Judas asked Jesus, "Teacher, surely it isn't me?" Jesus said, "Yes, it is you. What you are about to do, do quickly!" As soon as Judas had taken the bread, he left. And it was night.

The apostles did not understand why Jesus had said this to Judas. Because Judas was in charge of the money bag, some of them thought Jesus was telling him to buy what was needed for the Passover Feast, or to give some money to the poor.

Then Jesus took a loaf of bread, gave thanks to God, broke the bread, and gave the pieces to his apostles. He said to them, "Take and eat, for this is my body given for you; eat it in remembrance of me." The apostles ate the bread. Then Jesus took the cup of wine, gave thanks to God, and gave it to his apostles. He said, "Drink from this cup all of you, share it among yourselves. For this is my blood of the new covenant, which is poured out for the forgiveness of sins. I tell you the truth: I will not drink wine until that day when I drink it new with you in my Father's kingdom." And the apostles all drank from the cup.

Then once again the apostles began to argue among themselves about which one of them was considered the greatest in the kingdom of God. Jesus said to them, "Non-Jewish kings exercise power over the people, and those who rule with authority over them call themselves Benefactors. Benefactors were prominent people who bestowed gifts on their citizens to gain loyalty. But you are not to be like them. Instead, the greatest among you will be like the youngest, and the leader will be the one who serves others. For you know that the master who eats at the table is greater than the one who serves him. But I live among you as the one who serves. You will eat and drink at my table in my kingdom and sit on thrones judging the 12 tribes of Israel."

Jesus quietly got up from the table, removed his outer clothing, and wrapped a towel around his waist. He then filled a bowl with water, and began to wash the feet of his apostles, and dried them with the towel. Jesus came to Peter, who said to him, "Lord, are you going to wash my feet?" Jesus said, "You do not know now what I am doing, but later on you will understand." But Peter said, "No! You will never wash my feet!" Jesus said, "You will never be my disciple unless I wash your feet." Peter cried out, "Lord! Then wash not just my feet but my hands and my head as well!"

After washing his apostles' feet, Jesus put on his outer clothing and returned to his place at the table. He said to his apostles, "Do you understand what I have done for you? You call me your 'Teacher' and 'Lord,' and you are right. For that is what I am. Now that I have washed your feet, you also should wash one another's feet. I washed your feet to give you an example to follow. I tell you the truth: A slave is not greater than his master, and a messenger is not greater than the one who sent him. Now that you know my teaching, you will be blessed if you do it. For the Son of Man is glorified and God is glorified in him. My dear children, I will be living with you only a little longer. You will look for me, but where I am going, you cannot come. I give you this new command: Love one another. As I have loved you, so you must love one another. By your love everyone will know that you are my disciples."

Flustered, Peter asked Jesus, "Lord, where are you going?" Jesus said, "Where I am going, you cannot follow now, but you will follow me later." Peter said to Jesus, "Lord, I am ready to go with you to prison and even to death! Why can't I follow you now? I will die for you!" Then Jesus said to Peter, "Will you really die for me? I tell you the truth Peter, before the rooster crows today, you will deny that you know me three times. Peter, Peter, listen to me. Satan has asked to sift you like wheat. But I have prayed for you, so that your faith will not fail. And when you repent and return again, be sure to strengthen your fellow brothers."

Then Jesus said to his apostles, "Do not allow your hearts to be troubled, but believe in God and believe also in me. For my Father's house has many rooms. If this was not true, I would not have told you. I am going to prepare a place for you. I will return and take you to be with me." Thomas said to him, "Lord, we don't know where you are going, so how can we know the way?" Jesus said, "I am the way and the truth and the life! No one comes to the Father except through me. If you really know me, you will also know the Father. From now on, you do know him and have seen him." Philip said to Jesus, "Lord, all we ask is that you show us the Father, and that will satisfy us." Jesus said, "Philip, I have been with you a long time, and you still do not know me. Whoever has seen me has seen the Father. So why do you ask me to show you the Father? Don't you believe that I am in the Father, and the Father is in me? The words that I speak to you are not on my own authority, but the Father lives in me and does his work through me. Believe me when I tell you that I am in the Father and the Father is in me; or at least believe on the evidence of my miracles. I tell you the truth: Whoever believes in me will also do the works I do, and they will do even greater works than I do, because I am going to the Father. And I will do whatever you ask in my name, so that the Father will be glorified in the Son. You can ask me anything in my name, and I will do it. If you love me, you will obey my teaching. I will ask the Father, and he will send you the Holy Spirit of truth. The Holy Spirit is the counselor to help you and be with you forever. This world cannot receive the Holy Spirit of truth, because it does not see him or know him. But you know him, because he lives with you and will be in you. I will never leave you as orphans, but I will come back for you. Soon, this world will not see me anymore, but you will see me. Because I live, you also will live. On that day you will know that I am in my Father, and you are in me, and I am in you. Whoever obeys my teaching is the one who loves me. The one who loves me will be loved by my Father, and I too will love him and reveal myself to him."

Then Jude said, "But, Lord, why are you going to reveal yourself to us, but not to this world?" Jesus said, "Whoever loves me will obey my teaching. My Father will love him, and we will come to him and make our home with him. Whoever does not love me will not obey my teaching. My teaching is not my own, it belongs to the Father who sent me into this world. I tell you all these things while I am still living among you. But the Holy Spirit—the Counselor—who the Father will send in my name will teach you everything and will remind you of everything I have told you. I leave you my peace; my peace I give you! I do not give to you the passing peace that this world gives. Do not allow your hearts to be troubled and do not be afraid. You have heard me say to you, 'I am leaving you, but I am coming back for you.' If you love me, you should rejoice that I am going to the Father. I tell you now before I leave you, so that when I do leave you, you will believe. I will not tell you much more, because Satan—the ruler of this world—is coming. He has no power over me, but he comes so that this world will learn that I love the Father and do exactly what my Father has told me to do."

Jesus asked his apostles, "Did you need anything when I sent you on a mission journey without a moneybag, backpack, or sandals?" They said, "No." Jesus then said, "But now if you have a moneybag, take it, and also a backpack, and if you don't have a sword, sell some clothes and buy one. For it is written in *Isaiah 53:12*, 'And he was counted with the rebels.' I tell you the truth: This passage must be fulfilled in me. Yes, what is written about me in the Bible is about to be fulfilled." Jesus' apostles said, "Look, Lord, here are two swords." Then Jesus said, "That is enough!" After singing a song of praise to God, Jesus said to his apostles "Stand up and let us leave this place." They were reclining around a low table, so they stood up. Jesus and his apostles left the upper room, and he led them toward the Mount of Olives.

As they were walking toward the Mount of Olives, Jesus frightened his apostles when he told them, "This very night all of you will fall away from me, for as it is written in *Zechariah 13:7*, 'I will strike the shepherd, and the sheep of the flock will be scattered.' But after I rise from the dead, I will meet with you again in Galilee."

Jesus continued to teach saying:

"I am the true vine, and my Father is the gardener. He cuts off every branch in me that doesn't produce fruit. He prunes every branch that does produce fruit, so that it will produce even more fruit. You are already clean because of the teaching I have spoken to you. Live in me, as I also live in you, because no branch can produce fruit separate from the vine. Just as the branch must remain in the vine, so neither can you produce fruit unless you remain in me. I am the vine, and you are the branches. If you live in me and I live in you, you will produce much fruit, but apart from me you can do nothing. If you do not live in me, you are like a branch that is thrown away and dries up. And dried branches are then gathered and thrown into the fire and burned up. If you live in me and my words live in you, ask me for whatever you desire, and it will be done for you. The Father is glorified when you produce much fruit, proving that you are my disciples.

"As the Father has loved me, so I have loved you. Now live in my love! If you obey my teaching, you will live in my love, just as I have obeyed my Father's teaching and live in his love. I tell you these things so that my joy will be in you and that you will have abundant joy. This is my commandment: Love one another as I have loved you. The greatest act of love is this: To lay down your life for your friends. You are my friends if you obey my teaching. I no longer call you servants, because a servant does not know what his master is doing. Instead, I call you friends, because everything I have learned from my Father I have made known to you. You did not choose me, but I chose you and appointed you, so that you will go and produce fruit that will remain. Whatever you ask in my name the Father will give you. This is my command: Love one another!

"If the world hates you, remember that it hated me first. If you belonged to this world, it would love you as one of its own. But you do not belong to this world, because I have brought you out of this world.

That is why the world hates you. Remember what I taught you: 'A servant is not greater than his master.' If they persecuted me, they will persecute you also. If they obeyed my teaching, they will obey your teaching also.

"If I had not come into this world and spoken to them, they would not be guilty of sin; but now they have no excuse for their sin. Whoever hates me, hates my Father also. They have seen my miraculous works, and yet they still hated both me and my Father. This happened to fulfill *Psalm 35:19*, 'They hated me for no reason.' When the Holy Spirit of truth comes, who I will send to you from the Father, he will bear witness of me. And you my apostles also must bear witness of me, because you have been with me from the beginning.

"I tell you all these things so that you will not fall away from the faith. For the Jewish religious leaders will excommunicate you from the synagogue. In fact, the time is coming when those who kill you will think they are murdering you in the service of God. They will do these things to you because they have not known the Father or me.

"But now I am going to him who sent me into this world. Now you don't need to ask me, 'Where are you going?' But because I have said that I am leaving you, your hearts are filled with sadness. I tell you the truth: It is for your good that I am going away. Unless I go away, the Holy Spirit will not come to you; but if I go, I will send him to you. When the Holy Spirit comes, he will convict this world concerning sin and righteousness and judgment. I have much more to teach you, but you are not ready to accept it now. But when the Holy Spirit comes, he will guide you into all of God's truth. He will not speak on his own authority, but he will speak only what he hears. He will tell you what is yet to come. He will glorify me because it is from me that he will receive what he will tell you. All that belongs to the Father is mine. That is why I said the Holy Spirit will receive from me what he will tell you.

"In a little while I will leave and you will see me no more, but then after a little while you will see me again." Confused, his apostles said to one another, "What is he talking about? They kept asking, "What does he mean by 'a little while'? We don't understand what he is saying." Jesus knew that his apostles wanted to ask him about what he was saying, so he said to them, "Are you asking one another what I meant when I said, 'In a little while you will see me no more, but then after a little while you will see me again'? I tell you the truth: When I leave, you will cry and mourn, but this world will rejoice. You will mourn, but your sorrow will become joy. A woman giving birth has great pain at the time she is giving birth, but right after she gives birth she forgets her pain because of her great joy for her new baby born into the world. In the same way, your hearts will be filled with sadness when I leave, but when I come again your hearts will be filled with joy, and no one will be able to take this joy away from you. In the day that I come again, you will no longer ask me any questions. I tell you the truth: My Father will give you whatever you ask in my name. Ask and you will receive, and you will have abundant joy.

"Although I have been teaching you using stories, the time is coming when I will tell you plainly about my Father. For the Father loves you because you have loved me and have believed that I came from God. I came into this world from the Father, and now I am leaving this world and returning to the Father." Then Jesus' apostles said, "You are now speaking in plain language and not in stories. We can see that you know all things and that you do not need to have anyone ask you questions. This is why we believe that you came from God." Jesus said, "Do you now believe? I tell you that a time is coming, and in fact has now come, when you will be scattered. You will leave me alone and go to your own home. But I will not be alone, because my Father will be with me. I tell you these things so that in me you will have my peace. In this world you will have trouble. But take heart, be strong! For I have overcome this world!"

After teaching his apostles, Jesus looked up to heaven and prayed: "Father, my time has come. Glorify your Son, that your Son can glorify you. For you have given him authority over all people, so that he can give eternal life to whoever you have given him. Now this is eternal life in the kingdom of God: That they know you, the only true God, and me, whom you have sent into this world. I have brought you glory on earth by finishing the work you gave me to do. And now Father, glorify me in your presence with the glory I had with you before the creation of the universe. I have revealed your name to the people you gave me out of this world. They were yours, but you gave them to me and they have obeyed your word. Now they know that everything you have given me comes from you. For I taught them the words you gave me and they believed. I pray for them. I am not praying for the world, but for those you have given me, because they are yours. All I have is yours, and everything you have is mine. And I am glorified in them. I am leaving this world, but my disciples are still in this world. Holy Father, protect my disciples by the power of your name—the name you gave me, so that they will be one as we are one. While I was living with them I protected them and kept them safe by the name you gave me. None of them has been lost except Judas who was destined to destruction, so that your word would be fulfilled. I am now coming to you, but I say these things while I am still living in this world, so that they will have the fullness of my joy within them. I taught my disciples your word and the world has hated them, because they are not of this world any more than I am of this world. My prayer is not that you take them out of this world but that you protect them from Satan, the evil one. Make them holy by the truth, for your word is truth. As you sent me into this world, I have sent my disciples into this world. And for them I sanctify myself, so that they too will be holy in truth. I not only pray for my disciples, but also for whoever will believe in me through their message, so that they all will be one. Righteous Father, just as you are in me and I am in you, may they also be one in us, so that this world will believe that you sent me into this world. I have given them the glory that you gave me, so that they will be one as we are one—I in them and you in me—so that they will be brought to complete unity. Then the world will know that you sent me into this world, and that you have loved them even as you have loved me. Father, I want those you have given me to be with me, so that they can see my glory—the glory you gave me because you loved me before the creation of the universe. Father, although this world does not know you, I know you, and my disciples know that you have sent me into this world. I have revealed your name to them, and I will continue to make it known, so that the love you have loved me with will be in them, and I will live in them."

CHAPTER 24

After Jesus finished praying, he walked with his apostles across the Kidron Valley to a field of olive trees called Gethsemane. When they arrived at Gethsemane, Jesus said to his apostles, "Sit here while I go to pray. I pray that you will not experience temptation." Then Jesus took Peter, James, and John along with him. He became deeply grieved and troubled. Jesus said to them, "My heart is overcome with sorrow to the point of death. I feel as if I am going to die. Stay here and keep watch and stay awake with me."

Jesus slowly walked a short distance from them. He dropped to his knees and then fell with his face to the ground. Jesus prayed: "Abba my Father, everything is possible for you. If it is your will take this time of suffering from me. But not my will, but your will be done. I want to do your will! Then an angel from heaven appeared to Jesus and gave him strength. Experiencing deep agony, Jesus prayed with greater energy, so that his sweat became like drops of blood falling to the ground. Then Jesus stood up from praying, walked back to Peter, James, and John and found them sleeping, because they were tired from sorrow. Jesus asked them, "Why are you sleeping? Couldn't you stay awake and keep watch for one hour? Get up, watch, and pray so that you will not fall into temptation, for the spirit is willing, but the body is weak." Jesus went away and prayed a second time. He prayed the same words that he prayed the first time. When he went back Peter, James, and John, he found them sleeping again because they were tired. They did not know what to say to Jesus. Jesus went away again and prayed a third time, saying the same words as he prayed before. Then Jesus went back to them and said, "Are you still sleeping? Enough! The time has come. Look, the Son of Man is delivered into the hands of sinners. Get up! Let's go! Here comes my betrayer!"

While Jesus was still speaking, Judas Iscariot arrived leading a large crowd of soldiers. The soldiers were sent by the Jewish religious leaders. They were carrying lanterns and torches, and armed with clubs and swords. Judas knew where Gethsemane was because Jesus had often met there with his disciples. Judas told the soldiers this signal: "The one I kiss on the cheeks is Jesus. Grab him, arrest him, and then lead him away under your guard." Going immediately to Jesus, Judas said, "Teacher!" and kissed him on the cheeks. Jesus asked him, "Judas, are you betraying the Son of Man with a kiss? My friend, do what you came to do."

Jesus knew what was going to happen to him. He asked those who were about to arrest him, "Who are you looking for?" They said, "Jesus of Nazareth." Jesus said, "I AM!" They stepped back and fell to the ground. Jesus asked them again, "Who are you looking for?" They said, "Jesus of Nazareth." Jesus said, "I told you that I am the one you are looking for; let my disciples go." This happened so that the words he had spoken would be fulfilled: "I have not lost any of those you gave me."

When the apostles of Jesus saw that he was being arrested, they became alarmed and shouted, "Lord! Should we attack them with our swords?" Standing nearby, Peter took out his sword and sliced off the right ear of a servant of the high priest. Jesus shouted, "Stop! Put your sword away! I must drink the cup of suffering that the Father has given me. All who fight with the sword will die by the sword. You know I could call on my Father, and he would immediately send me armies of angels. But if I did, how then would God's word be fulfilled that says it must all happen this way?" Then Jesus touched the ear of the servant and healed him.

At that time Jesus said to those who had come to arrest him, "Am

I leading a rebellion that you have come out with swords and clubs to arrest me? I taught every day in the temple courts, and you did not arrest me. But now the Bible must be fulfilled! This is your time—a time when the authority of darkness has come." All this happened so the words of the Old Testament prophets would come true.

Then the group of hardened soldiers with their military commander stepped forward, grabbed Jesus, and arrested him. As Jesus was being arrested, all the apostles ran away and deserted Jesus.

CHAPTER 25

From a distance Peter and John followed the guards who took Jesus to the palace of Annas. Annas was the high priest from AD 6 through AD 15 and remained the patriarch of the high priesthood. He was the father-in-law of Caiaphas the high priest that year. Because John knew the workers at the palace, he went into the courtyard, but Peter stayed outside the gate. John spoke to the servant girl guarding the gate, came back, and brought Peter inside the courtyard.

It was late in the night, and Annas interrogated Jesus about his disciples and his teaching. Standing his ground, Jesus said to Annas, "I continually taught in Jerusalem's synagogues and in the temple courts. I did not teach anything in secret. Why are you questioning me? Ask the people who heard my teaching. Surely they know what I taught." When Jesus said this, one of the officers of the high priest standing there hit him in the face. He demanded, "Stop speaking to the high priest that way!" Jesus said, "Tell me what I said wrong; I spoke the truth, why did you hit me?" After being interrogated by Annas, the guards bound Jesus and took him to the palace of the high priest Caiaphas, for the Jewish religious council had gathered together.

Peter followed Jesus from a distance to the palace's courtyard of Caiaphas. When the temple guards arrived at the palace, they started a fire in the middle of the courtyard and sat down together. Peter walked into the courtyard and sat down with the guards and began warming himself by the fire because it was cold. He was watching to see what would happen. At that time one of the servant girls of the high priest walked by and saw Peter. She looked him in the face and said, "You were with Jesus the Nazarene from Galilee! This man was with Jesus! Aren't you one of Jesus' disciples?" But Peter denied it saying, "No, I am not one of his disciples. I don't know what you're talking about. Woman, I don't know Jesus!" Then Peter got up and walked out to the courtyard's gate. A little later at the gate another servant girl saw Peter and said to those standing around, "This man is one of the followers of Jesus of Nazareth." Peter again denied it and said, "I do not know this man Jesus!" After about a hour those standing nearby said to Peter, "Yes, you are one of the followers of Jesus! You are from Galilee, for you talk like a Galilean." Then one of the high priest's servants who was standing alongside Peter—a relative of the man whose ear Peter had cut off—said to him, "Yes, I saw you in Gethsemane with Jesus?" Again Peter denied it. Then Peter began to call down curses on himself and he swore to them, "I don't know this man Jesus that you're talking about!" Immediately, while he was speaking the rooster crowed. Now being held in the courtyard, Jesus turned and looked straight in Peter's eyes, and he remembered what Jesus had told him, "Before the rooster crows, you will deny that you know me three times." And then Peter went outside, broke down, and cried bitterly.

The Jewish religious council was looking for evidence against Jesus from false witnesses, so that they could have him crucified by the Romans. Although many false witnesses came forward, they could not find any crime with which to condemn Jesus to death. They brought in many false witnesses, but their statements contradicted each other. Then two false witnesses came forward and lied saying, "We heard him say, 'I will destroy our temple made with human hands and in three days I will build another one not made with hands.'"

Frustrated, the high priest Caiaphas confronted Jesus saying, "Are you the Messiah, the Son of the Blessed One? Aren't you going to answer these charges? What are you going to say against the testimony of these men?" Jesus did not say anything. Then Caiaphas stood up and said to Jesus, "I charge you under oath by the living God, tell us if you are the Messiah, the Son of God!" Jesus said, "Yes, as you have said. As it is written in *Psalm 110:1*, from now on you will see the Son of Man enthroned in authority at the right hand of the Mighty God, and coming on the clouds of heaven." In disgust, Caiaphas tore his clothes and yelled "We do not need any more witnesses! Everyone has heard him. He speaks blasphemy against God! Caiaphas asked the other religious leaders, "What should we do?" They condemned Jesus and said, "He is guilty! He deserves to be put to death."

Then the guards took Jesus and began mocking and beating him. They spit in his face. They blindfolded him, hit him with their fists, and slapped him. They said to Jesus, "Prophesy to us Messiah! Who hit you?" They shouted insults at Jesus over and over again.

At sunrise on Friday morning, the religious council met again, and had Jesus brought before them. They said to him, "Tell us, are you the Messiah?" Jesus said, "Even if I tell you, you will not believe me. As I told you, from now on the Son of Man will be enthroned in authority at the right hand of the power of God." They confronted Jesus, "So, are you claiming to be the Son of God?" Jesus said, "Yes, as you say that I am." The religious leaders said, "We do not need any more evidence. We have heard him say it." So they made plans to have Jesus put to death.

When Judas Iscariot saw that Jesus was condemned to death, he was overcome with remorse and gave the 30 silver coins back to the religious leaders. Judas said to them, "I have sinned, for I have betrayed an innocent man." They replied, "We do not care what you did, that's your problem not ours." So Judas threw the money into the temple and went away and hanged himself. Then the religious leaders picked up the coins and said, "It is against Jewish law to put this blood money into the temple treasury." So they used the money to buy a potter's field to serve as a burial place for foreigners. That is why the location of Judas' suicide was called the "Field of Blood."

CHAPTER 26

Determined to have Jesus crucified, the members of the Jewish religious council rose and had the hands of Jesus bound behind his back. They then led Jesus from Caiaphas' palace to Pontius Pilate, the Roman governor of Judea. When the religious leaders arrived at the palace of Pilate, they remained in the large courtyard, for if they went inside a non-Jewish palace they would become ceremonially unclean and could not eat during the Passover Feast.

Because the religious leaders would not enter the palace, Pilate went outside to meet them. He asked them, "What charges do you bring against this man?" They said, "We wouldn't have brought him to you if he was not a criminal. We have interrogated him and have found him guilty of misleading and deceiving the nation of Israel, refusing to pay taxes to Caesar, and claiming that he is the Messiah, a king!" Pilate said to them, "Take him and judge him by your own law." But the religious leaders said, "You know that it is not lawful for us to put anyone to death."

Pilate took Jesus inside his palace and said to him, "Don't you hear the charges they are bringing against you? The religious leaders have accused you of many things." But Jesus did not reply, not even to a single charge. Pilate was totally amazed and asked Jesus, "Are you the king of the Jews?" Jesus said to him, "Yes, as you have said. Is this what you believe, or did others tell you this about me?" Pilate said, "I am not a Jew. It is your religious leaders and your own people that handed you over to me. What did you do?" Jesus said, "My kingdom is not of this world. If my kingdom were of this world, my disciples would have fought against my arrest. But my kingdom is from another world." Pilate said, "So you are a king!" Jesus said, "You say that I am a king, but I came into this world to tell people the truth. Whoever belongs to the truth listens to my teaching." Then Pilate said, "What is truth?"

Pilate went outside of his palace and announced to the religious leaders and the crowd of people, "I find no legal grounds to declare this man guilty of a crime." But they insisted, "Jesus is inciting the people to rebel all over Judea with his teaching. He started in Galilee and has now come to Jerusalem." When Pilate heard that Jesus was from Galilee, a region governed by Herod Antipas, he sent Jesus to Antipas who was in Jerusalem during the Passover.

When Antipas saw Jesus, he was very pleased because he had wanted to meet him for a long time. From everything that he had heard about Jesus in Galilee, he hoped to see him do some sort of miracle. Although Antipas asked Jesus many questions, he remained silent and gave no answers. During Antipas' interrogation of Jesus, the religious leaders were standing there, viciously accusing Jesus of many things. Then Antipas and his soldiers ridiculed and mocked Jesus, and sent him back to Pilate. Although they had been enemies, Pilate and Antipas became friends that day.

When Jesus had been returned to Pilate, he called together the Jews and said to them, "You brought Jesus to me as one who was inciting a rebellion among the people. I have examined him, and I have not found him guilty of the criminal charges that have been brought against him. Herod Antipas did not find him guilty either. He has done nothing to deserve death. Therefore, I will have him punished and then let him go free." Then Pilate went back inside his palace.

A short time later, Pilate went outside of his palace to reason with the Jews who were gathered in the courtyard. While Pilate was sitting on the judge's seat, his wife sent him this message: "Don't have anything to do with this innocent man, for I suffered in a dream today because of him." Then Pilate said to the crowd of Jews, "I do not find this man guilty of the charges you have brought against him. But since it is your custom for me to free one Jewish prisoner every Passover, do you want me to free the king of the Jews or Barabbas?" For at that time the Romans had a very well known prisoner named Barabbas. Barabbas was in prison for starting an insurrection against Rome in Jerusalem and for murder.

The religious leaders stirred up the crowd and so they yelled, "we want you to release Barabbas!" They shouted, "Do not free Jesus! We want you to free Barabbas!" Away with Jesus! Release Barabbas to us!" Then Pilate said to them, "What should I do with Jesus who is called the Messiah, the king of the Jews?" They shouted, "Crucify him!" Pilate asked them, "Why? What crime is he guilty of?" But the crowd shouted even louder, "Crucify him!" Pilate said to them, "Why? What crime has he committed? I do not find him guilty of any crimes deserving death. Therefore, I will have him punished and then set him free."

Pilate had Jesus punished. The soldiers took Jesus into Pilate's palace and gathered a company of soldiers around him. They stripped Jesus of his clothes, put a purple robe on him, and then twisted together a crown of thorns and pushed it down on his head. They put a staff in his right hand. They knelt in front of him and mocked him shouting, "Hail, king of the Jews!" Falling to their knees, the soldiers pretended that they were worshiping him. Again and again they hit him on the head with a staff, spit on him, and slapped him in the face.

Then Pilate went outside his palace again and said to the Jews gathered there, "Look, I am bringing Jesus out to you. Jesus came outside wearing the crown of thorns and the purple robe. Pilate said to the Jews, "Here is the man!" As soon as the religious leaders saw him, they shouted, "Crucify him! Crucify him!" But Pilate said, "You take him and crucify him, because I do not find a legal basis for a charge against him." The religious leaders said, "Our law says that he must die, because he claimed to be the Son of God."

When Pilate heard that Jesus claimed to be the Son of God, he became afraid. He went back inside his palace with Jesus and asked him, "Where did you come from?" But Jesus did not answer him. Pilate said, "Do you refuse to answer me? Don't you know that I have power to free you or to crucify you?" Jesus said, "You would have no power over me if it were not given to you from God above. Therefore, the one who handed me over to you is guilty of a greater sin."

Once again, Pilate went outside his palace and tried to convince the Jews to let Jesus go free. But the religious leaders kept shouting, "If you let Jesus go free, you are no friend of Caesar." When Pilate heard this, he brought Jesus out and sat down on the judge's seat. Pilate shouted to the Jews, "Look, here is your king!" But the Jews shouted back, "Take him away! Crucify him!" Pilate said, "Should I crucify your king?" They shouted, "We have no king but Caesar!"

When Pilate saw that he was getting nowhere and that the crowd was getting out of control, he took water and washed his hands in front of the people saying "I am innocent of this man's blood; he is now your responsibility!" The crowd shouted, "Let his blood be on us and on our children!"

Wanting to please the religious leaders and the people, Pilate released Barabbas. Sitting on the judgement seat, Pilate then sentenced Jesus to crucifixion. He ordered the Roman soldiers to severely flog Jesus. After his flogging, Pilate handed Jesus over to the soldiers to be crucified. The soldiers led Jesus outside the walls of Jerusalem. As they were going, the soldiers met a Passover pilgrim named Simon from the city of Cyrene in North Africa, who was walking into Jerusalem from the country. The soldiers grabbed Simon, put the crossbeam of Jesus' cross on him, and forced him to carry it behind Jesus.

A large crowd of people followed Jesus, including women who were mourning and crying for him. Jesus turned to the women and said, "Daughters of Jerusalem, do not weep for me; weep for yourselves and for your children. For the time is coming when you will say, 'Blessed are the childless women, the wombs that never gave birth, and the breasts that never nursed!' Then they will say to the mountains, "Fall on us!" and to the hills, "Cover us!"' Jesus once again warned them about the Roman destruction of Jerusalem and the temple that took place in AD 70.

CHAPTER 27

The Roman soldiers led Jesus outside of the walls of Jerusalem to the "Place of the Skull," which is known as "Golgotha" and "Calvary." The words Golgotha and Calvary mean "skull," for it was a place of execution, with skulls and bones scattered around the area from past crucifixions.

The soldiers stripped Jesus of his clothes and crucified him about 9 a.m. They also crucified two criminals alongside Jesus—one criminal hung on a cross at his right side, and the other criminal hung on a cross at his left side. Looking up at Jesus, the soldiers mocked him shouting, "If you are the king of the Jews, save yourself!" The soldiers offered Jesus some sour wine to numb his pain, but he refused to drink it. Then the soldiers took Jesus' outer clothes and divided them into four parts—one part for each of them. Jesus' undergarment was seamless—woven in one piece from top to bottom—so the soldiers said to one another, "Let's not tear it. Let's throw dice to decide who will get it." This happened to fulfill *Psalm 22:18*, "They divided my clothes among them and cast dice for my clothing." Then the soldiers sat down to keep watch over Jesus on the cross. Hanging on the cross, Jesus prayed, "Father, forgive them, for they do not know what they are doing."

Following the command of Pilate, the soldiers nailed a sign on the main stake of the cross above Jesus' head with the Roman charge against him, it read, "THIS IS JESUS, THE KING OF THE JEWS." The sign was written in Aramaic, Latin, and Greek. In protest, the Jewish religious leaders went and said to Pilate, "Do not write 'The king of the Jews.' Write that Jesus claimed to be 'the king of the Jews.'" Pilate said, "What I have written, I have written."

The people walking by Jesus hanging on the cross yelled words of insults and shame at him. They shook their heads in disgust and shouted, "You were going to destroy the temple and build it again in three days. If you are the Son of God come down off the cross and save yourself! Sneering at Jesus, the people and rulers standing by watching yelled, "He saved other people; let him save himself if he is God's Messiah, the Chosen One."

The religious leaders also mocked Jesus among themselves. They shouted, "He saved others, but he can't save himself! Let this Messiah—this king of Israel—come down from the cross. If he comes down from the cross we will believe in him. He trusts in God, so let God rescue him if he is the 'Son of God.'"

At that time the two criminals who hung next to Jesus shouted insults at him. Then one of the criminals shouted, "Aren't you the Messiah? Save yourself and us!" But feeling guilty, the other criminal rebuked him and said, "Don't you fear God? You are under the same sentence of crucifixion. We are being punished justly, for we are getting what we deserve. But he has done nothing wrong." Then he said to Jesus, "Remember me when you come into your kingdom." Jesus said to him, "I tell you the truth: Today you will be with me in paradise."

When all the people who gathered to witness Jesus' crucifixion saw what had happened, they beat their chests in sorrow and went away. Jesus' women disciples watched him hang on the cross from a distance, but his mother Mary stood near the cross. Jesus looked down at her and the apostle John standing nearby. He said to her, "Mother, here is your son," and to John he said, "Here is your mother." From that time on John took Mary into his home.

Darkness covered all the land from noon to 3 p.m. It was as if the sun stopped shining. About 3 p.m. Jesus yelled out *Psalm 22:1*, "Eloi,

Eloi, lama sabachthani," which in Aramaic means, "My God, my God, why have you abandoned me?" When the soldiers standing nearby heard Jesus, they said, "Listen, he's calling for Elijah." Immediately one of them ran and got a sponge that he filled with sour wine and put the sponge on a stick and lifted it up to Jesus to drink. But the others said, "Leave him alone. Let's see if Elijah comes to save him by taking him down from the cross." Later, knowing that everything had now been finished, so that God's word would be fulfilled, Jesus said, "I am thirsty." So a soldier once again dipped a sponge into a container of sour wine and lifted it to Jesus' mouth. When Jesus tasted the sour wine, he cried out with a loud shout, "It is finished! Father, I commit my spirit into your hands!" Then Jesus bowed his head, took his last breath, gave up his spirit and died. At the exact moment, the inner curtain of the temple—separating the Most Holy Place from the Holy Place—was torn in two from top to bottom. And then the earth shook and the rocks split and the tombs broke open.

A high-ranking Roman soldier was standing in front of Jesus and saw how he died. When the Roman solider and the guards with him felt the earthquake, they trembled in fear and proclaimed, "He was a righteous man! It is true, he is the Son of God!"

The next day was the Sabbath and the religious leaders did not want dead bodies hanging on the crosses. So they asked Pilate to have the legs broken of the crucified men to hasten their deaths and take their bodies down. Then the soldiers went and broke the legs of the two men who were crucified with Jesus. But when they came to Jesus and found that he was already dead, they did not break his legs. Instead, a soldier pierced Jesus' side with a spear, and a flow of blood and water poured from his side. This happened to fulfill what is written in *Exodus 12:46*, "Not one of his bones will be broken," and what is written in *Zechariah 12:10*, "They will look on the one whom they have pierced."

CHAPTER 28

There was a rich man named Joseph from the town of Arimathea in Judea. He was a prominent member of Jerusalem's religious council and was waiting for the kingdom of God to come. Joseph was a good and righteous man. Although he was a disciple of Jesus, he kept it a secret because he was afraid of the religious leaders. He strongly opposed the religious council's decision to have Jesus crucified.

Joseph boldly went to Pilate and asked him for the body of Jesus. Pilate was surprised to hear that Jesus was already dead. When Pilate learned from a Roman solider that Jesus was dead, he ordered that his body be given to Joseph.

After Joseph received the body of Jesus down from the cross, he went and bought some high-quality linen cloth. He then wrapped Jesus' body in a linen cloth and covered it with fragrant oils according with Jewish burial customs. Then the religious leader Nicodemus—also a member of the religious council—met Joseph. He was the one who had earlier talked with Jesus under the darkness of night. Nicodemus brought a mixture of oils that weighed about 75 pounds. Because it was late on Friday, Joseph and Nicodemus laid the body of Jesus in a new tomb cut into the rock, The new tomb was located in a garden near where Jesus was crucified; it was a tomb that had never been used before. Then Joseph and Nicodemus rolled a large stone in front of the tomb's entrance and went away.

The women disciples of Jesus followed Joseph. The women sat near the tomb and saw how they laid Jesus' body inside. After seeing the tomb of Jesus, the women went home. They rested in obedience to the Sabbath law of Moses and prepared fragrant spices and oils to put on Jesus' body.

The next day on Saturday, the religious leaders went to Pilate and said, "Sir, we remember that when the deceiver Jesus was alive, he said, 'After three days I will rise from the dead.' So give the order for your soldiers to seal the tomb for three days. Otherwise, his disciples will come and steal his body and tell the people that he has risen from the dead. This lie will be a great deception." Pilate said to them, "Take some guards and make the tomb as secure as you want." So the religious leaders went and sealed the entrance, and had the soldiers guard the tomb.

CHAPTER 29

The sun was rising on Sunday morning, and the women disciples—Mary Magdalene, Mary the mother of James and Joseph, and Salome the mother of the apostles James and John walked toward the tomb of Jesus. The women brought fragrant oils they had prepared to anoint the body of Jesus. As the women were walking to Jesus' tomb, they asked each other, "Who will roll the large stone away from the entrance of the tomb?"

As the women disciples were walking, there was a violent earthquake when an angel of the Lord came down from heaven. The angel rolled back the entrance stone of the tomb and sat on it. The angel's appearance was like lightning. His clothes were bright white like snow. The guards saw the angel and shook in fear. They became like dead men.

When the women disciples arrived at the tomb, they found the large stone had been rolled away from the entrance. The women entered the tomb and found that it was empty. They were confused because the body of Jesus was not there. Then suddenly two angels appeared and stood by them inside the tomb. They were wearing bright shining clothing that looked like lightning. One angel was sitting on the right side where the feet of Jesus had been. The women were filled with fear and bowed their faces to the ground.

One of the angels said to the women, "Do not be afraid! Why are you looking for the living among the dead? I know you are looking for Jesus the Nazarene, who was crucified. He is not here; he has risen from the dead as he said he would. Come and see the place where his body once was. It is now empty. Remember how Jesus told you when he was with you in Galilee, 'The Son of Man must be delivered into the hands of sinful men, be crucified, and raised from the dead on the third day.'" And the women remembered what Jesus had told them. Then the angel said, "Go quickly and tell Peter and the other disciples: 'He has risen from the dead and is going ahead of you into Galilee. There you will see him again, just as he told you.'"

Shaking and filled with amazement, the women disciples ran from the tomb of Jesus to tell the apostles and the other disciples everything the angel had said. The women were filled with joy, but they did not tell anyone else because they were afraid. When the women disciples arrived, they told everything to the apostles. But the apostles did not believe the women, because they thought what they said was nonsense.

Mary Magdalene said to Peter and John, "They have taken the Lord's body out of the tomb, and we do not know where they have moved him!" So Peter and John ran toward the tomb of Jesus. Although both were running, John outran Peter and reached the tomb first. He bent down and looked inside at the strips of linen lying there, but he did not go into the tomb. Then Peter arrived and went immediately inside the tomb. He saw the strips of linen lying there, and the cloth that had been wrapped around Jesus' head. Then Peter went away, wondering to himself what had happened. Then John, who had reached the tomb first, also went inside the tomb and saw that it was empty. But Peter and John still did not understand from the Old Testament that Jesus had to rise from the dead. Then they went back to where they were staying.

CHAPTER 30

The women disciples had followed Peter and John to the tomb of Jesus, and after they left, they were all alone. Mary Magdalene, the one who had seven demons cast out of her, was crying outside of the tomb. As she cried, she bent over to look inside the tomb and saw two angels dressed in white. They were seated where the body of Jesus had been laid. One was sitting where Jesus' head had rested, and the other was sitting where his feet had been. The angels asked Mary, "Woman, why are you crying?" She said, "They have taken my Lord's body, and I do not know where they have taken him."

Distraught, Mary Magdalene turned around and looked outside the tomb and saw Jesus standing there, but she did not recognize him. Jesus asked Mary, "Why are you crying? Who are you looking for?" Thinking Jesus was the gardener, Mary said, "Sir, if you have taken my Lord's body away, tell me where you have laid him so I can go get him." Jesus said to her, "Mary!" She turned to him and shouted out "Teacher!"

Jesus then walked toward Mary and the other women disciples and said, "Greetings!" The women came to Jesus, fell down, held his feet, and began worshiping him. Jesus said, "Do not hold on to me, because I have not yet ascended to the Father. Go to my disciples and tell them, 'I am ascending to my Father and your Father, to my God and your God.'" Do not be afraid, tell my brothers to go to Galilee; they will see me there."

Mary Magdalene and the women disciples ran from the tomb of Jesus to tell the apostles the good news. When she arrived they were mourning and weeping. Then Mary Magdalene told them that she had seen Jesus alive. Mary said, "I have seen the Lord!" Then she told them everything that Jesus had said to her, but they still would not believe her.

After the women had left the tomb of Jesus, some of the soldiers went into Jerusalem and told the Jewish religious leaders everything that had happened. Then they devised a plan and gave the soldiers a large sum of money. They told them, "You must lie and say, 'His disciples came during the night and took Jesus' body while we were sleeping.' This lie will persuade Pilate and will keep you out of trouble." So the soldiers took the money and did as they were told. And this false story has been told many times among the Jews to this very day.

It was Sunday afternoon, and two disciples of Jesus—Cleopas and another man—were walking from Jerusalem to the village of Emmaus, which was about seven miles from Jerusalem. As they were walking, they talked about the crucifixion of Jesus in Jerusalem. Then Jesus came up and walked alongside them, but they did not recognize him, because Jesus appeared to them in a different form. Jesus asked them, "What are you talking about?" They stopped. Their faces were very sad. Cleopas said, "Are you the only one in Jerusalem who doesn't know what happened?" Jesus said, "Tell me." They said to him, "We are talking about Jesus of Nazareth! He was a prophet. He was powerful in word and deed before God and all the people. But our religious rulers delivered him over to the Romans to be sentenced to death, and they crucified him. We were hoping that he was the Messiah—the one who was going to redeem Israel—but he was crucified three days ago." The women disciples amazed us, for they went to Jesus' tomb early this morning, but they didn't find his body. They told us that they had seen angels. The angels told them that Jesus was raised from the dead and that he is alive!" Then Peter and John went to the tomb and found it empty just as the women had said, although they did not see Jesus."

Jesus said to them, "You are so foolish. Are you so slow of heart not to believe all that the prophets have written! Didn't the Messiah have to suffer and then enter his glory?" Jesus explained to them everything that Moses and the prophets had said about the Messiah. As they approached the village of Emmaus, Jesus acted like he was going to walk farther, but the two men begged him, "Stay with us, for it is almost night." So Jesus stayed with them. When Jesus was eating with them, he took a loaf of bread, gave thanks to God, broke it, and began to give it to them. The two men's eyes were opened. And they recognized that it was Jesus. Then Jesus immediately disappeared. The two men said to each other, "Our hearts were burning within us while he talked to us on the road and explained the Bible to us!" They got up and went back up to Jerusalem, and found the apostles and the other disciples gathered together. The apostles told the Emmaus disciples, "It is true! The Lord has risen from the dead and has appeared to Peter." Then the two men told the apostles that Jesus had appeared to them on the road to Emmaus, and that they only recognized him when he broke bread.

It was now Sunday evening, and the apostles were together in a locked room of a private house in Jerusalem because they feared the religious leaders. They were talking about the crucifixion of Jesus and eating. Suddenly, Jesus appeared and stood among them. He said, "Peace be with you!" Then Jesus rebuked them for their lack of faith, because they were so stubborn that they refused to believe the women disciples who had seen him alive after his resurrection. The apostles were startled and terrified. They thought they were seeing a spirit. Jesus said to them, "Why are you troubled? Why do you have doubts? Look at the marks on my hands, side, and feet. Touch me and see. A spirit does not have flesh and bones." Jesus showed them his hands and feet, but they still did not believe. Jesus asked them, "Do you have anything to eat?" They gave him a piece of cooked fish, and Jesus ate it in front of them. Jesus said to them, "Remember, this is what I told you would happen. Everything must be fulfilled that is written about me in the Bible." Then Jesus opened their minds so they could understand the Bible. Jesus told them, "This is what is written: The Messiah had to suffer and be raised from the dead on the third day. Then repentance for the forgiveness of sins must be proclaimed in my name to all nations, beginning in Jerusalem. You are all eyewitnesses of all these things. I am going to send you the Holy Spirit who my Father has promised. Stay in Jerusalem until you have been anointed with power from heaven. As the Father has sent me into this world, I am sending you." Then Jesus breathed on them and said, "Receive the Holy Spirit! Go into all the world and proclaim the good news of God. Whoever believes and is water-baptized will be saved. But whoever does not believe will be condemned." Then Jesus left.

Now Thomas, one of the apostles, was not there when Jesus first appeared to them. So the apostles told him, "We have seen the Lord!" But Thomas said to them, "I will not believe unless I see and touch the nail marks in his hands, and put my hand into his side." Then on Sunday a week later, the apostles were once again gathered in the locked room, and Thomas was with them. Jesus came and stood among them and said, "Peace be with you!" Then Jesus said to Thomas, "Touch the nail marks on my hands and the hole in my side. Now stop doubting and believe." Thomas shouted, "My Lord and my God!" Then Jesus said to him, "You believe in me because you have seen me, but blessed are those who have not seen me and still believe." Then Jesus left.

When the week-long Passover Feast was over, the apostles left Jerusalem and traveled to Galilee as instructed by Jesus. When they arrived, Peter, Thomas, Nathanael, James, John, and two other apostles were all together. Peter said to them, "I'm going fishing." The others said, "We're going with you." So they got into the boat and fished all night, but they did not catch any fish.

As the sun was rising early in the morning, Jesus stood on the northwest shore of Lake Galilee, but the apostles did not recognize him. Jesus shouted to them, "Friends, haven't you caught any fish?" They said, "No!" Jesus said, "Throw your net to the right side of the boat and you will catch fish." When they did what Jesus said, they caught so many fish that they could not lift their net into the boat. Then John said to Peter, "It is the Lord!" As soon as Peter heard that it was the Lord, he wrapped his outer garment around him and jumped into the water. The other disciples followed in the boat towing the net full of fish. When they landed, they saw fish being cooked on a fire and some bread. Jesus said to them, "Bring me some of the fish you have caught." So Peter climbed back into the boat and dragged the net onto the shore. The net was full of large fish, but it did not tear. Jesus said to them, "Come and eat breakfast." Jesus took the bread and fish and gave it to them.

After they had finished eating, Jesus took Peter aside and asked him, "Do you love me more than the other apostles?" Peter said, "Yes, Lord, you know that I love you." Once again, Jesus asked, "Peter, do you love me?" Peter said, "Yes, Lord, you know that I love you." Peter was sad because Jesus kept asking him whether he loved him. He said to Jesus, "Lord, you know everything; you know that I love you." Jesus looked into his eyes and said to Peter, "Then follow me and take care of my sheep!" Peter turned and saw John following them. Peter asked Jesus, "Lord, what is going to happen to him?" Jesus said, "What is it to you if I want him to stay alive until I come again? You just follow me!" Then Jesus left.

The apostles traveled to the Galilean hillside to meet with Jesus again. When they saw Jesus, they worshiped him; but some of them were not sure that it was him. Jesus walked to them and gave them the great commission. He said, "All authority in heaven and on earth has been given to me. Therefore, go and make disciples of all nations, baptizing them in the name of the Father and of the Son and of the Holy Spirit, and teaching them to obey everything that I have taught you. I tell you the truth: I am with you always, to the very the end of the world!"

When Jesus and the apostles were back in Jerusalem, Jesus led them to the area of Bethany on the Mount of Olives. He raised his hands, blessed them, and was taken into heaven and enthroned in authority at God's right hand. Then the apostles worshiped Jesus and went back to Jerusalem with great joy. They continually met to praise God at the Jerusalem temple. They went out and proclaimed the good news of God everywhere, and the Lord Jesus confirmed the message of salvation with miracles.

This is the end of the amazing story of Jesus' life and teaching. You can read the rest of the story of the mission of Jesus' apostles and the early church in the book of Acts.

GLOSSARY OF TERMS

Born Again: The biblical phrase "born again" refers to experiencing a renewal of our hearts and minds through the ministry of the Holy Spirit. The born again experience is an act of God, not the result of human effort. When we surrender our lives, accept the eternal forgiveness of Jesus Christ, and turn our lives over to God, we experience an internal supernatural change brought about by the love and grace of God. The immediate born again experience leads to a personal relationship with God and to a life-long process of the transformation of our whole person.

Christ/Messiah: The Greek word "Christ" and the Hebrew word "Messiah" are equivalent. Christ or Messiah are not personal names, but are titles meaning the "anointed one" of God. The promised Christ or Messiah of the Old Testament would usher in the Kingdom of God that was fulfilled in the coming of Jesus Christ.

Eternal Life: The biblical phrase "eternal life" refers to experiencing the life of God. Eternal life is equivalent to the kingdom of God. Just as the kingdom of God has a present reality of fulfillment and a future reality of completion, so does eternal life. When we are born again we experience the eternal life of God now, but we only experience the fullness of eternal life after the second coming of Jesus.

Father God: Jesus refers to God as the Father. Father does not mean that Jesus was the literal offspring of God. Father was not God's name. Rather, Father is a new revelation of the personal and relational nature of the eternal, transcendent God.

Feast of Tabernacles: The seven-day long Feast of Tabernacles was held in September/October each year in Jerusalem. It was a time for remembering and celebrating God's provision during Israel's journey from Egypt to the Promised Land.

High Priest: The High Priest, who was an aristocratic Sadducee, ruled over the Jewish Supreme Council (Sanhedrin) and all the activities of the Jerusalem temple. The High Priest was the only one who could enter the Holy of Holies once a year on the Day of Atonement. Caiaphas was the High Priest during the time of Jesus.

Holy Spirit: The Holy Spirit is the personal presence of God.

GLOSSARY

Jewish Supreme Council (Sanhedrin): The supreme religious and political council of the Jews was called the Sanhedrin. During the New Testament period, it is believed that the Sanhedrin was composed of seventy-one members including religious members of the Sadducees, Pharisees, and ruling elders. It enforced the religious laws regulating Jewish worship, and legislated the day-to-day affairs in Jerusalem and throughout Judea.

Kingdom of God: The good news of the kingdom of God is that the dynamic rule or reign of God invaded history in the person of Jesus Christ. The kingdom of God is the supernatural revelation of God in Jesus Christ. It is not a static realm. The rule and reign of God has two dimensions: It is a present reality (already) in the first coming of Jesus, and the future reality (not yet) of a new heaven and new earth after the second coming of Jesus. The kingdom of God is not the church. The church is the steward of the kingdom of God. The kingdom of God was the primary theme of Jesus' teaching and proclamation during his ministry.

Old and New Testaments: The word "testament" means covenant. The Old Testament consists of the first 39 books of the Bible. The old covenant stands for the original promise of God to the descendants of Abraham prior to the coming of Jesus Christ. When Jesus came into the world, he inaugurated a new covenant with God. The New Testament consists of 27 books of the Bible. The entire Bible has 66 books.

Passover and Feast of Unleavened Bread: Passover is the first day of the seven-day long Feast of Unleavened Bread that was celebrated by Israel in March/April of each year in Jerusalem. Passover commemorates Israel's exodus from slavery in Egypt. God's judgment bypassed the houses of Israel when they sacrificed a lamb and marked their doorposts with its blood. This is why Jesus was called the "Lamb of God' who takes away the sin of the world. Jesus was crucified on Passover and rose from the dead three days later. On the evening after the Passover, God told the Hebrew people exiting Egypt not to take leavened bread. In remembrance of the Exodus from Egypt, Israel celebrated the feast by cleaning their houses of yeast and eating unleavened bread called Matzo.

Pharisees: The Pharisees—meaning "separated ones"—were a major Jewish religious group that followed the Old Testament and the Jewish oral traditions that were called the Traditions of the Elders. All the Teachers of the Law of Moses were Pharisees. The Pharisees were very influential in promoting a strict religiosity among the common people of Israel, especially in the synagogues scattered throughout the land of Israel. They believed in the supernatural, angels, and life after death.

Repentance: Repentance is a heart-centered turning away from one's life of sin, and turning to God's love, grace, and forgiveness in Jesus Christ.

Sadducees: The Sadducees were a Jewish religious group consisting of high priests, chief priests, aristocratic families, and rich merchants. The aristocratic Sadducees claimed the power status of birth and social elitism. The Sadducees dominated the activities of the Jerusalem temple and its priesthood. The Sadducees did not believe in the supernatural, angels, resurrection, or life after death. The Jewish High Priest was a Sadducee.

Sabbath Day: The Sabbath day was from sunset on Friday evening to sunset on Saturday evening.

Son of Man: Over and over again, Jesus identified himself as the "Son of Man" during his life and ministry. Jesus self-identified as the Son of Man in Daniel 7:13-14, "In my vision at night I looked, and there before me was one like a son of man, coming with the clouds of heaven. He approached the Ancient of Days and was led into his presence. He was given authority, glory and sovereign power; all nations and peoples of every language worshiped him. His dominion is an everlasting dominion that will not pass away, and his kingdom is one that will never be destroyed."

Son of God: Son of God was a title for the Messiah. It did not mean that Jesus was a literal male offspring of God.

Synagogues: At the time of Jesus, local synagogues were small separate buildings or a special room in private homes. The common people met in synagogues especially on the Sabbath day for Bible reading, teaching, and prayer. Jesus ministered throughout the synagogues of Galilee.

Temple Complex: The Jerusalem temple complex consisted of a series of structures, courts, chambers, and the central sanctuary that included the Holy Place and Holy of Holies.

GEOGRAPHICAL GLOSSARY

Aenon: Located on the west side of the Jordan River in the Wilderness of Judea across from Bethany. Jesus ministered in the region of Aenon during his last journey from Galilee to Jerusalem.

Arimathea: The exact location of Arimathea is uncertain; it is one of the towns northwest of Jerusalem. Joseph of Arimathea was the person who buried Jesus.

Bethany, Mount of Olives: Located on the east slope of the Mount of Olives, about 2 miles east of Jerusalem. Mary, Martha, and Lazarus lived in Bethany. During Jesus' ministry in Jerusalem, he would spend the night in Bethany.

Bethany, East of the Jordan River: Located on the east side of the Jordan River, about six miles east of Jericho and five miles north of the Dead Sea. The public ministry of John the Baptist took place in the region of Bethany. It is considered to be the original location of the water-baptism of Jesus. This was also the region where the Israelites crossed the Jordan River into the Promised Land (Joshua 2).

Bethlehem: Located five miles south-southwest of Jerusalem. It was the birthplace of King David and Jesus.

Bethphage: Located near the summit of the Mount of Olives, less than a mile east of Jerusalem.

Bethsaida: Located on the northeast coast of Lake Galilee. It was the original hometown of Peter, Andrew, and Philip before they moved to Capernaum on the northwest coast of Lake Galilee.

Bethsaida Plain: A fertile area located along the northeast coast of Lake Galilee. It was about five square miles. Jesus fed the 5,000 on the Bethsaida Plain.

Cana: Located about eight miles north of Nazareth. Jesus turned the water into wine in Cana.

Capernaum: Located on the northwest coast of Lake Galilee, about two miles west of the upper Jordan River. Today at the excavated site you can visit a large limestone synagogue that dates from the late 100s to 200s. It was built on top of the synagogue where Jesus taught. The family house of Peter is located about 100 feet from the synagogue on the main street. Capernaum was the home base of Jesus' ministry in Galilee.

Caesarea Philippi: Primarily a non-Jewish territory located about 25 miles north of Lake Galilee near Mount Hermon. King Herod the Great built a white marble temple to the god Pan in honor of Caesar Augustus. Later, Herod Philip rebuilt the town of Panion to become the capital of his territory. He renamed Panion Caesarea Philippi after Caesar Augustus and himself. It was in Caesarea Philippi that Peter declared that Jesus was the Messiah.

Decapolis Region: The southeast region of Lake Galilee where a league of ten free Greek cities existed. Jesus fed the 4,000 in the region of the Decapolis.

Ephraim: Located about 15 miles north of Jerusalem. Jesus traveled to Ephraim during his last journey from Galilee to Jerusalem.

Emmaus: Probably Nicopolis located about 20 miles west of Jerusalem. Jesus appeared to two of his disciples in Emmaus after his resurrection.

Fortress of Machaerus: Located in the region of Perea on the east side of the Dead Sea in the modern nation of Jordan. This is where John the Baptist was imprisoned and beheaded.

Galilee Region: Galilee was about 45 miles north-south and 25 miles east-west, with a population of about 300,000 living in about 200 villages and towns. A majority of Jesus public ministry was in the region of Galilee.

Gaulanitis Region: Located north and east from the northeast coast of Lake Galilee. It was governed by Herod Philip. Caesarea Philippi was located in the region of the Gaulanitis.

Gennesaret Plain: A crescent-shaped fertile plain located along the northwest coast of Lake Galilee between Tiberias and Capernaum. It is about five miles long and two miles wide.

Geresenes (Gaderenes) Region: The southeast territory of Lake Galilee near the town of Gerasa (modern Kursi). It was likely near Gerasa that Jesus delivered a man from a legion of demons.

Gethsemane: A cultivated area located near the bottom of the west slope of the Mount of Olives opposite the Temple Mount. In Hebrew, Gethsemane means "oil-press," for olive oil was made there. Jesus was arrested in Gethsemane.

Garden Tomb: The traditional site of Jesus' burial. However, this tomb was created in the 700s BC and couldn't have been the new tomb of Jesus.

Gordon's Calvary: The traditional site of Jesus' crucifixion. Gordon's Hill is a rocky hill located near the "Garden Tomb" just north of Jerusalem's old city. It was probably not a hill at the time of Jesus, for it is the product of modern quarrying operations. Because Golgotha was called the "Place of the Skull," people claim that one can see the shape of a human skull in the cliff face of Gordon's Hill. However, it is unlikely that it was called the Place of the Skull based on appearance.

Hills West of Lake Galilee: Throughout his ministry, Jesus often withdrew from the crowds of people in order to spend time in prayer along the ridge of hills west of the coast of Lake Galilee. It was here that Jesus taught the Beatitudes, Sermon on the Mount, and gave the great commission to his apostles.

Idumea Region (Edomites): An ancient region between the Dead Sea and the Gulf of Aqaba, bordering the land of ancient Israel. The kingdom of Edom was located in the southern area of the modern nation of Jordan. The Edomites later migrated into the southern Negev region of the Kingdom of Judah. King Herod the Great was an Edomite.

Jericho: Located near the Jordan River in the Wilderness of Judea. Jesus ministered in Jericho on his last journey from Galilee to Jerusalem.

Jericho-Jerusalem Road: The winding road from Jericho to Jerusalem was about 18 miles long and ascended about 3,000 feet through the dry desert of Judea.

Jerusalem: Located on the Judaea mountains in central Israel. The Old City of Jerusalem is surrounded on three sides by steep valleys: The Hinnom on the south and west, and the Kidron on the east. Today the walled Old City of Jerusalem is divided into the Christian Quarter, Muslim Quarter, Jewish Quarter and Armenian Quarter.

Jordan River: Originating at Mount Hermon, the Jordan River is about 156 miles long. It flows north-south through the Lake Galilee and down the Jordan Valley to the Dead Sea. Today it is the border between Israel and the modern nation of Jordan.

Judea Region: Judea gets its name from the tribe of Judah that was located in southern Israel. The core of Judea was the upper hill country that extended from Bethel in the north to Beersheba in the south.

Lake Galilee: Lake Galilee is heart-shaped and freshwater. It is about 700 hundred feet below sea level, and is 13 miles long and 7 miles wide. Lake

GEOGRAPHICAL GLOSSARY G

Galilee has high hills on its west and east sides. Because Lake Galilee was located in a geographical bowl, it experienced strong downdrafts and sudden windstorms.

Magdala (Port of Dalmanutha): Magdala is the hometown of Mary Magdalene. It was located about six miles south of Capernaum on the Plain of Gennesaret. Dalmanutha was possibly the port of Magdala.

Mount Gerizim: Mount Gerizim forms the south side of the valley in which Nablus (Old Testament Shechem) is located, while the north side of the valley is Mount Ebal. Mount Gerizim is known as the mountain of the Samaritans, and it remains sacred to Samaritans today.**Mount Hermon:** A mountain cluster with its summit straddling the border between the modern nations of Syria and Lebanon. The transfiguration of Jesus probably took place on the lower hills of Mount Hermon.

Mount of Olives: A mountain ridge located just east of Jerusalem and is separated by the Kidron Valley. The Kidron Valley served as the eastern border of Jerusalem. The Mount of Olives was technically not a part of Jerusalem proper.

Nain: Located six miles southeast of Nazareth. Jesus raised a man from the dead in Nain.

Nazareth: Located about 12 miles southwest of Lake Galilee; it was a small village with a population of about 500 to 1000 people. Nazareth was Jesus' hometown.

Palace of High Priest Caiaphas: High Priests Annas and his son-in-law Caiaphas probably lived in different wings of the same palace that had a common courtyard. The traditional site of the palace of Annas and Caiaphas is the Church of Saint Peter in Gallicantu located on eastern slope of Mount Zion. The term "gallicantu" means Rooster's Crow in Latin, signifying Peter's three denials of Jesus. The Jewish trial of Jesus took place at the palace of Caiaphas.

Palace of King Herod the Great: Located at the northwest corner of the city walls of Jerusalem, near the Tower of David and the Jaffa Gate. The Roman trial of Jesus took place in Herod's palace.

Place of the Skull (Golgotha, Calvary): The location of Jesus' crucifixion was outside Jerusalem's city walls. It was named the 'Place of the Skull' because it was a place of crucifixion, with skulls and bones scattered around the area. The words Golgotha and Calvary mean "skull," The Place of the

Skull was located near a major road, since crucifixion was intended to be a public spectacle. The Place of the Skull was probably located within the area now occupied by the Church of the Holy Sepulcher in the Christian Quarter of the Old City of Jerusalem. This area was outside the walls of Jerusalem during the time of Jesus.

Perea Region: Perea was primarily a Jewish region. It occupied the eastern side of the Jordan River Valley, from about one third the way down from Lake Galilee to about one third the way down the eastern shore of the Dead Sea. Perea was governed by Herod Antipas and is today in the modern nation of Jordan. Jesus ministered throughout Perea during his last journey from Galilee to Jerusalem.

Pool of Bethesda: A large two-pool complex near the Sheep Gate next to the modern Church of Saint Anne in the Muslim Quarter of Old Jerusalem. Jesus healed a blind man by having him wash his eyes in the Pool of Bethesda.

Samaria: The central region of the land of Israel, between Galilee in the north and Judea in the south; with the Mediterranean Sea on the west and the Jordan River on the east. Samaria extended about 40 miles from north to south and 35 miles from east to west.

Sychar: Identified with the modern village of Askar on the slope of Mount Ebal. Located about two miles northeast from Nablus (Shechem in the Old Testament). Jesus ministered to the Samaritan woman in Sychar.

Syria Region: A non-Jewish region north of Galilee, between Damascus and the Mediterranean Sea.

Tabgha (Seven Springs): On the northwest coast of Lake Galilee, the cove of Tabgha had warm mineral springs that flowed into Lake Galilee. These warm springs attracted schools of fish. This cove was a favorite fishing area during the time of Jesus. It was probably at the cove of Tabgha that Jesus called the fishermen Peter, Andrew, James, and John, and where Jesus met with his apostles after his resurrection.

Temple: Israel's King Solomon built the first Jerusalem temple about 950 BC on the traditional site of Mount Moriah. Solomon's temple stood for about 360 years until the Babylonians destroyed it and took most of the Jews into exile. Fifty years later the Jews returned from Babylon and rebuilt the temple in 515 BC. King Herod the Great rebuilt and expanded the temple complex. Jerusalem and the temple were destroyed by the Romans under Emperor Titus in AD 70. The temple has never been rebuilt again.

GEOGRAPHICAL GLOSSARY

Temple Mount (Western or Wailing Wall): The Temple Mount is the massive masonry platform occupying the south-east corner of Jerusalem's Old City. It was constructed by King Herod the Great. Today the Temple Mount is under Muslim control, so non-Muslims have limited access. The Mount of Olives overlooks the Temple Mount from the east. On the Temple Mount today is the Islamic monument of the Dome of the Rock built in AD 691, and the Al-Aqsa Mosque built in the late AD 700s. Known as the "Wailing Wall," the Western Wall of the Temple Mount was the retaining limestone wall of the temple complex. Because the Temple Mount is today under Muslim control, the western wall is a place of prayer for the Jewish people.

Tiberias: Located on the western shore of Lake Galilee, about 10 miles south of Capernaum. Herod Antipas governed the regions of Galilee and Perea. He built his Galilean capital city of Tiberias about AD 18 and named it after the Roman Emperor Tiberius.

Tomb of Jesus: Probably located in the area occupied today by the Church of the Holy Sepulcher in the Christian quarter of the Old City of Jerusalem. There are numerous first-century rock-cut tombs in the area. This area was outside the walls of Jerusalem during the time of Jesus.

Tyre and Sidon: Non-Jewish cities located in northwest Phoenicia, a region that bordered Galilee to the west along the coast of the Mediterranean Sea. During his Galilean ministry, Jesus would leave Galilee and minister in the region of Tyre and Sidon.

Upper Room: The location of the Passover meal and the Last Supper was an upper guest room in a private home in Jerusalem. The guest room was reached by an outside stairway. This upper guest room became known as the "Upper Room." Based on the early chapters of the book of Acts, the apostles used the Upper Room as a temporary residence or regular gathering place. Since the AD 300s, the traditional site of the Upper Room has been identified with the room located in the compound of David's tomb. It is located in the southern part of the Old City of Jerusalem on Mount Zion.

Wilderness of Judea: The desert region located east of Jerusalem to the Jordan Valley, measuring about 75 miles north-south and about 10 miles east-west. The public ministry of John the Baptist, and Jesus' temptation after his water-baptism, took place in the Wilderness of Judea.

REGIONAL MAP

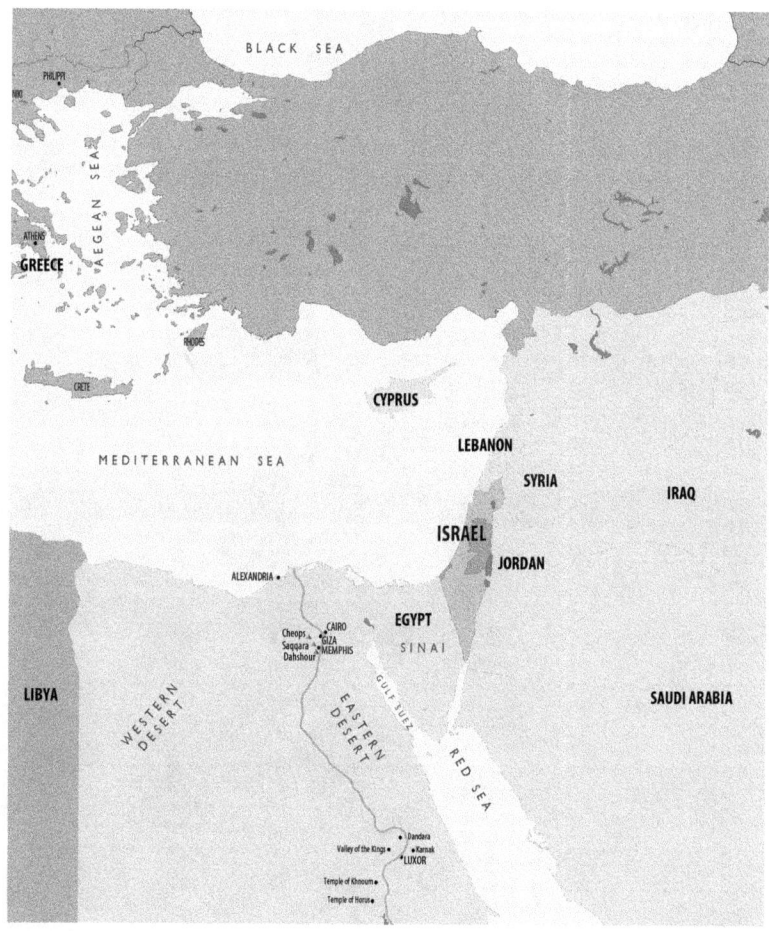

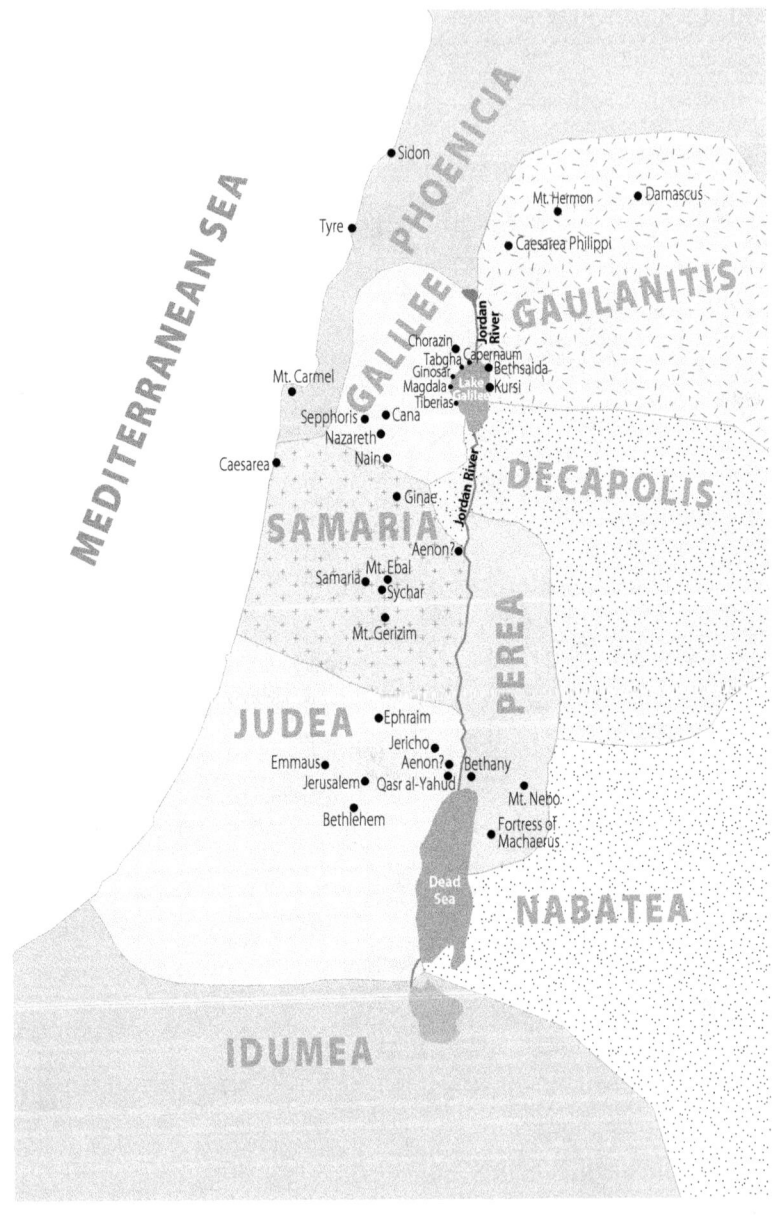

The Old City of Jerusalem

OTHER BOOKS BY ANDREW JACKSON ON AMAZON

THE INTERNATIONAL ENGLISH BIBLE
A New Testament Translation

THE CHRISTIAN SAINTS OF TURKEY
(Available only in Turkey)

A GUIDE INSIDE THE EARLY CHURCH OF ASIA MINOR
300 Profiles

ISTANBUL
A Guide Inside the Early Church of Constantinople

THE LOST LAND OF THE BIBLE
Prayer Pilgrimages Through Turkey

THE WAY OF JESUS
Living a Life of Grace and Hope Toward Others

MORMONISM EXAMINED
Comparing the Teaching and Practices of Latter-Day Saints with Biblical Christianity

www.ingramcontent.com/pod-product-compliance
Lightning Source LLC
Chambersburg PA
CBHW060516100426
42743CB00009B/1344